This book belongs to:

Barbara Hannah

BEYOND
THE ANDES

BEYOND THE ANDES

My Search for the Origins of Pre-Inca Civilization

Pino Turolla

HARPER & ROW, PUBLISHERS

NEW YORK

Cambridge   London
Hagerstown   Mexico City
Philadelphia   São Paulo
San Francisco 1817 Sydney

To Renée, who shared the arduous years and
provided invaluable assistance

BEYOND THE ANDES. Copyright © 1980 by Pino Turolla. All rights reserved.
Printed in the United States of America. No part of this book may be used
or reproduced in any manner whatsoever without written permission
except in the case of brief quotations embodied in critical articles and
reviews. For information address Harper & Row, Publishers, Inc., 10 East
53rd Street, New York, N.Y. 10022. Published simultaneously in Canada
by Fitzhenry & Whiteside Limited, Toronto.

FIRST EDITION

Designer: Janice Stern

Maps by *Bernard H. Wagner*

Library of Congress Cataloging in Publication Data

Turolla, Pino.
  Beyond the Andes.

  1. Indians—Origin. 2. Indians of South America—
Amazon Valley. 3. Indians of South America—Andes.
4. Turolla, Pino. 5. South America—Description and
travel—1951– 6. South America—Antiquities.
I. Title.
E61.T9 1980   980'.01   75-25069
ISBN 0-06-014369-X

80 81 82 83 10 9 8 7 6 5 4 3 2 1

Contents

PART V   LEGACY OF THE ANCIENTS

MAPS

Prologue

The river at this point deep within the jungles of Venezuela widened to form a large, quiet pool. The water was very still, with reflections of the sky and the foliage on the far shore shining vividly on the surface. It was a fine day, and the area was as pleasant as a sylvan meadow.

But the depths of the water were dark and murky with silt, and I knew that I would be diving blind when I went down to the bottom. There were also snags and branches in the water, which meant there was a chance of being entangled and trapped below the surface. So I picked a dead tree trunk that was standing vertically in the water about 10 meters from the shore. For my first dives, I decided, I would use this trunk as a marker, following it to the bottom, gathering the specimens I needed there, and then following it back up to the surface.

My companions and guides, Antonio and Ramirez, sat on the bank and watched as I put on my skin-diving gear. They were fascinated with the flippers; they had never seen anything like them before. When I stepped into the water, I felt their eyes on my back and I was aware that in their minds it must almost have seemed that I had transformed myself into some strange water animal. Keeping a tight grip on the pail that I would use to collect my specimens, I swam out to the tree trunk and dove to the bottom.

I could see clearly for no more than a foot or two, but I could feel the tree trunk along my leg. I began moving quickly around, scooping samples of sediment off the bottom into the pail. When it was filled, I transferred it to my right hand and gave a full, heavy stroke backward with my left to start myself toward the surface.

So suddenly that I felt as if my whole body had been hit, a penetrating, slicing, tearing sensation struck and gripped my left hand and wrist. It took a second for my mind to clear itself of the shock. But I knew I had to get to the surface immediately. I couldn't see a thing. I had twisted and wrenched so violently trying to free my hand that I had stirred up the sediment on the bottom and the water was completely dark. And my chest was beginning to burst. I was free-diving and had extended my breath to the utmost in filling the pail. With the shock and the exertion of fighting this thing, my oxygen consumption had shot up. I had to have air. I thrust my right foot down to the bottom to give a push and get myself moving upward quickly. Suddenly, with the same slamming impact, I felt the tearing sensation in my right heel. Now both my wrist and my foot were being held in viselike grips.

I dropped the pail and, using my right arm and left leg, swam with all my force. My mind was so jumbled that I had no conception of how far I was swimming; I was simply struggling upward, not knowing when I would reach the surface. Without the flippers, I am sure I would not have made it. Finally I broke through to the air and sucked in a huge gulp. I twisted my body and pulled my left arm up, and only then was I able to see what was happening. The thumb side of my left hand, down to my wrist, was in the mouth of a huge fish.

I looked down into two large, green eyes that stared murderously at me as the fish thrashed and strained to force its teeth deeper into my hand. I was wearing a wristwatch and band, and had it not been for them, I think those teeth would have gone all the way through my hand. I hit the beast repeatedly on the head with my right hand, but it didn't let go. I couldn't get my shoulders high enough out of the water to strike it with full force. Beneath the surface the second fish still had my right foot in its savage grip.

Finally I reached down with my right hand, flexed my forefinger, jammed the knuckle into the corner of the fish's mouth, and then twisted my hand, using my finger as a lever. The blows to the fish's head must have stunned it; I was able to force its mouth partly open and tore my hand free. The blood was gushing out, and the water around me began to turn red. I kicked with my left foot at the fish gripping my right heel. I banged it several times on the head, and finally I was able to rip my heel out of its mouth. My brain was in such tumult it seemed there was nothing but flashes of blinding light streaking back and forth in my head, but I remember feeling a knot in my stomach as I realized that there were probably many more of these fish in the water, and by now there was a lot of blood to attract them. I had to get out immediately.

I whirled my head around and located the shore, where Antonio and Ramirez were sitting calmly on the lovely white sand. I thrashed my way toward them, coughing and gulping; I had taken in a lot of water. Finally I hit bottom and tried to rise to my feet, but I stumbled and fell back into the water. "Antonio, help!" I yelled. But he made no gesture or movement to help me. At last I reached a rock that stuck up out of the shallow water and grabbed it. Antonio and Ramirez were still sitting placidly on the shore.

I sat in the shallow water, hanging on to the rock, and looked down at my hand. I couldn't believe what I saw: a huge gash between my thumb and palm, from the front all the way around to the back side of my hand. My thumb was hanging loose at a funny angle and I could see daylight through the gash. Blood was gushing out like water from a faucet and my foot was completely opened at the heel. I suddenly realized that I no longer had my underwater watch. It was gone.

At last Antonio got up from the shore and came toward me. "Out, out, out!" he said, and I struggled to pull myself out of the water. He looked at my hand and said, "Sit down, sit down! I didn't know there were aimara in these waters."

I held my left hand in my right and looked at him, unable to believe what had happened to me. "Aimara?" I said. "What kind of fish is that?"

"Aimara are very dangerous fish," Antonio answered. "Big fish, very voracious, like piranha—only bigger."

"But you said there were no fish here!"

"I didn't know," Antonio said. "We don't know aimara in these waters." He looked at my hand again and at my foot. Then he said, "You sit, sit down! If you don't die in five minutes, I can help you."

I was stunned. "Antonio, what do you mean—die?"

"Perhaps the fish are poisonous," he said. "We don't know. We must wait. If you don't die in the next few minutes, I can help you."

I looked at Antonio with incredulity. The sound of his voice, and my voice, multiplied and reverberated in my head like thunder. I might die! I was so dazed that it began to seem none of this was really happening to me. I wasn't sitting on this shore; I was off on some other plane of existence, watching a man who only looked like me. It was an eerie, disorienting sensation. I was in a state of shock; still it was clear in my mind that with every beat of my heart, blood was gushing from my wounds. There was nothing I could do about it. It was as if I was hypnotized.

Antonio kept peering into my eyes, pulling down he lids and looking at them very intently. He looked repeatedly inside my ears. I could not understand what he was doing and time was passing like an eternity. I stared into Antonio's face anxiously. I relied on him totally. I was unable to make a decision by myself at that moment.

Finally Antonio said, "It's not poisonous." And with that, he moved behind me. I had no idea what was going to happen next. He put his hands around my head, his fingertips practically in front of my eyes. Then I heard him chanting incomprehensible words in a very low key, and I started to feel something very strange, as if a magnetic force was taking over my head. My eyes became heavy and began to close, even though I was fighting to keep them open, perhaps with the idea of seeing what was happening. Slowly the chanting became louder and louder, and I felt my body growing colder by the minute, and heavier. The blood from my hand slowly stopped gushing out. I don't know how long all this lasted, but I was conscious that at a certain point the flow of blood had stopped.

Then Antonio, speaking in the language of the Zape Indians, said somthing to Ramirez. He turned and ran into the jungle, and Antonio walked to the edge of the river where he leaned down to pick something up. I realized when he returned that he had his hands full of mud. Ramirez reappeared, holding a bunch of herbs. Antonio put down the mud, selected some of the herbs, and squeezed the leaves and a few of the roots between his fingers. In a little cup that he carried with him he made some kind of paste. Then before he was finished he said something else to Ramirez in Zape, and Ramirez immediately opened his pants and pulled out his penis. He came toward me, grabbed my hand, and urinated over my wound. Then he held my arm and hand, while Antonio poured the paste he had prepared, and the juice that remained on the bottom of this little cup, over my wound. He took my thumb, pulled it out straight, and laid it parallel to the other fingers. I didn't feel any pain—no pain at all. He picked up the mud that he had retrieved from the bank of the river and put it over the herbs and my wound. He looked around for a moment, and I, by intuition, knew he was searching for something to wrap my hand with. I pointed to the towel I had with me. He cut off a strip and wrapped my hand. Then he pulled out a bottle from his pack and said, "Drink this. It will give you back your strength."

I didn't question him or anything he did; I felt that I had to trust these men to know what to do. My foot was still bleeding badly, but they paid no attention to it. Finally, after they had finished with my hand, Ramirez pulled off my flipper and Antonio said, "Put your boots on."

"But I'm bleeding," I said.

"That too will stop," Antonio replied. Ramirez helped

put my socks and boots on. Then Antonio said, "It's time we left. We're going from here to Mato—the place where you'll be picked up by plane."

We got up and started out on the trail. It was, in one way, an incredible journey; I felt no pain in my hand or my foot. We walked for eight hours through the underbrush in order to reach the plateau where I was to meet the plane. Today I cannot remember my thoughts or feelings during a single moment of that long march. I was just walking, following Antonio.

When we arrived at the Mato landing strip, we found a small shack built some time ago. "Here you can wait," Antonio said. "You'll be sheltered if it rains. Don't worry, everything will be fine."

He sat me down and studied me very attentively. He observed my color and leaned over and lifted my eyelids to look into my eyes. He peered into my ears, checked my expression, and looked at my hand again. Then he turned and said to Ramirez, "You stay with him. I'll be back in a short time." And he left.

Ramirez helped me fix a bed to lie on. Next, he went down to a small creek to fetch some water—not for drinking, but to sponge off my face and arms. I kept asking him what kind of herbs he had gathered and applied to my wound. But he just smiled and said nothing. I suddenly felt very tired. My energy was drained and I wanted only to lie down and go to sleep. But when I told Ramirez this, he said, "No, no sleep. Wait for Antonio." The urgency in his voice told me it was important to listen to him and stay awake.

I prayed that Antonio would return very soon, and at last, about an hour later, he came back. He had with him a small wooden bowl filled with a white liquid; it looked to me like some kind of milk. "What is that," I asked him, "milk?"

"*Si, leche,*" he said. "Now you drink."

As I look back on the experience now, I remember that Antonio had a certain strange expression on his face when he said that. My attention drifted, my head rolled

back and didn't move. It wasn't that I didn't want to drink
the liquid. I felt so sick and deranged that I just wanted to
be left in peace.

"Now!" Antonio said, snapping me back to the present.
"You *must* drink this now!" He spoke very sharply. He
turned my head, put the cup to my lips, and I drank a
good portion of its contents. It didn't taste like milk to me,
but at that moment I wasn't capable of thinking clearly. So
I dismissed the funny taste as being the result of my disor-
dered mind and believed the liquid was what Antonio said
it was—*leche.*

I drank two cups of this liquid and then I lay down. Antonio sat nearby, looking at me and smiling. From time to
time he told me that everything would be fine. My eyes
started to feel heavy and the image of Antonio began to
disappear slowly in a fog. But I was conscious that he was
talking to me—about life in the jungle, about hunting
grounds, and about the big cats: *el tigre,* the jaguar. My
heart began to beat like a drum pounding inside my head,
and I fought a rising sense of nausea very strongly, feeling that to vomit in front of my companions would not be
proper. Slowly my heartbeat became more rhythmic; the
sound of the drum was a continuous roll, no longer intermittent.

I still felt the presence of Antonio. I heard his voice and
the sounds of what he was saying, but I was not aware of
the actual passage of time. I had the impression that I had
left my physical body, but I realized that this could not be
so, because I felt the trembling of my muscles. Slowly, the
voice of Antonio came to me more clearly and authorita-
tively. I could not see him, but I felt his voice commanding me, and I entered into a sensation of nothingness. I
was floating in a void. But then I began to see the animals
and the places in the jungle that Antonio was describing
to me. I saw a giant anaconda come out of the water and
slowly flow through the grass and the flowers. Then I saw
the jaguar running in slow motion, jumping over tree
stumps, his body curving and undulating as if it had no
bones, no firm substance. The animal stretched out and

became much, much longer, weaving slowly, gracefully, back and forth, like some long, spineless, unknown sea monster, swimming toward me through a shimmering kaleidoscope of colors, ominous but beautiful. I saw birds with colored feathers moving through space. And above all, I saw light from the sun playing through the trees in incredible, ever-changing patterns of colors and shapes. Then, darkness.

When my mind awoke again and I opened my eyes, I was alone and the sun was high in the sky. Only then did I realize that an entire day had passed. I no longer had a watch but I believed it was about three o'clock in the afternoon. I must have gone to sleep about eight or nine the previous evening and I had slept through the night and the following morning—some eighteen hours. I looked at my hand. It was still in the same condition as the day before, but the thumb now had a more natural color. Then Antonio arrived. He asked me if I had had pleasant dreams. I told him what I remembered seeing and he laughed and said, "It was pleasant dreams."

After an hour or two had passed, Antonio offered me more of the milk to drink. Then he said, "Now I must leave you and go back to my people." I didn't say anything or ask any questions—I drank the milk. As he left he pointed to the bowl and said, "You must take more of this." I watched him walk away out of my line of vision, and slowly the same sensations began to pass over me as the day before. Again I seemed to leave my body and look at myself with very critical eyes from some distance away. I had the same dreams of animals, and this time I felt I could predict their movements before they took place. Again everything ended in complete darkness.

When I awoke I was alone. It was dark and as I watched the stars overhead I felt a frightening sense of isolation. That night I prayed; it was perhaps the first time in many, many years that I really felt that, after all, there was a God.

The following morning as I lay there waiting for the plane, the conviction grew within me that I was going to lose my hand. I could take no encouragement from the fact that the color of my thumb looked a little better. In my mind's eye, I saw Antonio chanting, covering my hand with a little mud, plant juice, and urine, and then telling me, "You're going to be all right." How could I believe such a thing? The gash between my thumb and the palm of my hand looked as if somebody had taken a machete and sliced right down to the wrist. All the important structures must have been destroyed. And certainly the wound was going to become infected; the polluted water, whatever was in the mouth of the fish, the mud, and Ramirez's urine, all guaranteed that. I wouldn't be able to reach a doctor for days, and by that time the infection might have entered my bloodstream. How could I expect Antonio's chants and herbs to reverse the course of all these destructive forces? It was out of the question.

So I became resigned to losing my hand; that would be my fate. I didn't even think to pray for the hand. What I did pray was, "Please, God, don't let me die in this place, where no one will ever find me or know what happened." I knew that if I died there, within a matter of three or four hours a jaguar would come, drag my body off into the bush, and eat it. Then when the plane came to pick me up, the pilot would circle overhead and see no one. Even if he landed for a few minutes, when he saw no one there, he would lose no time getting back into the air. A bush pilot is very survival-conscious, and he would not prowl around in the undergrowth for a couple of days looking for some evidence of what might have happened to me. No—if I died there, no one would ever know the story. And that was what I couldn't bear.

I noticed that the wooden bowl had been left next to me, filled with more of the milky-looking liquid. So occasionally I drank some of it, and again time became meaningless and the same dreams returned, interlocking with my prayers. In periods of lucidity I thanked the Lord for letting me survive my ordeal this long.

On the third day, at about 10:00 A.M., the plane arrived. Under my breath I said, "Thank God!" when I first heard the engine. The pilot dropped down low and began to circle the landing strip looking for me. I could see that there were two men in the plane. I lifted myself to my feet, walked out of the shack, and signaled as best I could with a white shirt. The pilot landed, taxied up, turned the plane around at the end of the strip, and shut off the engine. Virgilio Quinones, one of my associates, climbed out. He was anxious to know what I had found on the Chiquao plateau, and rather than sitting in Caracas waiting for me, he had contacted the pilot and had come along with him to pick me up.

Quinones and the pilot walked over to me quickly; they could see that I was not well. I gave them a sketchy account of what had happened. Then the pilot asked, "Who prepared this pack over your hand?" When I told him "Antonio," he stared at me with a very strange look in his eyes.

"We've got to get him to a hospital quickly," Quinones said to the pilot. "Where is the nearest one?"

"Upata," the pilot said.

"Then let's go," Quinones said. They helped me into the plane, Quinones hastily grabbed my gear and shoved it in, and we took off.

As we climbed into the air, I looked down at the spot where I had lain for three days and I felt, deep within myself, that something strange, profound, and soul-changing had happened there. I had no clear idea of what it was. Perhaps, I thought at that moment, it was the emotional impact of the incredible adventure that had almost taken my life in a virtually unknown river in this immense green jungle. Or perhaps it was the unsettling effect of the delirium and shock caused by my wounds that had been sweeping over me the last three days. I couldn't put my finger on it. But I felt different. I was not quite the same person I was when we had hiked into this region a week ago.

Quinones and the pilot asked me again and again about my adventure, and I gave them more details of the attack. When I described Antonio's healing ritual, Quinones just looked out the plane window and shook his head quietly.

I said I felt sure I was going to lose my hand, but Quinones set his lips firmly and said, "Don't talk now. We'll be there in a little while."

After a flight of about an hour, we spotted the Upata airstrip and began our descent. When we landed, Quinones jumped out and found a little old taxi. He helped me into it, and we headed for the hospital. It proved to be a small provincial clinic, and there we were received by a young mestizo medic, Dr. Luber. He looked quickly at my hand and asked me what had happened. When he found out that Antonio had taken care of me, he said, "There's nothing I can do for you. Antonio has done everything."

I was perplexed. I spent half an hour with Dr. Luber while he cleaned the mud and herbs from my hand and checked the less serious lesion on my heel. Then he spread the wounds with a yellow antiseptic liquid and put clean bandages over them. I asked him many questions, but always his answer was: "I really don't know what to tell you. I only know that in the jungle around here, Antonio is well known for curing people. He is a very well respected shaman in Guiana. Everybody in this part of the country knows that he understands all the secrets."

I left the clinic in a state of confusion, disturbed about the incomprehensible thing that had happened to me, and very concerned over the possibility of infection in my hand. I realized that I had to fly back to my home in Miami immediately. The bush pilot took Quinones and me from Upata to Ciudad Bolívar, where we flew with Aero Postal to Caracas. There we headed directly for Quinones's hotel to make a call to the airport to see if I could get immediate passage to Miami. Then I called Renée, my wife, to tell her I was returning home shortly. My state was not normal; I recognized that something strange was going through me. And I later learned that Renée had sensed it, too, over the telephone.

I had had almost nothing to eat but Antonio's "milk" ever since the attack and was feeling a bit weak. Quinones settled me into the hotel restaurant, then took my gear upstairs to his room. He rejoined me and while we were eating, our call to the airport was returned; there was a seat on a flight that left in about an hour and a half, if I could get there quickly. We decided to leave at once. "Don't worry about your gear," Quinones said, "I'm coming to Miami in a couple of weeks, and I'll bring it to you then. We've got to catch a taxi immediately—can't take a chance on your missing that plane." With the condition I was in, it hardly crossed my mind that precious geological samples—the reason for my entire expedition—were in those bags in Quinones's room.

We reached the airport in time, and as I boarded the plane, slipped down the aisle to my seat, and heard the sounds of the engines warming up, I had a certain feeling that I had rejoined the world of the rational—that I was again in touch with things concrete and explainable. I tried to put the unsettling, mystifying events of the last few days out of my mind. What a relief it was to be on that plane heading for Miami, where there were doctors, hospitals, X-ray machines, and drugs with known properties. And yet, I was afraid it would be too late. By the time I landed in Miami and saw a doctor, it would be five days since the attack. I was afraid that no one would be able to do much after that length of time, and the thought came to me again, "I'm going to lose my hand."

It was early evening when I landed in Miami. Renée was waiting to meet me. She said she was there purely on intuition; she had checked and found that the airline I had told her I would use did not have a service between Caracas and Miami. Yet she had had a feeling that she should come to the airport at this time. That struck me as strange, but no more strange than everything else that had happened to me.

Renée saw the bandage on my hand and I told her I had been attacked by an aimara. But I said nothing of Antonio's healing, or of the delirium and the visions that had come over me while I was lying at Mato waiting for the plane. There were too many things I simply couldn't explain. So I kept silent.

I went to see Dr. Baer, our family doctor, and it was in his office that my experience came to its incredible climax. Dr. Baer examined my hand and studied it under a fluoroscope. There was no infection; I would not lose my hand. Dr. Baer told me that bones had obviously been broken but were already healed, and that the veins and nerves between my index finger and thumb had been cut but they, too, were now healed. He could not understand how it was possible, if all this damage had been done only five days before.

At that moment I felt it was pointless to hold back the story any longer. So I told Dr. Baer everything: Antonio's healing ritual, my growing cool and the stoppage of the bleeding, the herbal paste, the mud, the urine, the milk he fed me, my delirium and visions, the absence of pain, and the return of color to the thumb. I even told him that I felt I had undergone some fundamental, unexplainable transformation.

He listened to the story, rapt, but he could offer no rational explanation. Obviously, he was puzzled. I, too, was puzzled as I left his office. My hand had healed. I could not, intellectually, accept such a happening. I could not accept the fact that Antonio could do such things. I had never before had an experience remotely similar. But the realities of what I had gone through remained in my mind and could not be denied.

In the days and weeks that followed, my emotions lurched back and forth in many different directions. At times the thought flashed through my head: "Maybe I'm losing my mind! Maybe I was out of my senses down there, and none of it really happened." But then, there was my hand, with the ugly, vivid scar between the thumb and the palm—and it was healed. I had never before been interested in religion. Now I paced the house, talking erratically and obsessively about God. There was an unexplainable, gnawing sense of unrest and apprehension as I realized that my body had been—perhaps still was—in the grip of forces that I knew nothing about.

I groped for answers. I searched back into my past, retracing my steps, hunting for clues. The same questions rang again and again through my head. How did I get here? What had really happened to bring me to this point in my life?

PART I

The Search Begins

CHAPTER 1

The Past Unfolds

It started decades ago in the manor house of my ancestors, where I was born, which overlooked a small hamlet, Bacchia, high up in the shadows of snow-covered Alpine peaks near the Austrian border in a land called Istria. It was a land with a stormy history of rebellion and revolution against its eastern European conquerors who, at various times in history, swept down through the Alpine passes on their quest to control the land further south known as Italy. My grandfather—my father's father—lived in the manor house, the seat of the estate that had been my family's for several centuries. He was the Count, a title that passed later to my father and, upon my father's death, to me.

Grandfather was a large man—6 feet 5 inches, which at that time was extraordinarily tall by European standards. To my small eyes he seemed immense. And he was very strong. I remember during my boyhood the excitement of the "feria," the festivals in the Istrian towns and villages. Traditionally, one of the main events was steer carrying: the men competed to see who could lift the largest steer and carry it so many paces. Hoisting a larger steer than anyone else, Grandfather always triumphed. As I grew older, I began to appreciate other aspects of his character. He had a very open, inquiring intellect—perhaps more open than he needed for his place and time.

Visiting the manor house was always exciting for me. Grandfather called it the "Eagle's Nest." It was built high off the floor of a valley, against the side of a mountain—a situation that had provided effective defense in earlier centuries. The thick, heavy walls were made of the same stone as the mountain itself, so that the Eagle's Nest was very hard to see from the valley below. The house was my second home and the mountain was my playground. I learned to climb and ski almost as soon as I could walk. From my earliest years I was in awe of the majesty of mountains, and felt a deep respect for their dangers.

One day when I was about five, we were visiting Grandfather when a letter arrived from his younger brother, Umberto. The letter caused a flurry of excitement in the family. Umberto had left Europe for America many years before, and had been heard from only rarely. I remember sitting on Grandfather's lap that day and asking him about Uncle Umberto. We were in his library, a huge old room overlooking the valley below. Wood paneling covered the walls and ceiling, and thousands of books in shelves were ranged against the walls all around us. In the center of the room, next to Grandfather's chair, was a huge old mahogany table stacked high with books, papers, and documents.

As I sat on Grandfather's lap listening to him talk, and as I overheard other conversations in my family, images built in my mind of this uncle I had never seen and the strange country he had traveled to. Grandfather spoke of his younger brother, his only brother, with love and much hope. Umberto was smaller than Grandfather, "a scholar," restless, idealistic. I imagine he felt he had no place in Europe. My family didn't know whether he was in North America or South America—they made no such distinction. Umberto had simply "gone to America." To my mind, America was a place of mystery and adventure. The word evoked images of cowboys and Indians, the Gold Rush, a wild, trackless frontier. It was a place where strength and personal enterprise prevailed above everything. There was no consideration that Uncle Umberto might be doing menial labor, or that he might be living in strained circumstances. He was "in America," and that meant he was rich, successful, and had a life full of adventure. It was the dream of that generation, as it also became my dream, my hope. I wanted very much to go to America.

I asked Grandfather why Uncle Umberto had left, and he said: "Well, he believed in a new type of life. He felt he couldn't stay here any more—that life here seemed too uncertain and someday everything would crumble." Umberto may have seen well into the future. When he left, Istria was still part of the Austro-Hungarian Empire. Within a few years, as a consequence of World War I, it was ceded to Italy. Then within a few more years, after World War II, my family lost everything, and Istria was absorbed by Tito and made part of modern-day Yugoslavia.

But all that was a bit complicated for my small mind to absorb at the time, and so I asked Grandfather again why Uncle Umberto had left. He lifted me off his lap and went to the window where he looked out over the valley below to the ranges of Alps beyond. He had a dreamy, far-away expression on his face, and he said, "Maybe he wanted to follow the conquistadors."

The conquistadors . . .

It was traditional in families such as mine that young boys, after completing six years of primary schooling, were sent to a military academy. My father had done this, and decided that I would do the same. So at age twelve, with very mixed feelings, I said goodbye to my parents, was put on a train, and went off to begin my formal schooling in Gorizia, a small town in northeastern Italy.

It was a time of tremendous political turmoil in Italy. Mussolini had consolidated Fascist power and moved against the king, Victor Emanuel III. He had occupied Ethiopia, and was increasingly drawn into the expansionary plans of our belligerent neighbor to the north, Germany. My family was caught in the middle. My father and grandfather, and most of the other strong families in the Alps, were hostile to the Fascist ideology and to Mussolini's régime. Yet they never felt themselves directly involved with these political machinations. The Alps was our home; national politics were brewed far to the south in Rome, and we had very little sympathy, nor much desire, to be involved with the Romans.

But in a curious way, the Fascist influence stimulated my imagination if not my allegiance. At military school, we were told again and again that a small group of people, if they are determined and well organized, can influence the course of an entire nation, as the Fascists had done in our country. As an illustration, we studied the military campaigns throughout history that had been won by small numbers of troops against what appeared to be overwhelming odds. Most striking to me were the repeated stories of the conquests in America by Pizarro and Cortez. The subjugation of the Aztecs, and a few years later the Incas, fired me with unanswerable questions. How, I wondered, could large, rich empires, with hundreds of thousands of people and military leaders who were themselves legends, be overcome by a small force of perhaps 300 Spanish soldiers? The conquistadors, it seemed to me, must have had some power that was unknown to us. I didn't understand how they had done it, and it kept occurring to me that some day I would like to find out.

After only two years in military school, I found myself in the army. My experience in the mountains made it an easy transition for me—I entered a school for Alpine troops. I then became part of the Second Regiment of the Julia Division, which had been entirely recruited from Istria and the adjacent Alps. We were very proud of our regiment. We were bound together by our love for our birthplace, and we felt an idealistic satisfaction in being chosen to help defend our Alpine homeland.

But early in 1940, when I was still in my teens, I left my homeland. Our regiment was sent to join the Julia Division, which had already been sent to Albania, where the government was mounting a campaign against Greece. We were told that the Balkan campaign would be an easy military operation. Instead, the fighting became very bloody and we felt that we had been betrayed by Rome. But we fought on.

My youth was shattered one clear day when, in the middle of a scrimmage on the rocky slopes of Mali Bechisthit near the Greek border, a man suddenly rose out of a foxhole 20 meters in front of me and shot me with a burst from his machine gun. I can't recall exactly my impressions at that moment: I remember only a sense of astonishment as I heard the sound of the bullets cracking into my bones. Then I heard incredible musical sounds, like notes from a harp, and sparkling patterns in all the colors of the rainbow danced before my eyes as I dropped down, down, down until I hit the ground. I was aware that I was lying on my stomach, face on the earth. There was no drama, no cries—just the realization that something unfathomable was happening to me.

How long I lay there, I don't know—perhaps five or ten minutes. Everything was very peaceful. Then I heard the sound of steps, the crunch of boots on the rocky slope. Some of my comrades had seen me, and were at my side. From far away, a voice said, "Are you hurt?"

"Yes . . ."

I heard another voice say, "He's not dead yet."

They picked me up and carried me back to our lines, to a doctor. He looked first at my shattered arm, turning it one way and then the other, counting the bullet holes. Then he spotted a wound under my right arm, checked the bullet's trajectory through my chest, and saw the exit hole under my left shoulder blade. Shaking his head, he taped my arm to my thorax to immobilize it, and bandaged the wounds to stop the bleeding. Then my comrades carried me on a stretcher to a field hospital six or seven hours to the rear of our lines. There the surgeons checked me out, and immediately inserted a needle through my ribcage and withdrew blood and fluid from my right lung cavity. One of the doctors said, "You are very lucky to be alive. How far away was the man who shot you?"

"Something like twenty meters."

"Yes, very short range—that's what did it. The bullet was hot and partially cauterized the tissue as it passed through your body. Otherwise a lot more fluid would have built up in your lung cavity, your lungs would have collapsed, and you probably wouldn't be here."

I nodded. I felt very strange, thinking that except for the accident of my attacker's being so close, I would no longer be alive.

The surgeons put the pieces of my mangled arm back together, and I was taken by truck to the port city of Durazzo, Albania, where I was put on a Red Cross ship headed back to Italy—and another close brush with eternity. Halfway across the Adriatic, the ship was sunk by an English submarine. It was pandemonium. But again, luck was watching over me. My cabin mate had the use of his arms and helped me put on a life jacket. We then jumped overboard and were in the water as the ship went down. All around us were the crew and wounded men in lifeboats, clinging to debris, or just swimming. It was night and very dark. I could see very little but I heard voices, splashings, cries. It was a tapestry of the sounds of survival.

Another ship came to our rescue, and when we reached Italy, I was taken to a hospital in Francovilla, a small town on the shores of the Adriatic. I spent fifty or so days there, and then was given forty days' leave to recuperate. I spent the time in Florence, a city that I grew to love. Gradually my arm became more mobile, and as I began to use it, regained most of its strength. The memory of the sounds of bullets cracking into my bones and the ethereal harplike tones and brilliant colors that had passed before my eyes began to recede from my memory. It all seemed to have happened to someone else. Yet there remained with me the feeling that I had been close to something incomprehensible; there was a part of me that had been touched by an experience from some other world. That feeling would return years later after I was attacked by aimara in the murky waters of a river in Venezuela.

My convalescence over, I rejoined the Julia Division and fought briefly on the Russian front. Then I applied and was accepted for a newly formed force that would be trained in special techniques of warfare, including parachute and underwater training. I became one of the first instructors of this special force, and was assigned to a school that had just been established in Tarquinia. It was a most fortunate assignment. Tarquinia had been one of the more important cities of the ancient Etruscan culture. According to legend, men from this city founded a dynasty that ruled Rome throughout the sixth century B.C. During this same period, the city was in contact with the near eastern powers: a Phoenician urn of faïence was found in a Tarquinian tomb, bearing figures of Egyptian priests and slaves and the hieroglyphic name of the Pharoah Bocchoris, who ruled from 715 to 709 B.C.

I was fascinated—and with time, increasingly chagrined—to find that parts of the modern-day city of Tarquinia were built on a hill that had served as the cemetery of the ancient Etruscan city. The hill, called the Monterozzi, is actually a small plateau, and in good weather the Mediterranean is clearly visible from its western ridge. To the east beyond the valley of the San Savino is another plateau, called the Pian di Civita. Most Tarquinians reserved the Monterozzi for their tombs, perhaps because they wanted to provide their dead with the most beautiful prospect.

The airfield that served as the nucleus of our training station was built more or less parallel to the Monterozzi, just south of the modern town of Tarquinia, and as soon as I arrived there, I became aware of numbers of Etruscan tombs around its perimeter. They intrigued me, and I began spending some of my available free time crawling into the tombs and exploring their environs. I soon learned that further west on the Monterozzi plateau, there were a number of especially rich tombs with interior walls covered with fresco painting. I was astounded when I entered the first of these, the "Tomb of Hunting and Fishing," which dated from the end of the sixth century

B.C. This tomb consisted of two rooms, one leading to the next, and when I stepped into the first room and looked around, I saw a marvelous frieze on all four walls, filled with figures of dancers and musicians moving amid trees with delicate, almost lacy branches and foliage. The painting was exquisitely executed in a great number of colors— white tunics and beige, red, or umber robes; warm flesh tones and dark brown for the hair; green and a characteristic rich aqua for the foliage. The tomb had a gabled roof, and the pediment on each end under the gable bore a charming scene showing the return from the hunt. The effect was breathtaking.

When I walked into the inner room, my delight grew even stronger. The walls of this room bore some of the most original and powerful painting I had ever seen: flocks of birds in bright, vivid colors flying across the sky, with a man below ready to sling a net to catch them; young men fishing with nets from a boat bearing the characteristic Etruscan eye painted on the prow, an omen of good fortune; dolphins leaping and playing in the water, very realistically done; swimmers, and a young naked boy diving from a high rock into the water. There was a tremendous sense of exuberance and life. I had the feeling that the coastal plain and the Mediterranean had been very good to the ancient Etruscans.

As the weeks and months passed, I studied many other painted tombs in the area, and developed a tremendous admiration for the subtlety, the sensitivity, and the humanity of these ancient people. I was amazed that they had achieved such a high level of culture when Rome was still a series of hills covered by shepherds' huts. My exposure to these Tarquinian tombs, which have provided some of the richest archaeological knowledge available from the ancient world, and my repeated visits to see the sarcophagi, pottery, sculpture, inscriptions, and bronze artifacts gathered in a renaissance villa, now the Museo Archeologico Nazionale, stimulated my interest in ancient cultures. I began taking courses in archaeology and anthropology. It was a period of rapid intellectual growth for me.

But, at the same time, the business of war continued. Between parachute-training sessions I flew many missions to drop saboteurs behind enemy lines, and I learned the art of diving with the newly perfected self-contained breathing apparatus. The Italian special forces had introduced this new offensive tactic with great success, sinking several ships in the harbors of Gibraltar, Alexandria, and elsewhere. Underwater I discovered another new world, and the excitement of exploring a terrain completely unknown to most men, free of any constraining ties with the surface, filled me with a sense of wonder and exaltation.

On July 10, 1943, the Allies landed in Sicily, and with the invasion of the mainland two months later, Italy itself became a battlefield. Italy surrendered, and as members of the royal army under King Victor Emanuel, we were ordered to cooperate with the Allies in the struggle against the Fascists and the Germans. We—100 men selected from special forces—formed a squadron under the direct command of the British 13th Corps, and I took part with my squadron in many actions with British and American troops in the Italian campaign. After the liberation of Rome, the Germans retreated to the north, and my squadron was headquartered in Fiesole, a small town situated on a hill overlooking Florence. Fiesole had also been an important Etruscan center, and later it became an important Roman town. There is an amphitheater dating from Roman times surrounded by both Roman and earlier Etruscan ruins. It was ironic that amid the grim realities of modern warfare, my imagination was again captivated by the enigmatic Etruscan civilization.

My squad—fourteen men—was lodged in two houses immediately adjacent to the ruins. My window looked out over them, across the valley below. One night shots rang out from the ruins, waking us up. I summoned the squad to my house and we leaped out of the window. German infantrymen had infiltrated our lines and entered the lower portion of the Etruscan and Roman ruins. We were able to circle behind them; then we began a pursuit around the walls and through the rooms of these ancient structures. The action became bloody, and continued throughout the night. There were many casualties. Later, when I studied the layout of the ruins, I came to the conclusion that they had served as part of the defense perimeter of the ancient Etruscan settlement. Those stones, those walls, 2500 years later, had been put to the same service for which they were originally intended.

In the closing drive of the war, the Allies dropped my squadron behind the German lines in the Po Valley as a diversionary action to draw enemy defenses away from the point of the main Allied attack. We fought for weeks against an overwhelming concentration of German forces. We were considered expendable, and no attempt was made to keep us supplied. Many died, and when I and two of my men ran out of ammunition we were captured by German paratroopers. There was the formality of a tribunal, and we were sentenced to be shot as saboteurs the following morning. Miraculously, that night we were able to jump and dispose of our German guard. We escaped and made our way south to rejoin our unit.

When the war ended three weeks later, I was a very different person from the idealistic, mountain-loving teenager who had joined the Alpine troops. The day I left the military, the only token I had to show for all those years were incredible memories, many battle-wound scars, nine medals for military valor, 5000 lire—about $13.00—as a bonus, and an open railway ticket to any place in Italy I chose to go. I could not return home. Istria was occupied by the Communist army of Yugoslavia. My grandfather had died several years before, my father was in a small town in northern Italy with two of my sisters, and my mother was living on her family's estate in the French Pyrenees with my other sister. I did not know where to go or what to do with my future. Finally I decided to return to Florence, and to study anthropology and philosophy at the nearby University of Pisa. Two years later I moved to Brescia, in northern Italy, and enrolled in a journalism program at the Instituto Bonsignori—a choice that three years later proved to have been most fortuitous.

I made several trips to France to visit my mother, where many of the things from the old manor house, the Eagle's Nest, had been taken for storage. When I asked my mother to let me see them, she led me into storerooms filled with boxes, trunks, and cases containing souvenirs, family heirlooms, documents, and papers. In one trunk, I found two old books that had belonged to my Uncle Umberto. He had brought them from America to the manor house on one of his visits, and had left them there. One was an aged, fragile book with mottled covers and a black binding printed in 1853. It bore the title *Crónicas del Peru,* by Cieza de León. The other, with similar covers and binding, was the *Compendio de la Historia del Ecuador,* by P. F. Cevallos, dated 1885. They were charming and parochial accounts of the histories of these two countries, based as much on legend as on fact. Yet they exerted a strange fascination over me. I had in my hands the words of men who had actually lived in and written about the strange continent beyond the oceans that had stimulated my imagination for so many years.

My interest in the history of America—beyond my boyhood enchantment with cowboys and Indians, the Gold Rush, and the like—was further provoked in Spain. During this same period, the late 1940s, I went there several times, and I began visiting Spanish museums to study documents and artifacts from the eras of conquest and colonialism. But as fascinating as they were, they barely touched upon the origins of the ancient peoples of the Americas. Where had those great cultures come from? Why was so little attention paid to the real roots of the Aztecs, the Mayas, the Incas? And the question that had been on my mind since military school returned: How could Pizarro and his brother, with only 300 men, completely subjugate the great Inca nation with its tens of thousands of warriors?

While I was still studying at the University of Pisa, I learned of the existence of the Gruppo Archeologico Mediterraneo, and now came a fusion of the wartime skills I had learned with the special forces and my growing interest in archaeology. The Gruppo had received reports of classic era amphorae lying on the sea bottom between Leghorn and the island of Elba, and I joined a team of divers working to corroborate those reports. Indeed, we did find amphorae—hundreds of them, many still filled with wine and oil, the cargo they had contained when they went to the bottom 2000 years ago. We were able to discern the outlines of sunken ships, and photographed them for study by the experts. We also uncovered fragments of classic marble columns lying on the ocean floor. As we worked, we were supplied with numbers of books on both land and underwater archaeology, ancient trade routes, classic ship design, and the like. My knowledge grew by leaps and bounds, but I was even more stimulated by the adventure of an archaeological search and the excitement of an actual discovery. I decided to become an archaeologist; many years would pass before I in fact realized that ambition.

Life in those days was very difficult. Italy was a land in ruins ruled by the Allied military forces. Fledgling political factions fought among themselves for supremacy and control. Istria, the land of my ancestors and my childhood, was incorporated into Yugoslavia, and the Istriani who refused to live under the new rulers, through a law of political expediency, were declared stateless. A friend who had become an official of the International Refugee Organization reminded me of that fact. "As an Istrian you are stateless, aren't you?" he said. "You have the right to emigrate through our organization if you wish to."

An explosion of mixed feelings rushed through my brain: elation at the thought of leaving behind the chaos and turmoil that was all around me, but at the same time, sadness that such a decision would also mean leaving my family and friends. Before I realized it my lips had formed the word "America."

In answer to what I had just said, my friend replied, "You can go to Canada. It won't be difficult to arrange."

The procedure for emigration proved to be so simple, and things moved so fast, that I hardly knew what was happening. Within a very few weeks I had obtained the necessary documents from the civil and military authorities, had been processed for emigration by the IRO, and had been shipped to Bremerhaven, Germany, the embarkation center from which I would set sail for Canada.

Ironically, my introduction to North America was as a cowboy. When I arrived in Canada, I learned that all immigrants were required to do six months of service in some assigned task for the Canadian government—partly as repayment for the passage to Canada, and partly to give the newcomers a chance to learn the language and become familiar with Canadian life. I spent my six months on a cattle spread in Alberta, tending a herd of steers with four Indians. They were strikingly deficient in Italian, French, or Spanish, but we soon developed a sign language that worked very effectively, and we became good friends. At the end of my tour of duty, we delivered our steers to a railroad collection depot north of Diamond City, Alberta. The Indians and I then made our way to Calgary and attended the famous Stampede, my first direct encounter with the roping, steer throwing, and bonco busting that had filled my boyhood imagination.

It was my training not in archaeology but in journalism that determined the next step in my career. I was interviewed and offered a position with the Canadian Broadcasting Corporation's International Service in Montreal, and for the next few years writing and broadcasting became my major interests. I found Montreal to be an attractive cultured city. The lifestyle was European in flavor, and the French spoken throughout the city made it very easy for me to fit in. Montreal had many things to offer to a new Canadian, but one element that was lacking was a good opera season. I decided to do something about that and formed the Canada Opera Productions. One day the manager of the theatre where the performances were to be held introduced me to a young woman who had just joined the staff. A French-Canadian student at Bennington College who was working on her non-resident term program, she was extraordinarily attractive, open, very bright, and warmed me every time she smiled. Her name was Renée Patenaude and she was to become my wife.

Renée and I began meeting for lunch, walking together or sitting in the park. When her work term was over and she returned to Bennington, I began a regular schedule of driving the 250 miles there to spend weekends with her. The intellectual stimulation and the liberal approach to education that I found at Bennington were very conducive to my own thinking and writing. It became a habit to draft my weekly CBC program there. The trips to Bennington also gave me an opportunity to visit New York, its library and museums, and especially the Museum of the American Indian with its exhibits tailored to specific cultures of North, Central, and South America. The director of the museum, Dr. Frederick Dockstader, whom I later met and with whom, over the ensuing years, I would exchange observations and reflections on the history of cultural development in South America, was the author of several books and papers on the ancient American cultures. Although my career in journalism consumed most of my time, I had not forgotten my earlier enthusiasm for archaeology, and I read Dr. Dockstader's books with great interest.

My life took another peculiar turn when I devised a new concept in parachute design. The serious problems confronted by those of us who jumped during World War II were somehow still vivid in my mind. The conventional parachute was designed for a specific constant velocity, but unfortunately, the wind factor influenced the speed and kinetic energy of impact of landing. The chute, when encountering turbulence in the air, began to oscillate and rotate, causing the chutist to swing back and forth like a pendulum. If he hit the ground in the middle of one of those swings, his velocity of impact could be increased two- or three-fold. Most of the injuries incurred on landing happened that way.

The design I now began working on incorporated circular vents around the upper surface of the parachute and eventually evolved into a controllable canopy. These vents eliminated the pressure under the canopy, and by so doing, neutralized the lift, oscillation, and rotation of the chute itself. Consequently, the velocity on landing was constant. After many test jumps to perfect the design, I obtained a first patent, under the title "Turolla Control-Descent Parachute," in 1957, and a second patent in 1961. The United States Armed Forces became interested in this new concept and a test program was established. At the same time, an advanced study project was presented to the National Aeronautic and Space Administration for the possible application of the new canopy in their space program. The testing, conferences, and paperwork dragged on for years, and consumed a lot of my time and effort with no apparent result.

Then in 1969, when the first photographs appeared showing the splashdown of the Apollo spacecraft, I saw that the three parachutes used in its recovery system had incorporated the circular vents that were one of the features in my U.S. patent. At first I was shocked, and then pleased to see that my work was benefiting the dramatic and important space program. But legal entanglement soon began which, to this day, remains unresolved.

Another subject in which I became increasingly absorbed was the study of global temperatures and glacial patterns. Cyclic glacial patterns were an important part of scientific study in Canada, and I was exposed to much of this information simply by living there, reading about it, and discussing it with scientists and academicians. There seemed to be a possible connection between these glacial patterns and questions that still filled my mind about the early cultural history of the Americas. Through all the reading and museum investigations I had done, I sensed a vacuum, a great gap in knowledge about the origins of the early cultures of Peru and Mesoamerica. As my mind groped backwards, seeking insight into the conditions that confronted early man 10,000 years ago or more, it struck me that even when the glaciers were at their maximum extent over both the northern and southern hemispheres, there was a belt along the equator that was not iced over. Could this belt have been warm enough to allow people living there to develop the beginnings of a true culture?

Renée was an immense help to me in my investigations. She, too, became fascinated by the mystery surrounding these early cultures, and I discussed all my ideas with her. She began to concentrate on combing the literature and securing reprints of anything, from whatever scientific discipline, that might be relevant. But much of my time was then devoted to the test program for my parachute, and archaeology remained little more than a hobby until the harsh Canadian winters led me to search for a more suitable place to continue the tests. Miami, Florida, was an ideal choice. Not only was its climate suitable for year-round outdoor activity, but it was also a gateway to South America with excellent air connections to the major cities. It would be a perfect jumping-off point for trips to the continent that had fascinated me for so long. By this time Renée had graduated from Bennington College, we were married, and decided to establish our residence in Miami.

Although at first my major activity was the development of the related hardware for the parachute, I continued my research and study of the ancient cultures of the Americas. Then one day, by a fortuitous incident, I met a very unusual man, Dr. Cesar Valdivia, an Ecuadorian living in Florida for political reasons. The coincidence of his name amuses me still; the Valdivia culture, named for a small village on the southern coast of Ecuador, is the oldest culture generally known in South America. Dr. Valdivia was large by our standards, and huge by Ecuadorian; he was more than 6 feet tall and weighed at least 250 pounds. He was similarly big in wanting to help. We became good friends and he provided me with an entrée into Ecuadorian archaeology by putting me in touch with Captain Simon Plata Torres, the governor of the province of Esmeraldas, in northern Ecuador. Captain Torres had a good grasp of the major archaeological sites in coastal Ecuador and had himself done excavations on his own land.

By 1965, the years of reading, museum study, and discussion with experts had led to a conviction within me that I wanted to devote my time to an archaeological search for the roots of the great pre-Columbian cultures. I had become familiar with most of what was known of early South American cultural development—but that, I had discovered, was very little. There was no dearth of information about the Inca. But most of the early Spanish writings—and much of the modern material published—talked about the Inca as if they were the first to create notable culture in South America. At the time the Spaniards first set foot on the South American continent, the Inca Empire stretched from central Chile into southern Colombia—a span of 2500 miles. They called their empire *Tahuantinsuyo*, meaning the Four Quarters of the World, and they had achieved a high state of civilization. In the process of building their empire, the Inca had subjugated and conquered innumerable existing tribes and nations, impressing upon them their language, Quechua, and a religion based on the belief that the Inca ruler was the god-king descended from the sun. Consequently, the flourishing cultures that existed before the Inca conquest slowly declined and in many areas totally disappeared. Today, our understanding of these pre-Inca cultures is much broader; but as recently as 1955, everything seemed to be discussed in terms of the Inca.

To be sure, in specialized academic and museum circles, there was knowledge of other earlier cultures: the Chimu and Tiahuanaco immediately preceding the Inca, the Mochica and Nazca around 1000 years ago, and the Chavin before that. But discussions of these and a few other lesser-known cultures took place mostly in esoteric archaeologic journals, books, and seminars, and had not displaced the concentration on the Inca. As I reflected on this paradox, it seemed in a sense natural. When the conquistadors arrived early in the sixteenth century, they were interested only in pillaging the material wealth that, to their astonishment, seemed to abound everywhere. They had no interest in the cultural past of the Inca or that of their predecessors. The chroniclers and missionaries who followed the conquistadors established a

pattern, from their very first written reports, that was followed by many scholars in the succeeding two or three
centuries: that all cultural remains found in the Inca Empire were basically Incaico.

Much more was known of the great Mesoamerican cultures—the Aztecs, Toltecs, Maya, and others. But the Olmecs, now seen to be the mother culture of all the other
Mesoamerican societies, were just beginning to be discussed in 1955. Even today the origins, the antecedents,
of the Olmec are a complete mystery and the subject of
much dispute.

A fair amount of work had also been done in Colombia.
The national museum in Bogotá, I later learned, is quite
rich in materials that reveal a number of pre-Columbian
cultures, some of them dating back more than 2000 years.
Among the dominant pre-Columbian cultures, the San
Agustin, characterized by sophisticated underground funerary temple complexes and large stone monuments,
was fairly well known in archaeological circles. But in the
area of modern-day Ecuador very little had been studied,
and even less reported. I felt sure that there was much yet
to be discovered in Ecuador. Quito, its capital, had been
the capital of the northern Inca Empire, after it was divided into two parts before the death of the Inca
Huayna-Capac, in 1526. Before that it had been the capital of the mysterious Shyris nation.

In the 1890s a German archaeologist, Max Uhle, had
done pioneering work on the coastal plain of Peru, es-
tablishing the existence of several successive layers of migration and cultural development prior to the Inca. Later,
he investigated the high mesas surrounding Quito, and 12
miles from the city he unearthed a mastodon skeleton in a
cave associated with shards of both primitive and advanced types of pottery ware. For this signal achievement,
Uhle was rewarded with years of hoots and catcalls. It was
conventional knowledge at the time that the mastodon
had not survived after about 5000 B.C. and, therefore, it
was unthinkable that advanced pottery ware could be
found associated with it. Uhle was accused of having

faked the find. He was so stunned by the rebukes and criticisms that in later publications he sometimes omitted mention of the skeleton even when it was relevant. I was fascinated, however, by the idea that great animals such as the mastodon would have been moving back and forth through the Ecuadorian Andes.

In the early 1900s one of the very few archaeologists to emerge in Ecuador until recent years, Jacinto Jijon y Caamaño, did much work in the Ecuadorian highlands. Drawing on reputable investigations which he had also conducted in Peru, Jijon established that a number of distinct cultures had existed in Ecuador long before the Inca. The Inca had simply expanded their empire by conquest, traveling up the Andes from their center at Cuzco, in Peru, and taking control over new territory by force of arms. Jijon showed that long before this Inca expansion, pottery making, art, agriculture, and social organization had reached an advanced stage at many places in the Ecuadorian highlands. His observations and findings remain one of the very few sources of information on this area.

In the years following World War II, a banker from Guayaquil, Emilio Estrada, pursuing a personal interest, had become an accomplished archaeologist. In 1956, excavating on the coast of southern Ecuador, it was he who discovered the Valdivia culture, which dates back to 3500 B.C., making it the oldest pottery-using culture then known on the continent of South America. Estrada's work, as was true of Jijon's and others, was not generally known. The publications were small in scope and distribution—pamphlets printed under private auspices and distributed primarily to a small, select group of museums. One of these publications, *Cultura Valdivia,* was prepared after two Smithsonian Institution archaeologists, Betty Meggers and Clifford Evans, joined forces with Estrada to investigate further his original findings. I was immensely excited when I first came across this material. It established that the coastal plain of Ecuador was indeed very rich archaeologically.

However, even such extraordinarily motivated investigators as Estrada, Meggers, and Evans had not pursued
investigations in "the sierra," the Ecuadorian ranges of
the Andes and the high plateaus standing between them.
Their work was concentrated on the coastal plain. That
puzzled me. The great Inca cities, and many of the pre-
Inca cultures in Peru, had been located in the sierra. The
mesas—narrow plateaus of high land running north and
south between the parallel ranges of the Andes—extended like roadways from Peru through Ecuador and
into Colombia. In Colombia, too, evidences of high cultural development had been discovered in the mesas.
Ecuador also seemed to conform to the same cultural pattern, according to Jijon, but as yet no serious investigations had been undertaken. I felt certain that a determined search there would produce much.

Beyond the sierra to the east lies "the Oriente"—the
eastern slopes of the Andes and the beginning of the Amazon Basin. Of this huge area even less was known. Wasn't
there some chance of early cultural development in the
Oriente? Years before, as I searched various sources in
Canada, again and again I had come across references to
Colonel P. H. Fawcett, an English explorer who was active
in the Amazon around the turn of the century. Fawcett
had spent much time among the jungle people, described
them in great detail, and from many of them had heard
legends of the sacred cities of Manoa. Some of the adventures Fawcett described in his lectures and published journal, *Exploration Fawcett,* were so extraordinary that many
people doubted him and thought he was simply a story-
teller.

But I had always had the feeling, when reading this
journal, that Fawcett was telling the truth. It had the distinct flavor of being the record of a man who had been
there, and had actually undertaken each of the events described. Unfortunately, on his last expedition in 1925 during his search for Manoa, he disappeared and was never
heard from again. As I glanced at a map showing the
vastness of the Amazon territory, extending from Vene-

zuela through Colombia, Ecuador, Peru, Bolivia, and Brazil—an area of approximately 2,700,000 square miles, practically the size of the continental United States—I wondered how many secrets were still locked in that timeless land.

If I was going to pursue my archaeological search, Ecuador seemed the logical place to begin. So named because of its unique geographical position on the equator, Ecuador is a land of contrasts, transition, and mystery. Its broad coastal plain links the wetlands of southern Colombia, to the north, with the dry, desert-like land of northern Peru, to the south. To the east, behind the ranges of the Andes, lie the mysterious, low, swampy lands of the Amazon. Its size is comparable to the states of Nevada or Colorado, yet within this small area Ecuador is the most heterogeneous country on the South American continent. Almost every combination of climate, elevation, topography, and plant and animal life can be found there. The more I studied and compared the possibilities for man's survival and cultural development after the last ice age, the more I came to the conviction that this territory, lying on the equatorial belt, might have the greatest potential. Perhaps its geographic situation and its varied topography had given Ecuador the unique combination necessary to play a prominent role in the cultural prehistory of the Americas.

With Renée's support and encouragement, I decided that the next step was to go there myself, and in October of 1966 I was finally able to arrange my first visit. We had a tremendous feeling of jumping into something new and uncharted. Using our own resources, we knew that our first trips would have to be modest and tightly budgeted. But I felt confident that if my work was productive, support would be forthcoming from some quarter or other in the future.

The important thing was to get started.

CHAPTER 2

The Land of the Ancients

The captain's voice came through the loudspeaker: "Sorry, folks, we are in a holding pattern until the clouds clear enough to let us land in Quito." And a few moments later I learned from one of the stewardesses that if we couldn't land within thirty minutes, the flight would have to continue to its next stop—Lima, Peru. "No pilot would try to come down in this pea-soup weather," she said. "The approach is much too tricky through these high peaks surrounding the airport." Fine, I thought. On my first trip to Ecuador, a trip I had been dreaming about for years, I was going to land in Peru.

As we circled the city through dense clouds, I could rely only on my imagination for a picture of the land below. Ecuador, I knew, is cut up by these great ranges, or cordilleras, of the Andes Mountains, which run north and south parallel to each other, dividing the nation into three main regions: the coastal plain bordering the Pacific Ocean; the sierra, or mountain region; and to the east, the Amazon River Basin. The western range of the Andes, over which the road to the coastal plain crosses, and the central range are quite prominent on any map, and extend through the entire country, from Colombia in the north to Peru in the south. The third range, the eastern or "Oriental," is more fragmentary and is comprised of three sections, the names of which would become very important to me on later trips: to the south the Cordillera del Condor, which borders the valley of Zamora; north of

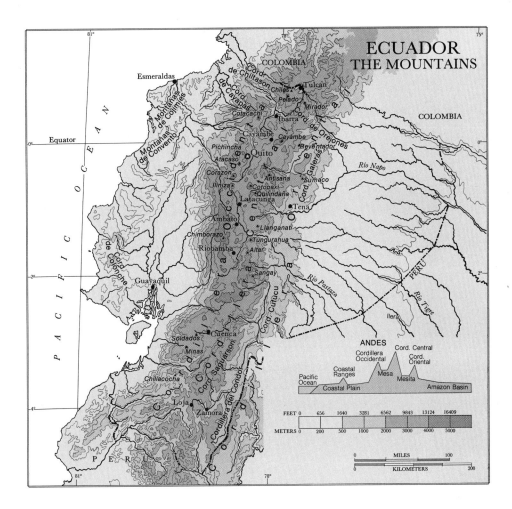

ECUADOR
THE MOUNTAINS

Esmeraldas

COLOMBIA

COLOMBIA

Equator

Tulcan
Chiles
Pelado
Cord. de Chiltason
Cord. de Cayapas
Cotacachi
Ibarra
Mirador
Cord. de Orejones
Cayambe
Cayambe
Reventador
Pichincha
Quito
Atacaso
Sumaco
Corazon
Antisana
Iliniza
Cotopaxi
Quilindaña
Latacunga
Tena
Ambato
Chimborazo
Llanganati
Tungurahua
Riobamba
Altar
Sangay
Río Napo
Río Pastaza
PERU
Río Tigre
Ilera
Cord. Cutucu
Guayaquil
Cord. de Colonche
Cuenca
Soldados
Minas
Cord. Sagtiatson
Chillacocha
Loja
Zamora
Cordillera del Condor
PERU

Montañas de Cojimie
Montañas de Convento

PACIFIC OCEAN

ANDES

Cord. Central
Cordillera Occidental
Cord. Oriental
Pacific Ocean
Coastal Ranges
Mesa
Mesita
Coastal Plain
Amazon Basin

FEET	0	656	1640	3281	6562	9843	13124	16409
METERS	0	200	500	1000	2000	3000	4000	5000

MILES   0   100
KILOMETERS   0   200

the Condor, the Cordillera Cutucu, which borders the Upano Valley; and further north, the Cordillera Galeras, which borders the Coca-Napo Valley.

Between these three great Andean ranges are high plateaus, or "mesas." In conventional usage, however, the term "the Mesa" designates the larger of the two plateaus, the long mesa between the western and the central cordillera. Quito and most of the important cities and towns of Ecuador, with the notable exception of Guayaquil, Manta, and Esmeraldas, are on the Mesa. Through it twists the newly built Pan-American Highway that travels from Colombia, through Ecuador, and down into Peru. The Ecuadorian portion of the ancient Inca Royal Road of the Sun took the same general route.

The Mesa is crossed periodically by ridges of volcanic origin, extending between the western and the central cordilleras like rungs on a ladder. These ridges divide the Mesa into valleys, each named after the largest river coursing through it. In spite of its elevation, the Mesa is the most densely populated area of Ecuador. It averages 3000 meters (9800 ft.) above sea level, and much of it is above 3500 meters (11,450 ft.). The highest peak in Ecuador is Chimborazo, a massive dormant volcano about 150 kilometers south of Quito, close to the Pan-American Highway. Chimborazo's elevation is 6267 meters (20,561 ft.), which is only 712 meters less than Mount Aconcagua in Argentina, the highest peak in all the Americas.

Twenty minutes went by as we circled Quito; then, suddenly, the silver gleam of the city against the green slopes of the volcano Pinchincha came into view through a hole in the clouds. We would be able to land after all. A few minutes later the big prop plane put down at Mariscal Sucre Airport. Walking the 100 meters to the immigration building, I immediately felt the effects of the altitude. We were at 9350 feet.

Surrounded by incredible snow-capped volcanic peaks, only 14 miles south of the equator, Quito is named after the ancient Quitu tribe whose name in the Indian tongue means "the beginning." The Quitu Indians believed that

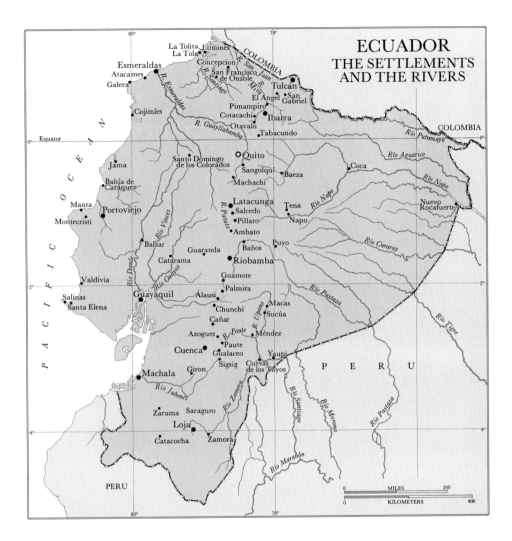

ECUADOR
THE SETTLEMENTS
AND THE RIVERS

COLOMBIA

La Tolita Limones
La Tola
Esmeraldas
Atacames Concepcion
Galera San Francisco
de Onzole
Tulcán
San
Gabriel
El Angel
Pimampiro
Cojimíes Cotacachi
Otavalo Ibarra
R. Guayllabamba Tabacundo

Equator

R. Esmeraldas
R. San Juan
Mira
R. Santiago

Río Putumayo

COLOMBIA

Río Aguarico

Santo Domingo
de los Colorados
Quito
Sangolquí
Machachi Baeza
Coca

Río Napo

Jama

Bahía de
Caráquez

Manta
Montecristi
Portoviejo

Latacunga
Salcedo
Pillaro
Ambato

Tena
Napo

R. Patate

Nuevo
Rocafuerte

Río Napo

Río Curaray

Balzar
Guaranda Baños
Puyo

Río Vinces

Catarama
Riobamba

Guamote
Valdivia
Palmira

Río Daule

Río Guayas

Guayaquil Alausí

Río Pastaza

Chunchi
Cañar
Macas
Sucúa

Salinas
Santa Elena

Río Tigre

Azogues
Méndez

R. Upano

R. Paute

Cuenca Paute
Gualaceo
Machala Giron Sigsig
Yaupi
Cuevas
de los Tayos

P E R U

Río Jubones

Zaruma Saraguro
Loja

Río Zamora

Río Santiago

Río Morona

Río Pastaza

Catacocha Zamora

Río Marañón

PERU

0   MILES   200
0   400
KILOMETERS

PACIFIC OCEAN

the center of the world was a mountain peak that today is known as "La Marca"—the Mark. Incredibly, this peak is less than 1 kilometer from the equator—Latitude 0-0-0—established by an official geodetic survey made in 1936. Quito, the capital of Ecuador, is also one of the oldest continually inhabited cities in this hemisphere, having survived volcanic eruptions, earthquakes, and conquests. Burnt to ashes by the Inca chieftain, Rumiñahui, in 1534, to deny it to the Spanish invaders, it was rebuilt by Sebastián de Belalcázar, a lieutenant of Pizarro, the conquistador. Today, inhabited by whites (mostly Spanish), Indians, blacks, mestizos, and mulattos, Quito is a city where the new and the old blend in harmony, and where Indian tongues and Quechua dialects mix with the Spanish language.

I checked into the modern Hotel Quito, recently rebuilt on a hill overlooking the city, and that afternoon I spoke on the phone with a cousin of Captain Simon Plata Torres, the governor of the province of Esmeraldas, who had invited me to visit him when I came to Ecuador. His cousin assured me that Captain Torres was expecting me in Esmeraldas, but in the meantime, he had mentioned my name to Father Julio Herrera, the head of the parish of Guapulo, a small village near Quito. He said that Father Herrera, who spoke English and was also interested in the ancient cultures of Ecuador, had offered me his assistance while I was in Quito. I was aware of the importance of contact with the clergy in South America, and took the initiative of calling Father Herrera to get acquainted. At his invitation, I went to Guapulo by way of a narrow, twisting road that descends into the valley behind the Hotel Quito and then becomes the head of a trail running eastward through the next range of mountains into the Oriente.

Father Herrera turned out to be the "procurador" of supplies for the Franciscan missions on the Galapagos, the group of islands lying 500 miles off the coast of Ecuador made famous by Charles Darwin. An intelligent and very knowledgeable man, he had been a friend of many governmental ministers and presidents over the years. As we discussed archaeology, he told me about a book on a culture called "Tolita"—a book that would prove to be pivotal in my archaeological search.

The next day, I visited the Casa de la Cultura in Quito to familiarize myself with the art and artifacts of the ancient cultures that had attracted my interest for so long. Surely here, I thought, I would find a valuable collection of the materials that had already been discovered—and clues as to where to start my search. I was sadly disappointed. From the outside, the Casa de la Cultura was impressive enough. It was a large, stone Spanish colonial building on one of the main squares of the city. But, I later learned, it was far from a center of disinterested archaelogical investigation. Traditionally, it was regarded by the government as a hornet's nest of subversion. It seemed to attract the sort of intellectuals and literati with independent modes of thought whose mere presence in groups larger than three always make the authorities distrustful and uneasy.

Inside, the Casa had meeting rooms, a dance school and small concert hall, a large display of native crafts and wares produced by the modern-day Indians, and a number of exhibits of colonial objects—paintings, spurs, and stirrups, armor and weapons, and clothing. But the ancient pre-Columbian cultures were represented only by a few artifacts displayed here and there throughout the building amid all the other material, with very little thought, and with virtually no accompanying explanatory material. I couldn't get over it. To the south, in Peru, an extraordinary and dazzling effort was being devoted to the investigation and presentation of both the Inca and pre-Inca cultures. And to the north, in Colombia, there was the marvelously rich National Museum in Bogotá. But here, at the center, in the country that I had come to suspect had played a major role in the prehistory of the Americas, the Ecuadorians seemed to have much more concern for their colonial, post-conquest history.

As I walked out of the Casa de la Cultura and stood on

the front steps, I felt rather alone. My hopes for finding some guidance here were gone. I sensed that if I was to have any success in my quest, it would be done with very little help from anyone else. But things have a way of taking a funny turn. Two days later, I had the occasion to meet a prominent nobleman, Conde Jacinto Jijon Caamaño, a descendant of the famed investigator Jacinto Jijon y Caamaño, who had an extraordinary art collection. I visited his home, was shown the collection, and was astounded. It was extraordinary indeed. The pieces there were so rich, so sophisticated, and obviously so ancient, that they confirmed my feelings about the potential value of Ecuador. I also realized that there must be many other Ecuadorians, men of intellect and influence, who were interested in the pre-colonial history of their country.

The lack of awareness that the majority of Ecuadorians appeared to have for the pre-Columbian cultures still puzzled me, however. I did not see how they could ignore the evidence of these cultures that existed right in the midst of their everyday lives. Overlooking Quito, on a large hill known as the Panecillo (which may not be natural), there stood in pre-Columbian times a Temple of the Sun. Today a mysterious cylindrical shaft, known as the Olla, built of bricks and stone and open to the sky, stands on the same ground. The purpose of this structure is not known; there is the possibility that a particular star or constellation, appearing in the opening on a particular day of the year, may have had significance. No one knows. The most attention it gets, as your nose will tell you from any point within 200 feet, is from passing citizens who use it as an impromptu lavatory.

After spending a few more days in Quito, it was time to go to Esmeraldas, a small city on the northwestern coast and the home of Captain Torres. It was my introduction to travel in Ecuador—and what an introduction. The roads to the coast proved to be more primitive than I could have imagined, but the bus alone was a memorable adventure. It was not an ordinary, colorless, anonymously regular busline, with vehicles leaving at scheduled intervals. The bus to Esmeraldas was a venerable vehicle, driven ("propelled," it seemed) by its owner, an old veteran who took it upon himself to operate this lone vehicle over this route as his sole means of livelihood.

We started out at six o'clock in the morning, and the driver would stop anywhere to drop off or pick up any man, woman, or child. Also welcomed aboard were assorted pigs, chickens, sheep, and geese—in fact, almost anything that moved, as long as it was accompanied by a human being. The need to urinate on the part of any of his passengers was similarly an excellent reason to stop, as was the appearance of any of a dozen little roadside stands along the way where the passengers could buy a beer and discuss the latest news while the bus waited for them patiently. Children were crying and yelling and running around. Baskets loaded with produce and goods to be sold crowded the aisle. The smells of food and perspiration were overpowering. After only a very few miles I had to repress forcibly the urge to get off and walk. There was a dramatic contrast between my fellow passengers and the educated Ecuadorians I had met in the last several days. Amid this sea of smells and noise swirling around me, I realized that Ecuador consisted either of a few people with position and money, or great numbers of these unremembered poor. One extreme or the other— very little in between.

Even the priests. I sat next to an aged padre in an old faded frock with a big grease stain down the front of it. Perhaps thinking of my boyhood in Italy, where the priest was often the best-educated man in the community, I struck up a conversation and told him I was interested in the archaeology of Ecuador.

"What do you mean by archaeology?" he asked.

"Well," I said, "you know—the study of the old things."

"Oh," he said, "Incaico." It was a response that I have since encountered many times from the preponderant majority of Ecuadorians. In their minds, anything at all that dates back before the conquest is Inca.

But I persisted: "Well, no. Things older than the Inca."

"But before the Inca there was nothing," the priest exclaimed.

"There had to be somebody here before the Inca," I said. "We know that they conquered other people."

"Ah, yes, I see. They were a bunch of savages."

With that, I realized there was very little point in trying to continue our conversation.

A few kilometers south of Quito, the road turned west and the bus started to climb up the Cordillera Occidental—the western Andean range. At this altitude, above 10,000 feet, it is not uncommon to drive through clouds. When we neared the San Juan Pass, a pile-up of vehicles forced us to come to a complete stop. The driver of a truck in front yelled that a landslide had occurred during the night, but that a crew was already at work clearing the road. This did not create any unusual reaction. It was a frequent occurrence.

The primitive roads of Ecuador are often obliterated by landslides, or cave in under heavy rains. Most of Ecuador's soil is of volcanic origin, which means it retains water poorly. Further, it does not compact and stay in place as well as loam or clay. This, combined with the steep slopes and the constant (sometimes torrential) rainfall, causes the steady formation of mud, tons of which periodically break loose and roar down the mountainsides. Every road in the country, particularly in the Oriente, has probably required clearing or reconstruction a number of times because the terrain on which it rests simply eats away and slides into the canyon below.

We waited at the San Juan Pass for two hours until the good news bounced from one vehicle to the next that the road was clear, and our bus became part of a convoy that slowly made its way through the pass. With the warming sun the clouds lifted and I could see, from the saddle of the pass, the white-capped peak of Volcan Corazon and through the mist, further southeast, the mighty volcano Cotopaxi, dressed in virgin snow. The Cotopaxi, the highest active volcano in the world, ranks second among the eight peaks exceeding 5000 meters (16,360 feet) in Ecuador.

Halfway between Quito and Esmeraldas lies Santo Domingo de los Colorados, larger than a village and an important crossroads between the sierra and the coast. The route from the capital splits here into three different directions: north to Esmeraldas, southwest to Manta, and south to Guayaquil. As soon as the bus pulled into the square, a wave of men, women, and children surrounded us, shouting and offering us food, souvenirs, tickets for the national lottery, cigarettes, and everything that a well-stocked bazaar could carry. Because of the time we had lost at the San Juan Pass, I hoped that we would not stay in Santo Domingo long. But our driver cleared his throat and announced, "Today, we will stop here for two hours." To the tumultuous inquiry of why, he replied matter-of-factly, "The usual mechanical problem." No one knew what that problem might be, but we accepted his explanation with resignation.

Twelve kilometers west of Santo Domingo is the village of San Miguel, and I knew that in the jungle nearby live the descendants of an ancient and colorful nation of Indians known as the Colorados. The life of these people hasn't changed very much from the past. The modern ways of Santo Domingo have not greatly influenced their archaic tribal system. Colorado men and women still dress in their distinctive way—a blue and white strip of cloth tied around the waist reaching to the knee, with the rest of the body nude. The men of the Colorado tribe can be distinguished from men of all the other jungle tribes by their hairdo, which they set themselves by applying red dye made from seed of the achioto plant mixed with the rubber-like juice of another plant. The result is striking: to the person who glimpses them for the first time, they look as if they have a big red leaf glued to their heads.

Today the Colorados live in peace, but at the time of the Spanish conquest they ferociously fought enslavement and massacred many of the Spaniards. Their cacique—

tribal chief—is also a powerful medicine man, and many whites living in Santo Domingo seek him out in times of sickness. In the legends of the Colorado Indians there are stories that tell of their ancestors, who built stone cities, temples, and dwellings thousands of years before the coming of the white man. Today, in the jungle where legends say there were such splendors, there remain only a few stelae, carved with undecipherable glyphics and symbols that the modern Colorado faithfully venerates. I hoped one day to be able to visit them.

When the bus was finally under way again, we headed northward toward the coastal plain and Esmeraldas. In the north and south of Ecuador, this plain is about 50 kilometers wide, but through much of the middle of the country it ranges up to 200 kilometers in breadth. There it is the broadest Pacific coastal plain to be found in South America. The route to Esmeraldas, however, consists almost entirely of twisting, jolting mountain roads made of gravel. When we finally reached a paved road, the driver turned around and said to me triumphantly, "Señor, I told you we were going to drive on some cement!" We were 2 kilometers outside of Esmeraldas.

We lurched into the city after a journey of eight hours. Esmeraldas, I soon noticed, was almost entirely a black community. I called Captain Torres, who greeted me warmly, and we agreed to meet the following day. Then I was directed to the Hotel Diana, the best that the city had to offer, I was told. After I checked in, a young black boy carried my baggage up to a room. When he opened the door, I was taken aback. The room was no more than 2 by 3 meters. There was a large bed in the middle, and at the foot of it, a narrow wooden box about 2 meters high. Inside this enclosure, I discovered a tube for a shower with a toilet underneath—no door on the wooden box, and no window in the room. There was, however, an opening under the ceiling all around the room, to let the mosquitoes in, and a steel rod extended from one wall to the other, its sole purpose to suspend a drape of mosquito netting over the bed. If this was the best the town had to

offer, there was no question of complaining. I tried to figure out how to take my shower. There wasn't much
choice. I sat down on the toilet and let the water drip
slowly over me.

In contrast to the hotel, the dinner I had that evening
was the best one could dream of—lobster is a common
dish in that part of the country. After dinner, I walked
down the main throughfare of the town and was engulfed
by a throng of black faces. It was the hour of the *paseo*—
promenade. Children played in the streets and doorways,
and young men eyed the passing girls while strumming
on their guitars. Everywhere there was laughter and singing. It was very hot; it's not rare for the temperature to be
as high as 90 degrees F. at nine o'clock in the evening.
The blacks of Esmeraldas are descendants of the African
slaves imported during colonial times to work the land.
After obtaining their freedom, they concentrated in this
region where the climate was similar to that of their native
land.

Although it is a provincial capital, Esmeraldas is not
much bigger than a country town. The buildings that one
can call modern stand side by side with houses built of
bamboo slats and plaster. Fishing, and the export of the
bananas and timber that grow in the tropical forests extending to the foothills of the Andean slopes, are the
main industries. The skills of the master boat builders in
this area are recognized throughout South America. It is a
family enterprise, and the skills are passed on from generation to generation. Boatyards dot the banks of the Rio
Esmeraldas, which flows southwest of the city.

Slowly, as the evening progressed, the streets emptied
and the people drifted back to their dwellings. I returned
to the Hotel Diana, hoping to have a good night's sleep. I
lay down in bed and found it impossible to turn to either
side. The springs were so weak that I might as well have
been lying in a hammock. But I was exhausted and soon
fell asleep.

The following morning I met Captain Torres, a short,
dark-skinned man in his sixties. Dressed in a black suit

with a white tie, he looked more like an old-time preacher than the governor of a province. His long fingers, with well-manicured nails, kept flicking at his jacket to remove the specks of ashes that continually fell from a cigarette that never left his lips; he was an inveterate chain smoker.

As we sipped thick black Ecuadorian coffee in a small café near the Hotel Diana, we were joined by Captain Torres's son-in-law, Democrito Caicedo, who played the role of both private secretary and business manager to the governor. This I discovered when we began speaking about archaeology. After the governor eloquently declared the importance of preserving the past, Democrito whispered to me that his father-in-law had recovered many artifacts from his extensive land holdings in the northwest corner of Esmeraldas Province, and he was interested in selling some of them. Captain Torres invited me to his house that evening so he could show me some of the pieces he had discovered, not only on his own property but from other areas as well.

That evening, after consuming a typical Ecaudorian dinner of fried pork and bananas with rice and beans, Captain Torres took me to a small house adjoining his larger two-story home. There he showed me several pottery artifacts from Atacames, an area on the coast south of Esmeraldas, and many beautiful little pieces, some of them gold, that he had found on an island called Tolita located at the mouth of the Rio Santiago about 70 kilometers northeast of Esmeraldas. He and his family occasionally went there, he told me, and they had found these pieces simply by digging into large tolas—the ancient burial mounds that dot the island. Looking at the beauty of these artifacts, and thinking of the ease with which they had been recovered on a family outing, I thought: "Such richness—and the rest of the world knows almost nothing about it."

Señor Torres then took out a little bag from which he produced a small gold bead, about the size of a BB. He told me to look at it very carefully. I saw that the surface of the bead was marked in some fashion, and reached into my pocket for my magnifying glass. As I looked through the glass, I was astonished. Circling the middle of the bead was a delicately wrought band of geometric design. I could hardly contain my excitement. A culture that could produce such fine work on such a minute scale had obviously achieved a very high level of craftsmanship. Captain Torres told me that many such beads had been found on Tolita, scattered in various places across the surface of the island. Standing there with the beautiful gold bead in my hand, I wondered: Who were the people who made this; where did they come from?

Captain Torres showed me several more artifacts in his collection, one of which was a pottery jaguar from Tolita. When I saw it, my thoughts turned eastward. The jaguar is a creature of the Amazon; it is not seen anywhere on the coast. Either the people who had made this piece came originally from the Amazon, or they learned of the jaguar from others who carried their knowledge westward over the mountains and down into the coastal plains.

Captain Torres also showed me artifacts that he and his family had found in the coastal area west of Esmeraldas, and Democrito, who had discovered many artifacts himself, offered to take me to see some burial mounds he had excavated near Cabo de San Francisco, south of the city. When I left them late that evening and headed back to the dreary Hotel Diana, I was very encouraged by what I had seen and heard. I wanted to explore both the coastal areas around Esmeraldas and the island of Tolita, and the burial mounds near Cabo de San Francisco would be a good place to begin. I knew that the cultures of Atacames, Esmeraldas, and Tolita had been classified by archaeologists as having developed in the period between 500 B.C. to A.D. 500, but very little else was known about them. Were they in some way related, I wondered? It seemed to me that if I could trace a relationship between the artifacts of these two cultures, it might provide some clues as to their origins and development.

During the next few days as I waited for Democrito to make arrangements for the trip to Cabo de San Francisco,

I was able to visit the Casa de la Cultura in Esmeraldas. It consisted of two dirty rooms on the first floor of an old building. The keeper of the collection, a young woman in her thirties, opened the door and proudly announced that the total number of pieces on the premises was 750. That was as far as her knowledge went. All piled up, helter skelter, in the corners and along the walls of these two dusty rooms were pottery vases, pots and bowls, human and animal figures, pieces of every description. There was no classification or categorization whatsoever. However, I could see that the Esmeraldas, Tolita, and Atacames cultures were well represented.

Ceramic mask with gold ornament on ear. Atacames.

Democrito and I left for Cabo de San Francisco on a beautiful fall morning in his beat-up panel *camioneta* (small truck). We followed a small road southwest from Esmeraldas along the coast, passing near La Rocas cove in Atacames. Democrito told me that a few years before, in the Atacames area, torrential rains had swelled a stream so that it undercut a high bank.. The stream bank caved in., revealing a tremendously rich burial ground. Instantly, the area was converted into an open museum, a storehouse of artifacts. But no attempt had been made to preserve the site or assemble the artifacts for archaeological study. Now they were scattered to the four winds. It was yet another example of the Ecuadorians' indifference to their pre-Columbian history.

Our destination was Tonchigüe, a small hamlet nestled between a low hill and the mouth of a small river emptying into the Pacific Ocean. There the road ended, but Democrito was hoping that the water level of the river would be low enough to cross it with the truck and continue driving on the rocky beach. But when we reached Tonchigüe, the river was impassable and we had to leave the truck behind. We took to our feet, after fording the river by mules borrowed from a local campesino.

We followed a foot trail that ran parallel to the coast, heading for Cabo de San Francisco, and on the way we met a black man named Ramon, a campesino, who lived along the trail. We were quite thirsty, and at first we thought we might be able to get some water from Ramon. I had second thoughts as I looked around at his place. Dirt and chicken droppings were everywhere. But his casa, a thatched-roof hut standing on thin stilts, was surrounded by tall coconut trees, and I asked Ramon if he could get us a coconut. Up the tree he went. I even had some misgivings about the coconut, coming from a tree that was so profoundly rooted in chickenshit, but thirst won out over scruples and I drank the milk.

As Democrito and I rested in the shade, I saw one of Ramon's pigs feeding greedily out of a stone *metate* (trough) nearby. Looking closer I saw that the trough was obviously hand-hewn, and that its sides were covered with carved marks. I asked Ramon where he got the trough, and he said, "Oh, up in the cemetery—not very far from here."

Democrito, seeing my interest, asked Ramon if he would show me this cemetery. He demurred, saying that there were many snakes there, but when I gave him a small tip, his fear vanished and we set out for the cemetery.

On reaching the area, it was evident that many excavations had taken place. There were no tolas; rather, the graves were relatively shallow, less than 2 meters deep. Originally, each of the graves had been closed over with wooden logs, on top of which was a layer of stone, and then dirt. The wood was guayacan, an extraordinary South American wood that is impervious to water and insects, making it virtually indestructible. Most of the guayacan was still intact, but with the passage of time the earth had settled somewhat, so that the top of each grave was slightly depressed below the level of the surrounding ground. These depressions were the tip-off for the *huaceros* (excavators) who visited the area. Democrito told me that they went around with heavy steel bars, ramming them down into the ground wherever they found a depression. If the bar went through, they began to dig. They occasionally find a few gold earrings or nose rings, but not much else that is of interest to them. There were many pieces of pottery lying around, some of which had doubtless been broken by the *huaceros* checking to see if there might be gold pieces inside.

When we returned to Ramon's house, we found that he had two nicely preserved clay vessels of a style similar to those of the Atacames culture. He kept salt in one and beans in the other, and probably appreciated the imperviousness to moisture of this fired pottery just as much as the original owner had, over 2000 years ago. They had obviously been recovered from the cemetery. Democrito asked Ramon, "Aren't you afraid of the spirit of the dead?"

"No, I'm not," Ramon answered. "I'm not an Indian." The blacks have very little day-to-day contact with the Indians, but they are familiar with their culture and beliefs. The Indians have a fear of any object that comes out of a grave, and most of them would not keep such a piece in their homes.

We still had several kilometers to travel before reaching Cabo de San Francisco, so we said goodbye to Ramon and got back on the trail. As we walked along, I could not get my mind off the trough Ramon's pig had enjoyed so thoroughly. I knew that the stone out of which it had been carved was of volcanic origin, and such a piece had to have come from the mountains. Who could have brought it to Esmeraldas: a culture that had suffered climatic or economic changes in the sierra, and had moved down to the coast? Or was it brought down as an article of trade, or perhaps retrieved by a coastal people who had great need for troughs to grind their corn in, but very little stone in their own area with which to make them? Did it have a ceremonial value that compelled some religious observants to carry it all that distance? The strange carvings on the trough lent some credence to that idea. Considering first the jaguar head in Captain Torres's collection, and now Ramon's volcanic stone trough, it seemed to me that the answers to my questions could only be found up in those mountains.

Democrito and I followed a twisting trail for several kilometers until, finally, we reached Cabo de San Francisco. Democrito took me inland to the burial ground and showed me the tolas that he and others had excavated. They were about 2 meters high and several meters long, and trenches could be seen in many of them where the excavations had taken place. Democrito described the clay pieces that had been found in these tolas, and we looked at some of the broken pieces of pottery that were lying around on the ground throughout the entire area. I could see that these shards were similar in style to pieces I had seen in the Casa de la Cultura in Esmeraldas and in private collections in Quito, and I began to think of how rich this burial ground must have been—how many pieces had come out of it, and had been carried to all corners of the country and even the world. I marveled at how incredibly productive these unknown, forgotten people had been.

By this time, it was quite late in the day and Democrito and I headed for the village of San Francisco, where we spent the night with friends of his. As I lay in bed before going to sleep that night, my head was swimming with impressions and with the awareness that each new clue, each new bit of information, led not to the answers I was seeking but only to more questions.

We got up early the next morning and began the hike back. After another coconut drink at Ramon's, we reached Tonchigüe, reclaimed the old truck, and gratefully heaved our weary bodies into the seats. However, our relief lasted only until we reached Sua, a small hamlet near a river that we had crossed safely the day before. On our way down the tide had been out, the river low, and the old truck had made it across without too much trouble. Now, however, the tide was in and an entirely different prospect faced us. Risking all, Democrito firmly shifted the gears, drove down into the high water—and got magnificently stuck.

It was then that I received a first-hand lesson in the buoyancy of the balsa-wood rafts once constructed by the

Ceramic figurine with head of an opossum and a human body. Cabo de San Francisco.

people of pre-Columbian coastal cultures. A number of young men came to our rescue with balsa-wood logs, which they forced under the truck. Finally, after much struggle and enough perspiration so that I now felt myself to be truly a member of the coastal community, we got the truck afloat and, carefully, against the current of the incoming tide, maneuvered it to the opposite bank. Democrito got in, put it into low, and converted it once again to a land-faring creature.

Back in Esmeraldas, I arranged to meet Señora Maria Gratia Nabon, a lady of whom Captain Torres had spoken highly. He told me that she was an experienced trader of artifacts, quite familiar with the numerous findings in this province, and I was curious to see her collection. Señora Nabon greeted me in the doorway of her simple stone-and-cane house. Neatly dressed in black, she loved to display her wealth in jewelry by wearing it at all times—day or night. The children on her street called her the *arbol de Navidad*—the Christmas tree. She graciously invited me to the upper floor—the cane part of the house—where she kept a number of remarkable pieces: pottery bowls, plates, hollow and solid figurines, masks, and mythic animals in the recognizable Esmeraldas style. She also had a number of pieces from Tolita. She and her two brothers had gone to the island many times to dig, she told me, and had found pieces on almost every occasion. I noted that all those on display were in a remarkable state of preservation.

Among her Tolita pieces, Señora Nabon pulled out several small pottery jaguar heads that riveted my attention. Here again in the artifacts of a coastal culture was this animal that existed only in the Amazon, on the other side of the Andes Mountains. I was electrified as I held one of these pieces in my hand. The clues were mounting, one upon the other, all pointing eastward to the Andes and the jungle beyond.

Señora Nabon told me that by far the greatest number of artifacts from Tolita had been recovered by an Italian whose family had lived in Ecuador for many years: Señor

Ceramic jaguar head. Tolita.

Donato Yannuzzelli, who was nicknamed *El Lupo* (the wolf). Yannuzzelli and his brother were in the banana export business, but many years ago he had received permission from the government to begin a gold placer operation on Tolita, and had brought in heavy placer equipment. Stories circulated that Yannuzzelli had recovered an immense amount of gold, and as part of this placer operation, regularly came across large numbers of artifacts. Señora Nabon wasn't sure he would be willing to see me, but she felt that if I could get through to him somehow, he might be helpful.

I was not able to see Señor Yannuzzelli, but I met once more with Captain Torres, Democrito, and their families. I was scheduled to return to Miami a few days later, so I made plans with Democrito for another trip in about three months, and he enthusiastically offered me his assistance again. Then I braced myself for the bus trip back to Quito.

On my return to the capital, I revisited the Casa de la Cultura, and the private collections I had seen earlier, to study the pieces, this time with better-informed eyes. I was struck again by the carved stone artifacts in these collections and wondered whether a relationship might exist between them and Ramon's trough. From the abundance of artifacts that had come to light in the many excavations in the Esmeraldas region, it was evident that its ancient inhabitants had reached a remarkable stage of development hundreds of years before the birth of Christ. They excelled not only in the art of pottery making but also in the art of working with precious metals: silver, gold, and platinum, sometimes in the pure stage, sometimes mixed with copper for hardening.

But that did not mean the cultures that mastered these arts had originated there. It takes time for a culture to progress from one stage of development to the next, and prior to the period generally ascribed to the Esmeraldas cultures, geological studies reveal that the environment of this region was not conducive to the development of societies capable of such a high degree of craftsmanship. For before 1500 B.C. this area was subject to continuous flooding from the network of hundreds of rivers flowing down from the highlands. Only by about 1000 B.C. did the soggy and swampy land become dry enough to permit the growth of small settlements. Thus its inhabitants had come from some place else. But where? I had already discovered clues linking the Esmeraldas cultures in northwestern Ecuador to the sierra and the Amazon Basin. Perhaps, I speculated, an investigation of the cultures that had flourished in the central and southern coastal areas would provide additional clues.

To solve the mystery, I now realized, would take many trips to Ecuador, and investigations in almost every corner of that diverse and difficult country. Moreover, I would have to bring to my search an understanding of all the disciplines of both anthropology and archaeology. Looking for artifacts would be the easiest part of the job; they existed by the hundreds of thousands all over the country. My search would have to go beyond that. I was interested in the cultures that had made them—and why. Each artifact was, after all, merely one small piece in a gigantic puzzle which, if properly assembled, could reveal the origins and development of the cultures they represented, as well as the physical, mental, and spiritual lives of its members. From the beginning of time, man has instinctively had visions of his own historical significance and has attempted to register his concept of life, his aspirations and ideals, on lasting monuments. The artifacts so carelessly excavated and so haphazardly collected in Ecuador were, I knew, the monuments of remarkable, but virtually unstudied and unknown, cultures.

As I flew back to Miami, my mind was filled with a crazy mixture of impressions. I was excited by the potential of my search in Ecaudor, but equally awed by the immensity of the work to be done.

CHAPTER 3

Tracking Prehistory

I spent only six weeks in Miami before returning to Quito, and there I was able to acquire the booklet about Tolita Island that Father Herrera had mentioned to me on my first trip. It had been published in 1941, and the author was Captain Jorge Ribadeneira, a geologist. As I began reading the booklet, and thought back on some remarks that acquaintances had made about it, it became evident that it had been written and published under the aegis of the Ecuadorian government to explode Donato Yannuzzelli's claim that Tolita was the site of natural placer gold. The booklet went carefully into the geology of the island and established that there was no naturally occurring gold placer there. However, there were ancient burial sites all over the island from which gold had been recovered in the form of manmade artifacts. The implications were clear to all who read the booklet. For years Yannuzzelli had been melting down gold artifacts found in these burial sites and casting them into ingots for sale. He had run his expensive placer equipment merely as a front.

Over the four or five years, beginning in 1935, in which Yannuzzelli had this little scheme going, he is said to have produced around 250 to 300 kilos of gold (550 to 660 lbs.), or more, and even today it makes me wince to think of the number of artifacts that must have been melted down and destroyed. Considering the fact that the ancient peoples of Tolita usually used very thin hammered sheets of gold, or copper plated with gold, to produce their pre-

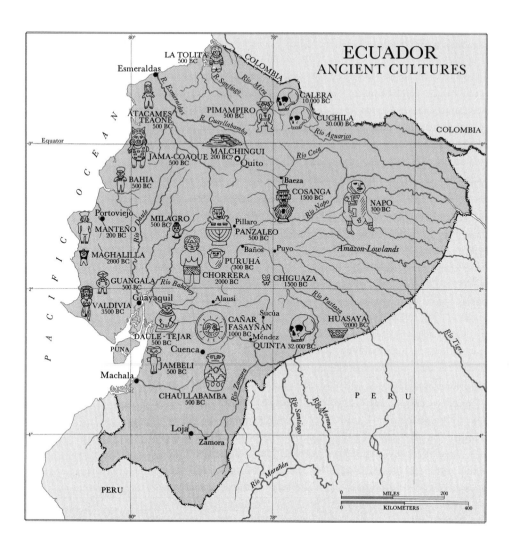

ECUADOR
ANCIENT CULTURES

LA TOLITA
500 BC

Esmeraldas

COLOMBIA

R. Santiago

Río Mira

CALERA
10,000 BC

ATACAMES
TEAONE
500 BC

PIMAMPIRO
500 BC

R. Esmeraldas

CUCHILA
30,000 BC

COLOMBIA

R. Guayllabamba

Río Aguarico

Equator

MALCHINGUI
200 BC?

Quito

Río Coca

JAMA-COAQUE
500 BC

Baeza

BAHIA
500 BC

COSANGA
1500 BC

NAPO
300 BC

Río Napo

Portoviejo

Río Daule

MILAGRO
500 BC

Pillaro

MANTEÑO
200 BC

PANZALEO
500 BC

Puyo

Amazon Lowlands

Baños

MAGHALILLA
2000 BC

PURUHÁ
(300 BC)

CHORRERA
2000 BC

CHIGUAZA
1500 BC

GUANGALA
500 BC

Río Babahoyo

Río Pastaza

Alausi

Guayaquil

VALDIVIA
3500 BC

Sucúa

CAÑAR
FASAYÑAN
1000 BC

HUASAYA
2000 BC

Méndez

DAULE-TEJAR
500 BC

QUINTA 32,000 BC

PUNA

Cuenca

Río Zamora

Río Santiago

Río Morona

JAMBELI
500 BC

Río Tigre

Machala

CHAULLABAMBA
500 BC

PERU

Loja

Zamora

Río Marañón

PERU

PACIFIC OCEAN

MILES   200
KILOMETERS   400

cious artifacts, Yannuzzelli had probably melted down hundreds, even thousands of artifacts before the government abruptly stopped his operation in 1942.

In spite of Yannuzzelli's wholesale destruction, Ribadeneira's booklet offered me great encouragement. It called Tolita "an archaeologic monument," and went on to describe thirty-seven large tolas that dot the southern part of the island, the majority of which were 4 to 6 meters tall, and anywhere from 10 to 30 meters long. I also learned that the island, as a result of alluviation, was covered only by an average of 1 meter of topsoil; it could not possibly have provided the amount of earth necessary to build such a number of tolas. It would seem then that the only other source for this material would be the mainland. I could hardly imagine how the people who built the tolas could have moved that much earth across the swift currents of the Rio Santiago, to say nothing of the skill and labor involved in making the number of gold and clay artifacts that had been found, and promised yet to be found, in this rich burial ground. Ribadeneira's booklet, and the photographs of the tolas it contained, kindled my mind and I itched to get back to Esmeraldas Province, where this island—and who knew what else—lay waiting.

From what I had just read, I had mixed feelings about contacting Yannuzzelli. But if what Señora Nabon had told me about him was true, he might have in his possession the largest private collection I had yet seen. I knew I had to meet him if at all possible, and having no more graceful way to proceed, I picked up the telephone and called him. I introduced myself, we talked for some minutes in Italian, and he agreed to see me in Esmeraldas. I think now that much of the credit for the success of that call was due to the Italian. Yannuzzelli opened up more readily to a man who spoke his native tongue.

A week later I was in Esmeraldas, standing before the home of Yannuzzelli—*El Lupo.* If Ribadeneira's booklet on Tolita had not given me an insight into the origin of that nickname, the man himself did. About sixty or sixty-five years old, he was rough, hard, and wily. But from the tone of our first conversation, I had the feeling that, in his own way, he was very pleased that a foreigner had heard about his archaeological activities. Of course I didn't mention the booklet, and when I expressed an interest in seeing his collection, he immediately pointed to his jeep and said, "Jump in." Yannuzzelli was a man of action.

He drove me to his country house a few kilometers outside of Esmeraldas where there was a small guest house which, he said, had been converted into a private museum. To me, after we had entered, it looked more like a warehouse. Shelves had been built over all the walls of a room about 6 by 5 meters, and I was speechless when I saw them. They were crowded with thousands of artifacts.

As I began to examine the collection, I discovered that most of the artifacts were clay pieces of the Atacames and Tolita cultures. There were figures both human and animal, pottery ware, flat and cylindrical stamps, ceramic molds for making figurines and jars, and many other pieces. And here for the first time I saw an obsidian mirror, a flat disc of the black stone, about 15 centimeters in diameter, that was polished so smoothly my reflection was quite visible as I gazed at the surface. It had taken a high level of technical skill to create such a perfect, polished surface.

Obsidian mirror, front and side views. Tolita.

Also among these artifacts were three pottery representations of what appeared to be a house, the same sort of representation that occurs in Peruvian art of a much later period. These pieces ranged in size from 30 to 35 centimeters long and 20 to 35 centimeters high, with roofs shaped in the fashion of an A-frame. Steps led up to a doorway in the front wall of each piece, which bore a very distinctive decorative design, the same design, I noted in later investigations, that often appeared on small clay seal stamps. I also noted later that many similar pieces had the small figure of a male seated in the doorway, wearing spool-shaped earrings and a necklace with a pendant that perhaps represented the emerald, which was reported, in the early Spanish chronicles, to have been venerated by the Indians as a sacred stone with healing powers.

Some authorities have described these objects as merely

representations of ordinary dwellings, or of temporary structures built on balsa rafts for purposes of migration. But I have come to believe, judging from the detailed craftsmanship, the decorative designs, and the ceremonial dress and appearance of the figures seated within the doorways, that they are representations of a shrine or the domicile of a priest or shaman. I have further come to believe that these pieces may depict the beginnings of the tradition of temple building over the centuries; as these ancient societies progressed from the leadership of a tribal shaman to that of the more powerful autocracy of a priest-ruler, so their shrines became larger and more elaborate, with higher bases and more and more steps leading up to them. Thus, ultimately, they evolved into the truncated pyramids topped by temples that characterize the Mochica culture of Peru, ca. A.D. 1–900, and the Mayan culture of Mexico, ca. A.D. 200–900.

Ceramic replica of shrine or priest's domicile. Tolita.

My eye was also caught by the tremendous number of pottery torsos with no heads, and heads broken off from the torsos, that lined Yannuzzelli's shelves. The remainder of each of these torsos was generally in good condition, and it came to me quite clearly that some sort of deliberate ceremonial decapitation had been performed on these pieces as they were placed in the burial mounds. I thought of the belief held by the Amazon Indians (and by many of the aboriginal peoples of the world) that the head is the site of very special powers, the seat of life. Among headhunters, this leads to the further belief that when they possess the shrunken head of an enemy, they possess his power. For the Tolita people, it occurred to me that the beheading of an artifact may have been considered a ritual reenactment of this belief. Its implications were strikingly displayed in a ceramic piece that depicted a shaman in full regalia holding a decapitated head in his hands, incorporating as a background the silhouette of a shrine. The perforation above the forehead indicated that the piece was probably worn as an amulet or as a symbol of authority.

Ceramic headless torso. Tolita.

The beliefs and rituals of decapitation were widespread and can be seen in artifacts from Bolivia, Colombia, and

Shaman with decapitated head in his hands. Tolita.

Stone monolith of shaman holding decapitated head. Tiahuanaco.

Mesoamerica. And it is now believed that the well-known Olmec colossal head from Mexico is a representation of the decapitated head of the chief of a losing team of the ball game pelota. The Olmecs, Zapotecs, and Mayans played pelota so seriously that the chief of the losing team was ritually beheaded by the high priest officiating over the game. This was a practice that was not merely represented in their art but actually performed: there is a large frieze on the inner wall of the ball court at Chichén Itzá that depicts the event quite literally, complete with jets of blood spurting upward from the severed neck arteries of the victim.

Among the other pieces in Yannuzzelli's collection was a stone mortar very much like the mortar I had seen under the snout of Ramon's pig in the region south of Esmeraldas, except that this one had no design carved on its outer walls. The pestle was also a stone, flat on the bottom and rounded on the top, of the sort that Indian women grasp with both hands and slide back and forth in the mortar to grind grain.

I spent some time looking at this extraordinary collection; then we walked back to the main house, where Yannuzzelli began to talk and little by little became more expansive. He said with a twinkle in his eye that he still had a lease firmly in hand from the government to use Tolita for cattle grazing. And he went on to tell me that the pieces in his collection had been found not only on Tolita but over the entire northern part of Esmeraldas Province, especially along the course of the Rio Santiago, the river that flows northwest to Tolita from the interior where its headwaters arise in the Cayapas range of the western Andes. I decided, right at that moment, that I had to make a trip up that river into the Cayapas Mountains, even though I knew that organizing an expedition to that remote area would not be an easy task. There were no roads; the only accessible route was by water, and arrangements had to be made well in advance.

Yannuzzelli's comments on the archaeological potential

Stone statue with decapitated head showing jaguar features. San Agustin.

Ceramic representation of Xipe-Totec holding decapitated head and staff. Zapotec.

of the Rio Santiago and Cayapas region coincided with impressions I had received from Ribadeneira's booklet, which stated that gold that occurred naturally in the coastal areas around Tolita would have to have been washed down by the rivers originating in the Cayapas Mountains. When I mentioned this to Yannuzzelli, he confirmed my impressions. "Yes," he said, "some Indians working up the Rio Santiago have found naturally occurring gold, and also a few small gold artifacts."

It was dark when Yannuzzelli and I drove back to Esmeraldas. My mind still reeled at the richness of his collection but I was appalled by the cost at which it had been assembled. Important archaeological sites had been
destroyed; countless thousands of artifacts had been shattered or sold. Such pillage was inevitable without government intervention. Nor was Yannuzzelli alone guilty. The
following day I called again on Señora Nabon, who
showed me several pieces that had been freshly unearthed
on Tolita. Her motives were a little more straightforward
this time; she said that she was looking for promising
buyers. I replied that I regretted I was not in this business
for commercial reasons. I also regretted that the excavations on Tolita still continued unchecked under the aegis
of free enterprise.

I mentioned to Señora Nabon that I was planning to
leave for Manta, a small coastal town some 280 miles
south of Esmeraldas in the province of Manabí, to further
my investigation of the coastal cultures. She suggested
that I contact Jorge Moncayo, whose family owned an an-
tique store in Guayaquil, and who had lived for many
years in Manta and was very knowledgeable about the ancient cultures of the central and southern coastal regions.
I called Moncayo, and we agreed to meet in two days' time
at Manta.

The trip to Manta is longer than the trip from Esmeraldas to Quito, and when I boarded the bus, I was
prepared for the worst. The first part of the journey retraced the now familiar road to Santo Domingo de los
Colorados. From there, however, we took what was for
me a new direction, southwestward to Manta. The road
had been paved with asphalt at one time for the purpose
of shipping bananas in this area, but the paving had not
been maintained, and every 10 or 20 feet, here and there,
across the entire width of the roadway there were gaping
potholes.

After a comparatively short distance, we began to see all
manner of trucks, buses, and cars by the side of the road
with blowouts or broken axles. Our driver then began

what can best be described as evasive action, a maneuver he continued for the next 200 kilometers. Swinging the wheel wildly, he lunged the bus maniacally from the right shoulder of the road all the way over to the left and back again, then down the middle or wherever he spotted a gap between the potholes. The drivers of trucks and buses coming from the opposite direction were similarly intent on dodging potholes, but I soon began to see that avoiding those vehicles was of secondary importance in our driver's mind, to be considered only at the very last moment. He apparently believed it was the responsibility of the drivers of the oncoming vehicles to avoid him.

A green wall of banana trees encased the road from Santo Domingo to the outskirts of Manta, and there were few gas stations on the way. So the driver carried extra cans of gas on the bus, and a young boy to help him refuel. When the gauge showed that the tank was getting low, he sent the boy up over the hood with one of the cans of gas to refill it. He did not bother to stop the bus for this operation. As we lurched along, the boy made a manful attempt to pour the gas from his can into the tank, and for the most part he succeeded. But he was not a miracle worker; gas came sloshing back over the wooden body of the bus, while the passengers simply moved their possessions out of the way and continued drawing on their cigarettes. I found myself hoping that the ancient gods who had protected their ancestors in pre-Columbian times were still with us. Perhaps they were, for about nine hours after leaving Esmeraldas, we reached Manta without so much as a flat tire.

The morning after my arrival, Jorge Moncayo came to my hotel to meet me. He was a short, good-looking gentleman, and we exchanged the usual pleasantries that are *de rigueur* in South American social relations. Then I told him more about my interest in the ancient coastal cultures, and he offered to take me that afternoon to the town of Bahía de Caráquez to meet a family who had uncovered many artifacts on their property. I was struck by his willingness to be of assistance. I thought of how slim

Mold-made figurine wearing nose- and earrings and necklace. Bahía.

Hollow figurine incorporating multiple-tone whistle. Bahía.

the resources were in the museums I had visited, and how indifferent the government appeared to be, and yet in Moncayo I had found another Ecuadorian who displayed a genuine interest and enthusiasm in the past.

I rented a camioneta for our use the next few days, then spent the rest of the morning wandering around the streets of Manta. For many years Manta was the only city in Ecuador that had a harbor with docking facilities, and it became the center of the coffee export business. There was a fine fleet of fishing vessels anchored in the harbor, and I could see people sailing small balsa canoes far out in the Pacific, handling them very expertly. In my subsequent years in Ecuador, I haven't encountered a town that I liked better.

Jorge and I met as arranged that afternoon and drove to Bahía de Caráquez, a sleepy fishing village at the tip of an inlet overlooking the Pacific. We went to the home of Jorge's friends, the Robinos family, one of whose sons, the eighteen-year-old Louis, was quite interested in artifacts. He had spent considerable time exploring the old burial grounds and tolas in the area, had probably done some digging himself, and had acquired a few pieces from the local *huaceros*. As I examined them, I saw immediately that they were quite different in style from the Tolita and Esmeraldas pieces I had become familiar with. But I remembered similar pieces in the private collections I had seen, as well as in the Casa de la Cultura in Quito and the Museum of the American Indian in New York.

Louis took Jorge and me to a burial ground southwest of Bahía de Caráquez. Most of the tolas had already been opened, and pottery shards were scattered around, some lightly covered by the dirt washed over them by recent rains. The pottery had probably been broken by the *huaceros*, who move quickly, checking the inside of every hollow object for gold. But among the shards, incredibly, there were two small pottery figurines, one mold-made and the other hollow, with arms outstretched—a stance I had seen in figurines from Esmeraldas and Tolita and was to encounter again in practically every other coastal culture. The posture of these pieces seems to suggest an act of supplication to the deities or a priest/leader, and in many, the palms are forward and the thumb uppermost. Around the neck of some of the figurines is the representation of a necklace with a rectangular pendant, perhaps depicting an emerald; in others, clay or bone-carved amulets are depicted. Plug or pendant earrings and nose rings are also common.

I learned that all along the coast, north and south of Bahía de Caráquez, are found not only burial grounds but also a number of refuse pits, indicating that large permanent settlements once flourished in this area. Unfortunately, due to the hot and humid climate, perishable materials like wood, fiber cloth, and animal skins have long ago disintegrated. Fragments of pottery, shells, bones, and artifacts are all that remain for an investigator to reconstruct and interpret these extinct cultures.

Female figurine with arms outstretched. Esmeraldas.

Louis, Jorge, and I set out to visit a number of landowners in this region, and I was shown numerous vessels and bowls, figures of deities, and other human and animal representations that had come not from one specific burial ground but from all over the coastal area. They had been excavated not with any purposeful archaeological intent, but as the result of landowners digging casually into whatever they encountered on their property. The incredible archaeological richness obviously extended up and down the entire coast.

Our first excursions were all quite close to the coast, along the road running north and south from Bahía de Caráquez. Then Louis, Jorge, and I headed inland to see what the terrain was like further into the interior. After 15 to 20 kilometers we discovered that the land was dry and sandy, and covered with dunes that seemed to go on forever. But I saw evidences of digging and realized that every one of these "sand dunes" had the potential of being a burial tola.

We spoke with some of the local campesinos, who confirmed that a profusion of ceramic artifacts had been uncovered from the "sand dunes." And occasionally, associated with them in the same burial site, were pieces of gold jewelry: nose rings or narizlieras, ear plugs, and

Clay figurine with arms outstretched. Tolita.

small amulets. I examined some of these pieces. The narizlieras measured about ¾ inch to 1 inch across and were examples of *depletion gilding*, where alloys of copper and gold, some also with part silver, were treated with acids to dissolve away the baser metals thereby concentrating gold at the surface. Their decorations were formed separately and then brazed in place. The craftsmanship appeared to be almost as highly developed as that seen in similar pieces from Esmeraldas and Tolita, and from practically all the coastal cultures. The art of depletion gilding, I learned later, had also reached a high level of sophistication in the Milagro culture that flourished at the foot of the Cordillera Occidental, extending to the coastal hills farther south from Bahía, from 400 B.C. to about A.D. 1200. The skill and imagination of these artisans, who also worked with silver and platinum, extended well beyond simple jewelry to more elaborate representations. Years later in Quito, at the newly opened museum of the Banco Central, I would be particularly struck by a gold mask from Tolita with rays of the sun depicted as snakes emanating from its core. What I found most intriguing about this piece was its similarity to a rendering from the Nazca culture of Peru at least 300 years later.

Gold narizliera. Bahía.

Nose rings of solid copper plated with gold (left); coiled platinum wire (upper right); and hammered gold wire (lower right). Bahía/Milagro phase.

Nose rings of solid copper plated with gold. Bahía/Milagro phase.

Gold amulet pendant. Tolita.

Gold mask. Tolita.

Gold mask. Nazca.

After our expedition to the interior, Jorge and I left the Robinos family and drove to the farm of a man Jorge knew, 25 to 30 kilometers southeast of Manta on the slope of the Cerro de Hojas. Here the countryside also looked very dry and sandy, the underbrush had the quality of sage, and everything was brown. The only animals we saw were donkeys and goats. When we arrived at the farm, Pepe Azueta, a portly and robust man in his fifties, showed us several artifacts he had found on his land. Among them there were small gold pieces, some of which were stuck together by corrosion; the thin layer of gold sheet on the surface of the pieces had broken away, exposing copper, which then oxidized.

Part of a stone seat supported by crouching human. Manteño.

In a small barn behind his farmhouse Pepe had an accumulation of pottery shards, urns, and an incredible number of stone pieces which, he said, he had found in various excavations through the years. My interest was drawn toward the stone pieces and, as I examined them, I could hardly believe what I saw. One piece in particular excited me. I recognized it to be part of a stone seat of a type similar to those originally discovered by the American archaeologist Marshall Howard Saville, who attributed them to the Manteño culture and described them in a 1907 report, "The Antiquities of Manabí, Ecuador." Many of the artifacts he discovered and collected in Ecuador are now part of the Museum of the American Indian in New York.

Of all the cultures that flourished about 500 B.C. on the coast of Ecuador, the Manteños are an enigma to most researchers because they were the only society that made extensive use of stone carving and construction. Centered in the area of Manta, from which they derived their name, their territory extended both along the coast and inland into the highlands. The famous seats or benches were originally discovered on the tip of a hill called Cerro Jamboncillo; others were later unearthed in burial grounds in Cerro Bravo and Cerro Hojas. These unique artifacts, carved out of solid blocks of volcanic stone, invariably take a U-shaped form supported by either a crouching human or jaguar-like beast. Once more, the

Stone seat supported by crouching jaguar. Manteño.

Pottery effigy of female in erotic position. Manteño.

jaguar could be seen as an important and prominent figure in the art of a coastal culture. Stone stelae depicting the female in an erotic position implying the importance of fertility and procreation were also discovered on the summit of Cerro Jamboncillo. A miniature clay effigy representation was found by Pepe in one of his excavations.

Another important and significant aspect of the Manteño culture was its veneration of the emerald as an object of the highest spiritual value, signifying the forces of light and health. In fact, ceramic figures of the shaman or healer found throughout the coastal area almost invariably show a representation of an emerald pendant. Further, the ancient chronicles reported that when the Spaniards arrived in the Manta area, at the principal ceremonial center they found the people worshipping a huge emerald "standing above the altar." The Spaniards stole the emerald, whereupon the enraged people slew the Spaniards, recovered the stone, took it into the interior, and concealed it. It has never been seen again. In Mesoamerica, in absence of the emerald, the Olmecs venerated the transparent emerald green variety of jade, which they sculpted into innumerable artifacts of all sizes and shapes.

Emerald necklace with triangular pendant depicting the head of a snake. Manteño.

There was another surprise in store for me at Finca Azueta. Pepe mentioned that he had recently found a very unusual piece. My interest stirred, I asked for more details, and he took Jorge and me into a room of his house where he brought out a metal blade that looked like an early axhead. Scrutinizing it closely, I was puzzled as to what the metal could be. Parts of the surface had a thin green patina, and where it had been cleaned it had the reddish look of copper, but it had been hammered into shape. Pepe remarked that he had never seen an axhead like this in his area. He, and other local people, had found axheads of stone, but nothing like this metal one.

Metal axhead. Bahía.

He agreed to show us where he had found the axhead and we started out on a walk of about an hour and a half from his house, going eastward, up into the hills. At last we came to a steep slope and Pepe gestured toward a horizontal opening in the hillside. That was where the axhead had come from. "How did you happen to be aware that there was anything there?" I asked.

Pepe answered, "Well, I was up here one day with some of my workmen gathering stone to use for a pen we were building for the goats. The land is so dry that there isn't much wood to work with—no poles or slats. Stone is the only material available.

"We had piled up a bunch of stone," he went on, "and were looking around for more when we spotted slabs of stone here, under the earth on the side of this hill. So we began pulling them out, and when we had them free, I could see that there was a big opening behind them. I began to dig into it, and in a little while I came across the burial remains. It was a bunch of bones, several pottery pieces, and the axhead. I sold the rest of the artifacts, but I kept the axhead because I'd never seen anything like it before."

"What happened to the bones?" I asked, thinking that they might be used to establish the date of the burial site.

"Oh, I didn't keep them," Pepe replied, "I had to get rid of them. My workers are very superstitious, and they're afraid of human bones. They think that a grave

Ceramic silvato (top); ceramic figurine wearing headdress of a style later seen in the Classic Mayan culture (bottom). Bahía/La Plata style.

has been desecrated. They don't know how old this stuff is."

Pepe told us that in this area it was quite unusual to find pottery figures complete with heads. He said that he did have a few complete pieces, however, and when we got back to his house, he showed them to us. They were all hollow figurines in the shape of a standing (or lying) human, with arms bent and hands held across the stomach, a posture that I was to encounter again and again during my investigations. They were *silvatos*, whistles, with a hole in the top of the head of each piece through which it could be blown and two acoustic parts set into the back. Two larger *silvatos* incorporated two fingerholes in the back and front lower part of the figurine, which when played sounded like an ocarina. I blew through several of the whistles and marveled that each one produced a different full and rich harmonic tone.

Remnants of three colors were visible on most of the *silvatos:* a uniform red over the head and torso, ocher on the face, and traces of white (probably kaolin) outlining the features. They were androgynous, but breasts were evident. A necklace, ear studs, and nose rings were also visible. A fragment of the pottery surface had broken away on the lower torso of one of the whistles, and I could see that its basic shape had first been modeled in very rough clay. Another piece had one of the acoustic parts broken, and looking closely, I saw that there was a pair of spherical resonance chambers, each communicating with one of the sound holes. Therefore, as the whistle was blown, the vibrating air leaving the ports excited sympathetic vibrations within the resonance chambers, adding harmonics to the tone, and providing a fuller, richer sound. What incredible technical mastery these people had; their expertise embraced even acoustics.

Because the eyes seemed to be closed in a deathlike state and the arms were folded across the stomach, these pieces suggested a depiction of mummification and use in funerary rituals. Usually, two or three are found in a burial site—sometimes one, and less often, more. The size varies, from small ones measuring 5 to 10 centimeters to larger ones of 30 to 35 centimeters. In some cases, a large *silvato*, a medium-sized one, and then a number of smaller ones have been found together in a grave—almost like finding a whole family buried.

Reflecting on this, I thought of the many cultures—particularly those that are very autocratic and are dominated by a strong priest or ruler—that had practiced the sacrifice of the entire family, and perhaps the servants also, and the interment of all of them along with the ruler when he died. But somehow I could not imagine the people of the Bahia culture performing that kind of sacrifice. Perhaps, through interment of a *silvato* representing each member of the family, the sacrifice was performed ritually, and the souls of the surviving family members could accompany the soul of the departed on his way to the other world.

Jorge had to return to Guayaquil, so we thanked Pepe and said goodbye. We climbed into the camioneta and started off, adjusting our bodies to the proper angle in the seats. One rear wheel of the small truck was a good 3 inches larger than the other, and the trip to Guyaquil was a most distinctive sensation. From time to time heavy rain battered the countryside, but the only hazard was bands of wild donkeys unexpectedly crossing the deserted road in search of new pastures.

When we reached Guayaquil—the capital of Guayas Province, inhabited by more than 700,000 people—Jorge suggested I stay at the Hotel Patria, a small residential hotel in the center of the city that, at that time, was a gathering place for many of its European residents. The owner, Mario Napolitano, always welcomed his new guests with a glass of good wine. Originally from Italy, he had emigrated to Ecuador fifty years before, following, in his own words, "in the footsteps of the conquistadors." A short, heavy-built man in his eighties, he could quote at length passages from the Spanish chronicles describing the exploits of Pizarro. But I was amused by the way in which he Italianized every important historical figure who

had taken part in the conquest of the New World. For
him, not only had Italian-born Columbus discovered
America but a score of Italians had conquered everything
else, and it was the Spaniards who had distorted the historical facts.

The next day Jorge and I took a short tour of the city.
Guayaquil is the largest industrial city in Ecuador and its
main seaport, although it is located 72 kilometers inland
on the banks of the Rio Guayas, which flows into the Pacific well south of the city. With every passing decade the
city finds itself even further from the sea, as the Guayas
River, carrying in its sweeping currents massive quantities
of sediment from the Andes, forms an ever larger delta.

Later in the day I met Señor Amador Navarro, a repre-
sentative in Guayaquil of one of the government ministries. It was a fortunate meeting, for Navarro was acquainted with the family of Emilio Estrada, the prominent
banker in Guayaquil who for many years, on his own initiative, had methodically undertaken archaeological investigations of the coastal area and had published several
booklets on these cultures for distribution to the academic
and the museum communities. They were rare, but
through Señor Navarro I was able to obtain a complete set
from the Estrada family, and they proved to be a great
help in expanding my knowledge of the coastal cultures
discovered and investigated by Estrada. Navarro also introduced me to a businessman, Andrea Salvador, who in
turn was later to lead me to a man who would figure
prominently in my future expeditions.

Salvador was an intense, likable man, married to a
young woman, Ingrid, the daughter of a German diplo-
mat. He had been educated in the United States, and
spoke English very well. I soon discovered, however, that
his interest in archaeology had a very special focus. He
was burning with the desire to find the lost treasure of
Atahualpa, the last of the Inca rulers.

Historically, it was reported that when Pizarro tricked
Atahualpa into captivity, he demanded a ransom in gold
for his release. His subjects complied and assembled a

roomful of gold. But Pizarro reneged, refused to release Atahualpa, and demanded a second ransom. This time the Incas collected an even larger amount of gold, and were on the point of delivering it, when they learned that Atahualpa had been killed by the Spaniards, who mistakenly believed the Incas were planning an uprising against them. At this, having learned well the lesson of Spanish perfidy, the Incas concealed the gold in an inaccessible place where it would be safe forever. The chronicles do not recount the location of the hiding place specifically; it is said only that the Inca leader, Rumiñahui, with 1000 Indians and scores of llamas carrying the gold, headed deep into the Llanganates, a remote region in the Andes. Thus was born the legend of the lost treasure of Atahualpa, and for centuries, dozens of expeditions have set out to find the Inca treasure. They have consistently returned empty-handed. The Llanganates is one of the toughest, most savage mountain systems in the entire Andes. There are very few trails and it is virtually unexplored.

His fascination with this legend had led Andrea into a more general interest in archaeology. He owned a large tract of land in the foothills of the Andes in the Oriente, flew his own small plane and, therefore, was able to pursue his search for the Inca treasure independently. But he was also knowledgeable about the artifacts of the pre-Inca cultures, and at his home in Guayaquil I saw the pieces he had collected over the years, many of which he had brought back from the Oriente. Among these were several stone pieces that intrigued me greatly. Some displayed characteristics similar to those to be seen in a more developed form in the pottery pieces of the coastal cultures. As I examined these pieces, the vague ideas I had previously had that the pre-ceramic stages of the coastal cultures might have developed in the Amazon now seemed to be corroborated.

Andrea also had a large number of pottery pieces in his collection, among them artifacts from the Esmeraldas, Tolita, and Bahia areas that I had become directly familiar with myself. And there were specimens from other cultures: in particular, the Valdivia, the oldest of the known Ecuadorian cultures (ca. 3500 B.C.); the little-known Machalilla culture, which existed about 2000 B.C. on the coast of Guayas; and the Chorrera (ca. 1800 B.C.), a rather widespread culture that had extended from the western footslopes of the Andes to the coastal plain. Many of the pottery pieces shared similar traits: outstretched arms, eye treatment, ear and nose ornaments, and headdress. A Chorrera figurine that displayed all these traits implied the possibility that many of the other coastal cultures may have devolved such representations from the Chorrera.

As I studied a greater number of stone pieces than I had yet seen in one place, alongside a very fine representation of the coastal pottery cultures, connections between the two began forming themselves quite naturally in my mind. Some of the stone pieces came from sites just east of the Chorrera area, and the close proximity of these finds seemed to suggest a relationship in the transition from stone to pottery.

After we had spent some time studying his private collection, Andrea took me to Guayaquil's Casa de la Cultura. It was not open to the public; Andrea had to look for the custodian and get the key to let us in. And as soon as we entered I saw why: two rooms full of dusty pieces in the same chaos I had seen in Esmeraldas. Only here the number of pieces was in the thousands. I saw artifacts from the major coastal cultures, including not only the north (Esmeraldas, Tolita, Atacames), but also the center (Jama-Coaque, Bahía, Manteño), the south (Guangala, Milagro, Machallila), and the oldest coastal culture of all—Valdivia. The incredible variety of styles and traits displayed by these pieces revealed different periods of development within all of these cultures: from the Formative to the Integration, an age span from about 3500 B.C. to A.D. 1000. But most of the pieces were in piles classified by the name of area of origin and nothing else. I was shocked as my gaze went around the room.*

Hollow ceramic figurine. Chorrera.

---

*It was only years later when Dr. Olaf Holm, a Danish archaeologist now living in Ecuador, assumed the directorship of the collection that proper classification was undertaken.

Bahía/La Plata style

Jama-Coaque

Guangala

Milagro

Pottery figurines of central and southern Ecuadorian cultures.

A beautifully molded two-headed figurine of the Valdivia culture attracted my attention particularly. It was an effective representation of the idea of the duality of man's nature, the concept of two identities or, perhaps, soul and body, the inner and outer self, the subconscious and the conscious. This belief in the duality of existence was familiar to the ancient cultures of America and often represented in their artifacts. I was also intrigued by another Valdivia figurine with an elaborate and well-defined coiffure, arms across the stomach and legs separated by a deep, narrow groove representing fertility.

Female figurine representing fertility (left), Valdivia; two-headed figurines: (center), Valdivia; (right), Tlatilco.

The people of Guayaquil lay claim to being residents of Ecuador's most progressive and cultural city. Yet those two cluttered rooms represented their appreciation of their own pre-Columbian heritage. They will spend hundreds of dollars for bronze spurs, stirrups, and swords from the Spanish colonial period, which they display proudly in their drawing rooms. But they have no comprehension of the richness of the ancient Ecuadorian cultures that lies all around them. As I met some of these people in the next few days, I steered the conversation again and again to the value of the artifacts of these ancient cultures. Their reactions were the same I had encountered elsewhere: a blank stare for a moment, then an animated look of sudden comprehension, and the statement, "Oh, you mean that Inca stuff." In their minds, everything that was there before the conquistadors was Inca.

The Catholic Church has helped to foster the ignorance of Ecuador's pre-Columbian heritage. Most of the early missionaries, and the priests in the century or two that followed them, passed off all of these artifacts as *infieles*—infidel works—the products of shameful paganism, only a step or two removed from the works of the Devil himself. This attitude has continued right down to the present day. Education in the country is overwhelmingly Catholic, and most grow up agreeing with the old priest I met on my first trip to Esmeraldas, that the people who were here before the Incas were just a bunch of savages.

Another reason why most Ecuadorians have not become interested in the pre-Columbian cultures is that they all know the story of how the Incas conquered other tribes and, to keep them in a weak and controllable position, regularly broke them up and moved the various segments to new locations, sometimes hundreds of miles away. Thus the preponderant majority, every time they encounter an artifact that is different and does not fit into the familiar patterns, think that it must have come from one of the tribes the Incas had dispersed, and they dismiss it without bothering to look further. In most cases, no thought at all is given to the possibility that it might stem from a culture older than the Inca, although it is well known that the Incas were a comparatively recent phenomenon, whose cultural expansion was based upon the knowledge they acquired from much older civilizations.

Of course, legends of lost Inca gold remain in the minds of many people, and Andrea Salvador was not the only one who devoted time to the search for the treasure of Atahualpa or to expeditions to solve some other mystery of the past. He told me a story that later would prove of crucial importance to my own quest. One day, several years before, he was approached in Guayaquil by an army officer; Andrea didn't remember whether he was a captain or a major. There was nothing mysterious about that. Many people in Ecuador knew of the wealth of Andrea's family, and somehow everyone who was looking for assistance came to him. The officer told Andrea that he had learned of the existence of a mysterious cave somewhere in the southern Oriente that he called the Cueva de los Tayos. According to him, this cave contained some form of megalithic carving or construction done by an ancient people. The officer wanted financial support from Andrea to mount an expedition into the Oriente to look for the cave.

Andrea was a little suspicious, his skepticism triggered by the name of the cave. Tayos are black birds that live throughout the Oriente, and he thought it was hardly likely that only one cave in particular would be visited by these birds. Therefore, nothing ever came of his conversation with the officer.

My interest in the story was captured for another reason, however. Since I had begun thinking of the possibility that the origins of the coastal cultures might be traced to the Amazon, caves loomed very important in my theories. Much of the land area in the Andes of the Oriente is too high to support timber, and if these areas were inhabited during the time when I felt that early cultures might have developed—4000, 5000, or even 7000 B.C.—then one of the most natural forms of shelter would have been caves. From my study of the geological history of the Andes, I knew that the period from 18,000 B.C. to 9000 B.C.—the time during which an early people might have been making the transition from primitive hunting and gathering to the more advanced technologies characteristic of higher culture—was a period of intense volcanic activity and telluric movement in this area. Caves would have provided good shelter against such movement, as well as the frequent landslides. Only recently has any detailed information begun to emerge on the climate in the Andes during this period. A general warming trend began about 20,000 B.C.; thereafter, for the next 10,000 years or so, both temperature and the moisture levels went through cyclic fluctuations. Caves would also have provided excellent shelter against the weather for an early people.

It seemed most unlikely that a mysterious army officer could lead me to a cave that had been inhabited by an ancient people, but I was intrigued by his story and asked Andrea to try to find his name and address. He promised he would do so, and some months later, he called me in Quito to tell me that the man's name was Major Petronio Jaramillo-Abarca.

The day after my meeting with Andrea, the shrill ring of the telephone woke me up in my hotel room. It was Jorge Moncayo inviting me to his home. There on his living room table and on the floor were at least fifty pieces of pottery—vases, plates, and figurines. The pieces had obviously come from the coastal area, and I asked how he had gotten them. "People come to see me in the store," he said, "campesinos or small landowners from the outlying areas. They find these things and bring them to me. And I take them on consignment."

Among the pieces was a hollow pottery figure of a seated male wearing spool earrings—a trait seen in the artifacts of many of the coastal cultures—with a very characteristic headdress that rose to a broad, flat top, forming a tray that was probably used for offertory purposes. It was from the Manteño culture in the province of Manabí, where I had been just a few days before. My attention was also drawn to several interesting clay masks with distinctive facial characteristics that are often seen on many of these Manteño pieces. Jorge said they came from a site not too far north of Guayaquil—Finca Doña Julia. I asked

Seated male figure with flat-topped headdress. Manteño.

him if he would take me there so I could see the site of origin. He agreed, and we decided to make the trip the following morning.

We left very early in order to beat the traffic that by
6:00 A.M. becomes clogged with trucks streaming into the
city, bringing the daily food supply to the markets. In
about an hour and a half we reached our destination, and
Jorge introduced me to "Lady Julia." The title "Doña" was
forgotten as soon as I laid eyes on her. I don't remember
ever having seen anybody so fat and so disheveled in my
life. Her breasts were huge and hung down from her
chest to below her waist. Hanging from a tree in her yard
I saw two long plastic bags tied together by a string of exactly the proper length to go around her neck. This obviously was Lady Julia's bra.

Doña Julia was so impressed that a "doctor" like me had
come to visit her that she took us immediately to the site
about a mile and a half away where the masks in Jorge's
house had been found. All I saw was a hole in the earth.
The excavation, as usual, had been done in haste, and all
the evidence of the overlying layers had been destroyed.
One object in particular stood out: an unusual female
figurine with characteristic traits similar to the late Chorrera
period that wore a strange and mysterious triangular-
shaped pendant, a rare feature I had not yet encountered. Another pottery piece, a head, depicted the face of
a shaman or brujo with deep incised lines on the cheeks
and forehead that indicated age, synonymous with wisdom, knowledge of the material and spiritual world, and
mastery of the forces of nature. Each of the ears bore
twelve perforations for earrings. It was the practice in
some cultures for the priest or shaman to wear an earring
for each lunar month of the year. The characteristic facial

*Female figurine with
triangular-shaped
pendant. Late Chorrera (?).*

renderings and their symbolic meaning were traits common to the artifacts of all the American cultures.

Before leaving, I asked Doña Julia if she had any children, knowing that Ecuadorians love to talk about their
children. "No, no children," she said. "But I have one *hijo
grande* (big son). Come, he's outside." So we went outside

and walked around the house, and there was a huge pig that you could smell a mile away. Doña Julia got down on her knees in all the dirt, put her arms around him, gave him a kiss on the head, and said, *"Mi hijo grande!"*

After having spent weeks in the parched provinces studying the artifacts of the ancient coastal cultures, surrounded by goats and burros, mounds of chicken droppings, and *hijos grandes,* I returned to Quito. Traditionally, every large South American city has a place, whether club, bar, or restaurant, where European expatriates gather in the evenings to meet new faces, exchange points of view, and drink to the glory of the past. In Quito such a place was "La Vieja Europa," an Italian restaurant. One evening I found it, walked in, and encountered Maya and Luky, the proprietors—two of the most remarkable people I've ever met.

Like a movie star, Maya greets her guests with one hand on her hip, the other in an elegant gesture up in the air, crying out: "Dah-lings!" She will say anything to anybody: the wife of the Polish ambassador, a French businessman, anybody. "Dah-ling! I must tell you, tonight you look awful! I must help you with this terrible problem you have with that old husband of yours!" Coming from Maya, everyone accepts it and loves it.

Maya would have liked to be a 6-foot-tall sex queen, a great movie star. Instead, she is about 5 feet tall and the owner of a restaurant. So she puts great drama into her life and her cooking. She steps into the kitchen in her mink mini-skirt and gold boots and reaches for spices, herbs, and condiments—poof, poof, poof! The smoke rises up into the air and fills the place. And in no time she steps back out like a painter, again with one arm in the air, and says, *"Voilà!* It is done." And you never tasted anything like it. Her husband Luky makes pizza—but such pizza as you never had in your life, because, again, it is something that is born at that moment.

La Vieja Europa became a sort of home away from home for me. At Maya's insistence, I ate most of my meals there while I was in Quito, and she compulsively introduced me to all sorts of people: engineers, doctors, European businessmen, ambassadors, foreign officials, and anyone who showed an interest in the ancient cultures of Ecuador. In that spirit, one night Maya introduced me to David Smith, an American engineer who matched the description of the proverbial tall Texan. He was married to an Ecuadorian girl from a prominent family, and was the president of a company that did exploratory drilling for oil. David was very interested in archaeology, and had several pieces he had purchased here and there that he wanted to show me. They were all pottery figures from the coastal area. I asked him if he had any stone pieces. He said, "No. But now that you mention it, I have had some stone pieces offered to me, but I didn't buy them. Once when I was in Puyo, and another time in Coca." Puyo is a village in the foothills of the east Andean mountain range, and Coca is a settlement at the confluence of the Rio Coca and the Rio Napo, deep in the Amazon.

"In both of these towns," David said, "I was approached by the locals with stone pieces for sale. One of them was a piece with carved human faces and a serpent on it. But I hadn't seen any of that kind of artifact before, and didn't know if it was authentic or not. So I didn't want to take a chance, and I didn't buy it."

"How much were they asking for it?" I asked.

"Oh, about three dollars."

I broke into laughter, and David said, "Yeah, I guess I was an idiot. I should have bought it. For that money, even if it had been fake, I could have used it as a doorstop."

That same evening, perched on the side of the balcony of my hotel room overlooking Quito, my vision blurred and what I saw was not the city but the Ecuadorian coastal plain stretching out before me. The patterns of the coastal cultures were starting to emerge more clearly in my mind, but where did they lead? There were so many promising directions to go, so many potential areas for exploration. The situation had been turned around completely from my first visit when the problem was to find a place to start.

Now the problem was to decide which of the many possibilities I should pursue next.

David's account of the stone pieces he had been offered, the stone pieces from the Oriente in Andrea Salvador's collection, and his story of the mysterious major and the Cuevas de los Tayos, all exerted a definite pull on me. But it seemed somehow that an immediate leap into the Oriente would be a bit premature, that more definite links between the coastal cultures and the Oriente had to be established first, and those links might be found in the intervening sierra. Best to take things one step at a time.

Finally, my memories of Ramon's stone pig trough, the stone pieces in Yannuzzelli's collection, and his description of the artifacts to be found in the Cayapas Mountains became uppermost in my mind. There, I thought, would be the best place to start the search for those intermediate links. I decided that my next expedition would be into the Cayapas, and I called my friend Democrito in Esmeraldas to see if he would accompany me. He was delighted, and we made preliminary plans for my return in about two months.

Representations of shamen with characteristic facial lines: (left), Zapotec; (right), Esmeraldas.

CHAPTER 4

The Cayapa Shaman

As the sun set behind the peaks of the mighty Andes, the guests at the Hotel Quito gathered in the cabana section for the usual cocktail hour. Sitting across from me at a small table was Philip Brooks, a lawyer who had flown with me from Miami on my third trip to Ecuador. A few weeks before when I mentioned to him that I was making the trip, he told me that he also had to fly to Quito to take care of some legal matter for a client; and after he learned that I planned an exploratory archaeological expedition into the Cayapas Mountains, he asked if he could join me. He had never been to South America and was very anxious to see for himself all the things I had told him during our conversations about Ecuador. Back home, however, we had rarely had the time to discuss in any depth my archaeological quest.

Here, as we sat quietly sipping Cinzano-on-the-rocks, he was curious to know why I had come so far to explore this particular area. I told him that a theory had been forming in my mind for some time that the well-known classic cultures in Peru and Mesoamerica were the descendants, the logical development, of a culture that was pre-ceramic. I explained that Ecuador—from what I had read and from what I had learned on my earlier trips—seemed to be of primal importance in the development of these great cultures and I wanted to explore the more primitive areas of the country to see if I could find evidence to substantiate this theory.

Philip found the idea fascinating, but he couldn't understand how I had come to this viewpoint. I told him that scholars today believe that the oldest known ceramic-using culture in the New World was in Ecuador—the Valdivia, dating as early as 3500 B.C. That one piece of information, I said, is crucial. If there was an elaborate culture at that early age, capable of advanced ceramic work, then obviously there had to have been prior stages of cultural development that may not have been ceramic at all.

Philip nodded thoughtfully, then said, "What do you think it was?"

"Stone," I said; "a very old stone-carving people. And I'm beginning to think that they may have originated in the mountains of the Oriente, or in the Amazon, and then came over the Andes westward, entering the coastal area."

I could see that Philip didn't put much credence in that theory. "Why do they have to have come from the Amazon?" he said. "Why can't they have come from the coast?"

"Early artifacts carved in stone are very rare in the coastal cultures," I said. "On the other hand, I have discovered a number of clues that seem to indicate that there was stone carving in the sierra and in the Oriente." I told Philip about Ramon's stone trough that could only have come from the sierra, and the similar trough in Señor Yannuzzelli's collection. I also told him of the stone pieces from Andrea Salvador's finca in the Oriente and his description of similar pieces found by the campesinos throughout the area bordering on the Amazon. I mentioned David Smith, the Texan in the Europa who had told me of being offered stone pieces in Napo, in the Amazon. And, I continued, these pre-ceramic, formative stages of cultural development—stone carving and whatever else we might find—probably took thousands of years. "The achievement of a high cultural level doesn't happen overnight," I said. "If we continue backward in time, we see that before the pre-ceramic stage of cultural development can begin, there would have to be an additional period of time—perhaps also a few thousand years—when people started to emerge from the primitive hunting and gathering stage, settled into villages, began to raise crops, and developed more stable social organizations. Maize has been documented in the Valdivia culture, dating around 3500 B.C. The process of domestication certainly had to have its beginnings a long time before that, possibly around 6000 or 7000 B.C. Thus we have to think in terms of 8000 or 10,000 B.C. for the beginning of this transformation from primitive hunters to agricultural village dwellers."

"But what makes you think that this transformation took place in Ecuador?" Philip asked.

I said it seemed to be a question of temperature and environmental conditions. "At that time, 8000 to 10,000 B.C., most of the world was still recovering from the ice age. The glaciers were withdrawing, but most of the North and South American continents were still pretty cold. And with culture, as with seeds, cold inhibits the process of germination. When you're spending eighteen hours a day keeping yourself from freezing or starving to death, you don't have the time, or the inclination, to sit down and think about the afterlife, study the stars and try to figure when the days will start to become longer, work out ways of writing down the names of the gods or the priests, or invent techniques for making ceremonial objects out of stone or clay.

"It's only where it is relatively warm, so that the hunting is good and crops can be grown, that there is enough comfort and leisure for some members of a tribe to begin to put their minds to these higher things. Only where it is warmer will a culture develop. And obviously, it was on the equator that the warm-up began first. Here on the equator, conditions were favorable for the germination of culture when it was still too cold elsewhere, north and south, for the people to do much but huddle in a cave by the fire and wonder what tomorrow would bring."

I told Philip that I wanted to investigate thoroughly this idea of an equatorial belt of cultural development, and that once we had explored the Cayapas range, I wanted to continue further into the Amazon, if that was where the clues seemed to lead, even though I realized that this trip would be the beginning of a long investigation that would probably take many years.

We started out for Esmeraldas early the next morning, and this time the bus trip was uneventful—no landslides and no delays in the schedule. However, Philip never stopped complaining. His 250-pound frame did not fit very comfortably into a seat built for people who rarely exceeded 160 pounds fully clothed. From time to time he succumbed to the heat and dozed off; and as I looked at him snoring, I wondered why this man, married with five children, used to taking vacations in comfortable American resorts, had decided to join me on this trip. Perhaps as a boy he had dreamed of such an adventure, just as I had, and this was his first opportunity to pursue his dreams. Whatever his reasons for coming, I was glad of his company.

At last we reached Esmeraldas, and within the tide of black faces waiting to meet the bus, smiling, yelling, and waving, I saw Democrito. He called a taxi, an old broken-down American Ford, to take us to the same dreary hotel I had stayed in before, the Hotel Diana, where he had already reserved two rooms for Philip and me. We discussed the plans for our trip, and Democrito told me there was a boat that left Esmeraldas late in the evening and in six hours reached a place called Limones. There we would change to an outboard-driven canoe and go up the Rio Santiago into the northeast territory of the province of Esmeraldas. We worked out the rest of the details and I gave Democrito a list of the things we would need. We agreed to meet again the following morning.

After a delectable lobster dinner, Philip and I went to bed, hoping to have a good night's sleep. It was not to be. At 3:30 that morning I was suddenly awakened by shouts from Philip's room. I jumped out of bed, opened my door, and there I saw some kind of Satanic spirit lurching around the hallway—all in white. It was Philip, enveloped in a mosquito net. I helped disengage him from the net and asked him what had happened.

He had been awakened, he said, by something dripping

on his face, and then he heard something flying around in his room. It startled him and he tried to jump out of bed, but he forgot about the net and got himself tangled up in it. It was like a nightmare; he couldn't understand where he was. We went back to his room and discovered what had happened. During the night, pigeons came into the room through the opening between the wall and ceiling to roost on the heavy steel bar that extended across the room overhead. And then, as pigeons do, they dropped their little notices on Philip to let him know they were there. We spent an hour having a drink, talking and laughing about the episode. Then we went back to sleep.

Democrito was at the hotel early the next morning. He advised us that the boat we would take, the *San Antonio,* was leaving at eleven that night, but because we were gringos, we would be able to board at ten in oder to avoid the crush of Ecuadorians who were expected to make the journey. The *San Antonio* was a fishing boat, he said, but it and the owner were so old that neither of them was able to go fishing any longer. So the owner had converted the *San Antonio* into a transport for the run between Esmeraldas and Limones, carrying passengers, cargo, and, of course, domestic animals.

Democrito came to the hotel to pick us up at 9:30 that night. We walked two blocks to the embarcadero, where a dugout canoe with an outboard motor took us out to board the *San Antonio,* anchored in the middle of the Rio Esmeraldas. The captain of the vessel, Don Marco, was a man in his sixties and he was happy to offer us the only cabin on the boat. The difference in the fare was about 50 sucres ($2.00) apiece. We thanked him and accepted his offer. But when he showed us the cabin, we were both amazed and apprehensive. It was a small cubicle that certainly had been built for pygmies, not for ordinary men. There were two bunks, each about 2 feet wide and 5 feet long, and I foresaw trouble when Philip tried to squeeze his large frame into that space.

We stepped out to walk around the deck but couldn't see much. We were more conscious of the smell: fish,

musky perspiration, old wood, and engine oil. But Don
Marco was a perfect host. He offered us trago—the Ecuadorian liquor distilled from sugar cane—and then said
that perhaps we should sit down in the pilot's cabin because the motor-canoes were coming. I wondered why,
but Democrito suggested that we do as Don Marco said.

We climbed into the pilot's cabin and waited to see what
would happen. We heard the engines of the canoes coming closer, and slowly out of the darkness a number of
dugouts came alongside the *San Antonio*. All of these canoes were full of people and goods, and as soon as they
touched the boat, we suddenly seemed to be in a scene
from an old movie, with pirates assaulting a helpless vessel. Everyone from the canoes struggled and scrambled to
climb aboard first to get a good seat. Men and women
jumped and clambered over the rails, passing up children
from hand to hand. Baskets filled with onions, tomatoes,
carrots, bread, and potatoes followed, and then pieces of
plywood, suitcases, and boxes tied with ropes, baby pigs,
ducks, plants, flowers. In the space of fifteen or twenty
minutes, this mass of humanity had crowded on board.
The entire deck, from stern to bow, was filled with people
sitting or lying, one against the other. For a moment I had
an image of the ships that once brought slaves from
Africa.

When the *San Antonio* was completely full, Don Marco
began smiling and singing. He was a very happy man; this
trip would mean good money to him. He turned to us and
said, "Gringo, you are good luck for me. This time my
boat is full." Then he turned to his first mate and said,
"*Vamos,* Pedro. Start the engines." The cough of the
engine mixed in with all the talk and laughter of the people on the deck. The only light on the boat was a bare
bulb hanging from the ceiling of the pilot's cabin.

I asked the boy at the wheel, "Where is the compass?"

"Señor, we don't use a compass on this boat. It broke
down two years ago."

Don Marco heard him and said, "This boat is so old and
she's made so many trips that she knows exactly where to

go. Don't worry. We'll be there at six in the morning."
The expression of incredulity on Philip's face made me
laugh.

The night was very dark and I thought that Don Marco
must truly know this route like the back of his hand to be
able to find his way. We sat on the roof of the pilot's
cabin, the night breeze moved across our skin, and we
heard the soft wash of the wake to the stern. A small
group of passengers began to sing and somebody yelled at
them to be quiet, it was time to sleep. The young singers
laughed, and the sound of their laughter mingled with
the snoring of small pigs and the crackling sound of
chickens.

At 1:00 A.M. Philip decided to try to get some sleep and
slipped into the small cabin. Democrito and I remained
on the roof, talking about what we expected to encounter
in the days to come. At least here we could breathe; the
breeze was freshening and breaking up the pungent
odors of the passengers and their livestock on the deck of
the San Antonio.

By 2:30 the wind had grown much stronger and the
swells were increasing on the sea. The San Antonio had
been rolling for some time when, suddenly, I heard a call
for help from Philip. He was stuck in his bunk and
couldn't get out. I climbed down from the roof and
helped him maneuver slowly out of the cabin. He didn't
feel very well and was afraid he might be seasick. He
wanted me to ask the captain where the toilet was. Don
Marco looked at me in surprise. "Toilet? We don't have
space in this boat for a toilet. That's a luxury, señor. This
is a fishing boat." A flash of understanding came to me. I
had been puzzled, when the passengers were boarding, to
see that each of them was carrying a small container. Now
I knew why.

It began to rain and the sea became rougher. Philip's
insides were being jostled back and forth mercilessly, and
he said he simply had to relieve himself. I suggested that
he might hang on to one of the stay cables of the mast,

stand on the rail, and extend his rear end seaward. He agreed that there was no alternative.

By 6:30 A.M. the wind and rain had stopped, and the sea quieted down. Slowly we approached the island on which the village of Limones is located. The island is very close to the mainland; it is a part of the delta of the Rio Santiago, which originates in the Cayapas Mountains. Ecuador's northern coastal plain is drained by a great number of rivers, which pour out of the cordilleras, including the Cayapas, and join to form the Rio Santiago. (Perhaps I should say *another* by the name of Santiago. I have gotten into the habit of calling it the Santiago Northwest, to distinguish it from "Santiago Southeast," the southernmost of the three "corridor" rivers in the Oriente.) This Santiago flows past Tolita Island into the Pacific at Limones, and is the river up which we intended to canoe on our expedition into the Cayapas Mountains. The Santiago, like other large rivers flowing into the Pacific, is navigable by canoe. Doubtless in ancient times, as today, they provided routes of communication from the coastal areas into the western foothills of the Andes.

Viewed from the *San Antonio,* the village of Limones looked like little more than a break in the uniform green color of the coastline: a small mass of houses, most of them built of bamboo, displacing some of the trees at the water's edge. Dozens of canoes, some with outboard motors, came out from the village to meet the boat. As soon as the *San Antonio* anchored, her passengers scrambled and jumped over the rail into the canoes, hustling their pigs, children, boxes, chickens, bags, plants, and baskets with the same frenzy as when they had come on board. In no time the boat was empty, and we stepped over the rail into one of the last of the canoes. As I looked back, nothing remained on deck but the smiling Don Marco and one or two chickens that had jumped out of their baskets. They were scurrying around, eating pieces of bread and biscuits that had been dropped by the passengers.

When we reached the shore, Democrito led us along the muddy beaten track that was the only thoroughfare going through Limones. At the far end of the village was the house of Señora Natalia, our destination. The two-story structure was built of bamboo slats and adobe, like all the other little houses of Limones. As we approached, we could see Señora Natalia standing squarely in the doorway, hands on her hips, waiting for us. A heavyset woman with a very dark complexion, dressed in black and high rubber boots, she appeared to be in her fifties. But I suspected that the hard frontier-like life in this lumber town had taken its toll. She welcomed us warmly, and offered us the upstairs of her house for the duration of our stay. It was a single room devoid of any furniture, so we hooked up the hammocks that we had packed with our gear to use on our trip up the river. They would serve us very well sooner than we expected.

Democrito left to see about renting a dugout canoe with an outboard engine for our trip. It was not as simple as looking for a sign that said: "Canoes for rent." Democrito had to find a man who owned one, and then he had to be patient and have a long conversation with him, while the man tried to figure out the situation. He would have to borrow his brother-in-law's dugout to use while we were gone, he said, or how would he be able to explain to his wife that he couldn't get her the vegetables she was counting on next week? And what would he do about the man whose pig he had promised to carry across the river? He told Democrito to go talk to the man with the pig, and if they could work out some other way to transport the animal, then come back and talk about his canoe. If not, too bad.

Democrito made all the necessary arrangements and even persuaded the owner of the boat, Juan, to take us upriver. The next problem was gas. He must have talked to fifteen or twenty people before he accumulated enough fuel for our trip, buying a pint here or a quart there from anyone who was willing to sell it. It was a time-consuming business. We had decided that our first objective would be a small village upriver called Playa de Oro (Gold Beach). It had been mentioned in Ribadeneira's book on Tolita, and looked to me like a good place to start my investigation. If the weather was good, we would be able to reach Playa de Oro in two days.

When our gear was packed and we were ready to leave, we thanked Señora Natalia for her hospitality and made our way down the muddy street to the bank of the river, where Juan was waiting with the dugout canoe. Twenty-five feet long, with a square stern to accommodate the outboard engine, the craft appeared very able to handle the swift currents of the Rio Santiago. Juan's expertise was immediately demonstrated by the manner in which he dispersed our gear and assigned us our places in order to balance the load. Once under way, he skillfully avoided all the branches, stumps, and debris that were floating down to sea. The water was very dark, obviously laden with silt and volcanic soil stripped from the mountains.

For hours Juan wove in and out, from the center of the river back to near the bank, selecting those areas where the current was less strong. Dozens of balsa-wood rafts passed us, usually guided by two men in front and one in the back, each with a long pole. They chose the areas of the river where the current was the swiftest, and steering adroitly traveled at a very fast rate. They were carrying vegetables of all kinds, bananas, domestic animals, and other goods down to Limones. Occasionally, we passed a balsa-wood raft being poled upstream close to the bank to avoid the strong current. It was obviously hard work and I was grateful that we had an engine.

The weather grew ominous as the day wore on; it began to rain and I wondered where Juan intended to stop for the night. We passed many small settlements and the people along the riverbank yelled hello and called out Juan's name when they recognized him. But he did not stop.

The vegetation along the river was luxuriant, and with the tall trees forming a green barrier on both sides, darkness came down quickly as soon as the sun dropped behind the hills to the west of us. Only then did Juan an-

nounce our destination. "We'll be stopping tonight at Casa
Ortiz," he said. "It's only about fifteen minutes upriver,
around the bend." When we reached it, Juan maneuvered
the canoe to the bank, we jumped out, and pulled it out of
the water.

A voice greeted us from the hill above, and two young
boys came running down to the riverbank, followed by
their father, Manuel Ortiz, Juan's friend. He helped us
carry our gear up to his small house. Then we lifted the
heavy outboard engine off the canoe and struggled up the
slope with it. Juan explained that leaving an engine outside, unwatched, was very risky here. I understood that;
an outboard engine is something very precious in this part
of Ecuador.

Standing in front of the house was a genial woman with
a beautiful smile. Señora Ortiz welcomed us graciously.
"*Los señores gringos* can sleep in our bedroom," she said.
"We will sleep with the children." We thanked her very
much, but refused and said that we would sleep on the
porch. Every house has a large porch, onto which the windows of the bedrooms and the kitchen open to catch the
fresh air and keep the house cool.

Appetizing smells were wafting through the kitchen
window. Señora Ortiz had prepared a tasty supper of
yucca, potatoes, corn, and a piece of delicious pork. As we
sat eating by the light of an oil lamp, both Señor and
Señora Ortiz were full of questions. They were very
curious to know what the devil two gringos were doing
going up the Santiago River in a canoe. I explained that
we wanted to visit the territory east of the Rio Santiago,
the area where the Cayapas Indians lived.

Señora Ortiz brightened up at this. "Oh, I'm a descendant of the Cayapas Indians," she said. "If you go upriver,
ask Democrito to try to find out where a very old Cayapas
named Pinuna lives. He was a friend of my grandfather.
Nobody knows how old he is; he doesn't know himself.
But if you can find him, he will be very useful, because he
knows the territory well. He has lived there many years."
We spent the rest of the evening digesting our supper,
drinking trago, and discussing the innuendos of Ecua-

dorian politics, a subject that everybody in this part of the country is interested in. By ten o'clock the fire was dying, and for our hosts, and us, it was time to go to sleep.

It was still raining lightly when we woke up the next morning. We said goodbye to the Ortiz family, loaded our gear into the canoe, and got under way. Our hope was to reach Playa de Oro by nightfall. But around 11:30 and later at 2:00 P.M. we had to stop and beach the canoe because the rain was coming down mercilessly, and Juan couldn't see where he was going. When we set out again, we had to bail water out of the canoe to keep it from settling too deeply into the river. Finally, Juan said we couldn't go much further; we would have to look for shelter. The only place nearby was Casa Cupa. We reached it a few minutes later and again beached the canoe, but as we approached the house, we were met by four male Cupas who did not seem very friendly. A certain air of tension and suspicion was reflected on their hard, unshaven faces. They held machetes in their hands and uttered not one word of welcome. Four women stood silently a few feet behind their men, the eldest holding three young children tightly to her. "I think they believe that we are from some government agency," Democrito whispered.

"Don't they see that we are not Ecuadorians?" I said.

"That doesn't matter," Democrito said. "They think that the central government plays all kinds of tricks on them to find out how many possessions they have, how much land they own, that kind of thing. So they are very suspicious."

Their attitude changed completely when I was introduced to the oldest member of the family and showed him my passport. "Oh," he said, "you are a Canadian!" He started to smile, as did his brothers and their wives. They invited us inside their house, pulled out a big bottle of trago, and we all drank together. There was no more reserve in the air.

Ceramic bowl. Cayapas range.

From that point on, the evening was very congenial and we talked about many things. When they learned of my interest in ancient artifacts, they mentioned that *infieles* had been found not far from there. I was immediately interested. "Have you found anything yourselves?" I asked.

"Oh yes, I have a big cup," one of the women said. She brought it out and showed it to me. It was a round, ceramic, platelike bowl with a short base, very dark, with no markings, and very ordinary. It was clearly a piece for everyday use.

Then I asked if they knew Pinuna, the old Cayapas Indian. "Oh yes," they said. "Everybody knows Pinuna. We don't see him ourselves, but we have heard about him, because he is one of the oldest Cayapas living in the north."

"Do you know where he lives?" I asked. They said they didn't, but that he had to live somewhere in one of the settlements near Piñan, a small village just below the paramo of Piñan, a bleak, broad, open plain in the highlands.

"The old Indians up there used to have some kind of temple for their ceremonies," one of the men told me, "but we don't know too much about it." I was intrigued by that piece of information. It seemed to substantiate my belief that I would be able to find some evidence of an ancient culture in the highlands of the Cayapas.

We set out again early the next morning, heading upriver in the direction of Playa de Oro. The current became much stronger as we ascended into higher land and got closer to the two affluents of the upper Rio Santiago, the Rio Angostura and the Rio Cojeria. We encountered more and more roots, tree trunks, branches, and debris in the water. Juan found it very difficult to maneuver, but by mid-afternoon Playa de Oro swung into sight on the right bank of the river. Dozens of people were on the riverbank as we approached the village. The entire population of about 200 people is black, descendants of slaves brought by the Spaniards from Africa to work plantations in Colombia. They fled during a revolution and settled here.

The chief of the village, Effe Martine, came forward to greet us, nodded when we explained our mission, and took us to the only available shelter, a bamboo hut that served as the schoolhouse. The walls were only about 3 feet high, and the space between the upper edge of the walls and the coconut-frond roof was completely open.

Through this space dozens of people, from all sides, watched us unpack and arrange our gear, smiling and commenting to each other on our every move.

We spent the rest of the afternoon with Martine, drinking some of the strongest trago I ever tasted. I asked him if he knew of any old burial grounds in this area. He said he didn't, but he had heard stories of such things further into the interior, in the paramo of Piñan. "We don't go into that area much," he said, "because it's the territory of the Cayapas Indians, and we don't want to have much contact with them." He explained that years before, a young black man from their village entered the Cayapas territory and came across an Indian girl. He raped her, whereupon the Indians started a tribal war against the blacks in retaliation. From that time on, the blacks had avoided the Cayapas territory. But when I asked Martine if he had heard of Pinuna, he said, "Yes, he lives near the paramo de Piñan."

We turned in that night with dozens of black faces still watching us over the low walls of the schoolhouse as we crawled into our sleeping bags. The next morning, we noticed many of the same faces engaged in serious discussion and we asked Martine what had happened. He said that the people were concerned because tomorrow was St. Joseph's Day—March 19—and the padre in the area, whom they had not seen for six months, had sent word that he would not be able to come that evening and perform the traditional mass. Their little chapel was nothing more than a bamboo hut with a few faded images of saints hanging on the walls, a wooden plank that served as an altar, and a rough-hewn wooden crucifix. But it was obvious that the ceremony meant a great deal to the villagers.

I asked Martine why, as the head of the village, he didn't read from the prayer book. "I don't know how to read," he said. "And besides, the book is in the Padre's language." He brought it to me, and I saw that it was in Latin and contained the same rituals that I had been familiar with when I was an altar boy. Democrito suggested that I read the prayers and before I had a chance to answer, Martine enthusiastically agreed.

By six that evening, the church had been spruced up and made presentable. The men, women, and children of the village, dressed in their finest, started to arrive, with looks of pleasure and expectation on their faces. Many carried wildflowers. We sang the hymns, I read the prayers and asked for the blessing of the Lord. The whole ceremony lasted about forty-five minutes. The villagers understood that I couldn't say the mass because I was not a priest, but they all felt the beauty of the ceremony. Afterward they prepared a small fiesta in the village square with food and a lot of trago, and everyone danced and sang until late in the evening.

When we awoke the next morning, Philip and I wanted to bathe, and we asked if there were dangerous fish or snakes in the river. We were told there was no danger; all the villagers washed themselves in the river, so we went in. We were startled by the temperature: in contrast with the tropical air, the water was incredibly cold, and made me aware of how close we were to the high ranges of the Andes, the source of the rivers that flowed into the Santiago.

As we were standing on the river bottom, Phillip suddenly said, "Look at my feet!" Our feet and lower legs were entirely covered with tiny flecks of gold. It was clear now why this place was called "Playa de Oro." It is probable that the precious metal was panned here thousands of years ago. It may have been one of the places from which the ancient inhabitants of the coastal region had acquired the gold used in the manufacture of the pieces found in the burial tolas on Tolita Island. Platinum, I learned, was found further south on the Rio Santiago. I asked Martine if the men in the village engaged in gold panning, and he said that only the women had the time to do so. They went down to the river to wash their clothes and while waiting for them to dry, they did some panning. The men had to work in the fields to plant or harvest; in their spare time, if they had any, they hunted and fished. Food was always their major preoccupation.

After a day of resting and bathing and another night's sleep, we arose very early and began our trek toward the paramo of Piñan. Juan and his outboard canoe had returned downriver after agreeing to meet us again in a week's time at Playa de Oro. Our route would now take us overland into the interior. Democrito led the way, followed by Marcos and Ivan, the son and the nephew of Martine, who had given them his permission to join our expedition, feeling that they would not get into trouble as long as they were with us. Philip and I brought up the rear of our procession, and the first few hours were quite difficult. The trail climbed steeply as it headed southeast from the village into the foothills of the Cayapas range. The heat was intense, and Philip and I had to push hard to keep up with Democrito and the young black boys who had been hiking in this country all their lives. By late afternoon we were in the highlands and the trail was less steep. Finally, we reached a small meadow near a creek where we decided to stop for the night. We pitched camp, Marcos and Ivan prepared a fire, and I fixed a supper of sardines, tuna, and eggs.

The boys now became curious. They had not been able to speak much in Playa de Oro; respect for their elders dictated that they not ask many questions. But here, around the fire, they felt free to ask us where we were from and what we were doing. I explained, and when I mentioned Pinuna, Ivan said, "Oh yes. I know where he lives. It's not far from the village of Piñan, on the edge of the paramo." I asked him how he knew that, and he said, "Oh, a few years ago two engineers from the central government went up into the paramo for some kind of inspection, and I helped them carry their gear. I heard about Pinuna then."

Marcos and Ivan stoked the fire for the night and we all settled down to sleep. The first night out in the open in a new, unknown area always makes a strong impression on my memory. I was acutely aware of the unfamiliar noises of the animals. The wind in the trees and the gurgling creek added their own soft sounds. I remember the stars shining overhead, the popping and flickering of the fire, and the breathing and stirring of the people around me. All this sharpened my own inner awareness—and my observations became almost spiritual. I began to think far into the future and to ask myself, "What am I doing here?" I felt that Philip, sleeping next to me, had perhaps asked himself that same question dozens of times. Each of us had our own reasons, and I found myself hoping that each of us would find what we were looking for.

The next day we continued to follow the trail, climbing steadily. When we began to meet a few Cayapas Indians on the trail, we knew we were in their territory. The Cayapas men wore only a shirt or tunic, covering them down to just below the waist. I later observed that when they talk to each other, they stand shoulder to shoulder rather than face to face. I discovered that there is a very practical reason for that. They urinate spontaneously, without announcement, whenever they feel the urge. So if you're standing in front of your companion, you're liable to get your feet wet.

We saw the Indian huts on the north side of the trail later that afternoon. In front of them stood two Cayapas women, perhaps in their twenties, dressed only in long skirts from the waist down. Marcos and Ivan looked straight ahead and did not glance at the girls, perhaps on instructions from Martine. We made a gesture of salute, but the women simply stared at us and did not respond.

That night we camped on a small plateau that looked inviting, but rain and high winds interrupted our sleep and we decided to move out and get back on the trail. Marcos and Ivan were able to see their way like cats in the dark, and by daybreak we had covered a fairly good distance. The rain stopped, but a cool piercing wind continued. In no time, our clothing and our packs were dry. Later that morning we reached a point called El Salto (The Falls), and from there, as we looked east, we could see the thatched huts of the village of Piñan. At a fork in the trail, we met a group of Cayapas Indians. They were very congenial and explained that the right branch, continuing southeast, led to the paramo, and the left branch headed east to the village. I decided to bypass the village for the moment; our interest was in talking to Pinuna. So we continued southeast.

By noon we had been on the trail for almost eight
hours. We were all tired and in need of some good food,
so we stopped and fixed a hot meal. Just as we were re-
packing, we saw an old Cayapas Indian coming down the
trail. We greeted him and asked if he knew where Pinuna
lived. He said, "Oh yes, he's my brother."

I was puzzled. "But we have heard he's very old and has
no family," I said.

"We don't have the same father," the Indian replied.
"He's my brother because of his mother's sister. Among
the Cayapas, men consider themselves brothers if they are
related in any way."

The old Indian offered to take us to Pinuna's house. He
turned and started back up the trail, and we followed. By
late afternoon we had reached a plateau above the
paramo of Piñan, and there our guide led us to a small
hut. Pinuna was not home. The old Indian said he was
sure he was not far away, and suggested that we wait for
him. "Every afternoon, Pinuna goes down to dig up some
yucca or potatoes that he grows not very far from here."
Then he left us, walking back in the direction we had
come from.

Philip, Democrito, and I settled ourselves on the
wooden floor of the narrow porch that framed the front
of Pinuna's hut, while Ivan and Marcos took charge of
our packs. Half an hour later, we saw Pinuna walking up
the path toward his house. He stopped 50 feet away and
stared at us. He was a very prepossessing-looking man,
quite erect, with a certain air of authority. It was impossible to tell his age. He was not dressed in the Cayapas style;
he wore the traditional heavy cotton shirt, but he was
clothed from the waist down in an old pair of trousers.

We all stood up, and Democrito and I walked down the
path to greet Pinuna and explain our reasons for being
there. I was sure he didn't understand; he was obviously
nervous about having so many strangers on his premises.
Nevertheless he invited us to stay, and after we had offered him some of our food, trago, and cigarettes, we sat
and talked. He told me he had lived in this area a very
long time, and when I asked him if he knew of any *infieles*

or old construction, he said, "Oh yes, there are *infieles,* but the spirits live in them. You have to be very careful because sometimes the spirits can enter your body and possess you."

"I think we are protected against such happenings," I said. "I would be very interested to see some of them."

He looked straight into my eyes and, after a long pause, said, "We'll see, we'll see." Then he turned in for the night.

Philip and I sat there a while longer, talking and enjoying the atmosphere of this strange place, so far removed from anything we knew. "My God," Philip said. "If my children could see me now." Then his mind turned toward more practical matters and he asked, "How are you going to finance all the work it will take to put together these expeditions and carry out the research you want to do?"

I said I didn't know at the moment. I might be able to associate myself with a foundation or university that had funds to support such research. But I wasn't sure that I could find one that would be interested in pursuing this particular theory of New World cultural origins.

"I know you," Philip said. "You want to stay independent. You'd be better off if you could somehow raise the capital yourself. What about that friend of yours in Miami who has connections in Venezuela? What's his name?"

"Virgilio Quinones?" I said.

"Yes, Quinones. You told me he said that friends of his in Venezuela knew an area where there are diamonds. And they wanted somebody like you, who knows exploration and can do underwater research, to go down and work with them. You're going to need a lot of capital. Why don't you do it? Get in touch with these people, spend some time in Venezuela, and see if you can find the diamonds. If you're lucky, maybe with a year's work or so you can come up with the resources to finance yourself for several years here in Ecuador."

It was an interesting idea, and when Philip and I turned in that night, I should have gone to sleep immedi-

ately—daybreak was only a few hours away—but I lay awake a long time thinking about it. I hadn't considered looking for diamonds seriously when Quinones first mentioned it to me. But now the possibility of supporting my research work in Ecuador through the Venezuelan venture began to excite me.

The following morning a mestizo—a half-blood Cayapas Indian—named Pedro Ozolo arrived from the village, having heard about my interest in the *infieles* from Pinuna's "brother." In his shoulder bag he had several small figurines of dark solid pottery that looked very old indeed. Some were strange mythic animal figures. Others were human, with very fine appliqué detail and characteristic traits I had seen in the coastal cultures. The depiction of warm clothing, caps, and headbands suggested that a much colder climate prevailed at the time the pieces were made. Today the region enjoys a temperate climate. I asked Ozolo where he had found these pieces, and he said vaguely, "Oh, in places around."

"You can tell him," Pinuna said. "I was ready to take the señor to where the *infieles* are found. You can trust him."

Ozolo then said that he had found the pieces on the paramo and offered to take us there. We finished eating, washed up, and started out with Ozolo and Pinuna in the lead, moving generally east across the paramo. After an hour or so we came to a series of small burial mounds, about 1½ meters high. From a distance, without knowing their specific location, they would have been difficult to find. Some of the mounds had been excavated. Ozolo pulled out the pieces from his shoulder bag again and showed me the specific mound that each had come from.

"How about the human remains—skulls and bones?" I asked.

"Oh, we don't touch those," Ozolo replied. I looked closely at the mounds and saw that, unfortunately, nature had taken its course and had disposed of any human remains there may have been. The few fragments that lay around crumbled in my fingers.

Rain interrupted further investigation. "We must go

Solid pottery figures. Cayapas range.

back to the house," Pinuna said. "When it rains on the
paramo, the wind comes up, and it can get very bad." We
started back; by the time we reached Pinuna's house the
sky was completely black, and it was pouring as if there
had been no rain for the last hundred years.

Ozolo left when the rain stopped and I promised that I
would try to get down to the village the next day to see a
stone piece that he had found on the paramo. That night
after supper, I asked Pinuna about the legends of the
paramo of Piñan. After sipping his trago slowly and staring at the fire for what seemed a long time, Pinuna said
that his people believed that the three volcanoes ranging
east to southeast from the paramo—Yana-Urco, Cotacachi, and Busag-Cocha—were great gods, each of
whom had given birth to a river. There is a small river
originating at each of these peaks; they all flow westward
into the Rio Guayllabamba, and ultimately into the Rio Esmeraldas.

The ancient people, Pinuna continued, believed that
when the laws were properly respected and all the religious days observed, the water in these rivers was clear
and beautiful for drinking. But when they were bad and
disrespectful, then the volcanoes erupted in flames and
lava and the rivers turned dark. That was a sign to the ancient people that they had to travel to a certain point in
the paramo of Piñan that looks out over a broad valley
and up toward these three great volcanoes. At this site
there was a small temple, where the priests offered sacrifices to appease the gods.

"Long ago, when I was a young man, I saw these ceremonies," Pinuna said. "The land was trembling, and the
gods were spitting fire and lava. My people were all chanting and walking in a procession with torches burning in
the night. After the chant, the priest performed a sacred
ceremony, and offered a human sacrifice to the gods.
Then the earth stopped trembling, and the gods stopped
spitting fire into the air."

I was fascinated to hear more of these legends, but
Pinuna stopped talking, moved to the door of his hut, and

stood gazing out toward the slope of the cordillera that was now in complete darkness. The flickering of the fire cast strange shadows as he turned from the door, walked to a corner of the room, lifted an old blanket, and from underneath retrieved a basket. He carried it near the fire and I knew that he wanted me to see its contents. He reached down, took out a number of small objects, and laid them on the floor. There were several well-polished black stones, three stone axes, potsherds with post-firing paint, and four short carved black wooden lances. It was clear to me now that Pinuna was a Cayapas shaman, and that these were the tools he used in the rituals.

He explained the significance of each piece. The Cayapas shaman believes that the ancient stone axes contain benevolent spirits that act as guides during a healing ceremony. The polished black stones and the ancient potsherds are also used during the ceremony: each piece is said to have a different spirit helper and each plays a significant role. The black wooden lances are used to cast spells on the bad spirits who inhabit the body of the diseased individual, and push them into one of the many rivers where they will eventually be carried down to the sea and lost forever.

I asked Pinuna where the stone axes and potsherds had come from. He looked toward the east and said, "Behind the sierra, from the *infiele* tolas." As he spoke, my eyes were riveted on the stone axes, and uppermost in my thoughts was the deep importance they represented. I knew that the Cayapas Indians had moved into this region in comparatively recent times, after tribal wars in which they defeated the ancient inhabitants. But according to their legends, they originally came from the high sierra, north of the equator in what is today known as Ecuador. The Cayapas are not inclined toward stoneworking, for they lack knowledge of the art. But, obviously, legends and traditions known to their shamans had driven them to search in ancient burial grounds for these implements that were used for ceremonial purposes rather than as tools of labor. It flashed across my mind that the metal ax

Stone axes. Cayapas range.

Pepe Azueta had shown me perhaps had the same significance, although it had been crafted by a more advanced culture.

The culture I was searching for in the Cordillera de Cayapas had indeed existed; the artifacts that Pinuna had recovered from ancient mounds seemed to confirm this. And I thought of the major rivers that today flow down to the Rio Esmeraldas—and of the Rio Santiago, which originates in this same area and flows to the island of Tolita. It would have been easy then, as it was now, to move along these rivers. It seemed quite likely that any ancient cultures developing in the Cayapas or adjacent sierras would have moved down these rivers and perhaps established themselves in the coastal areas.

The following morning Ozolo showed up early. He said he had decided not to wait; he was afraid we might change our minds and not come down to the village of Piñan to see his stone piece. He reached into his bag and pulled it out. It was an eroded piece of volcanic stone about 15 centimeters high, on which carvings of human features were still evident. Traces of carved mythic figures could also be seen on the sides and the back surfaces. The material of the piece and the atavistic style of the carving indicated that it considerably predated the pottery pieces I had seen that had been found on the paramo.

When I tried to pinpoint the location where this piece had been found, Ozolo would say only: "*Para allá* (That way)," in the grand, imprecise manner in which South Americans so often dispose of any question of direction or location. It may be that he himself didn't know; perhaps the piece had passed into his hands from somebody else. But he pointed to the east over the cordillera in the direction of the Cotacachi volcano, and the fact that he said it came from that region again jostled me into thinking of the possibility that ancient cultures had inhabited an area far into the Oriente.

I knew we would not be able to explore that region on this trip. The daily rainfall that at times became torrential, the swollen rivers, the rugged terrain, and the incredible

sea of mud would be major obstacles. Philip also reminded me anxiously that we had to keep our appointment with Juan, our boatman, in Playa de Oro. I told
Pinuna that we had to leave but that I would be back. He
nodded, and suggested a different trail that would take us
back to Playa de Oro more quickly. We left two bottles of
tra ᵎ and a few packs of cigarettes with him and said
goodbye.

*Primitive mythic figure
carved from volcanic
stone. Cayapas range.*

We met Juan as scheduled in Playa de Oro and set out
again on the Rio Santiago. But this time we were traveling
downstream with the current and our return trip went
very quickly. Just before we reached Limones, I persuaded Juan to stop at Tolita Island. I hadn't been able to
get out of my mind the image of all of the tolas on the
island, lying there unprotected as campesinos, entrepre-
neurs, families on outings, European collectors, mer-
chants—anyone—dug into them at will and carried off the
priceless artifacts. I knew that an immense amount of
damage had been done, but I wanted to see for myself if
anything of interest still remained.

As we approached the island, Juan said he knew a few
fishermen who lived there and did excavation when the
weather was too bad for fishing. He maneuvered the
canoe toward their houses, typical small wooden structures on stilts, and when we beached the canoe, two men
who recognized Juan came to greet us. I asked if they
would take me to a tola that had been excavated in the last
month or so, and one of them agreed.

We started out through dense jungle foliage, following
a trail leading toward the northwest part of the island
where the burial grounds are located. I later learned, con-
trary to what I had been led to believe, that the name
"Tolita" does not refer to the whole island but only to this
northwestern section where most of the tolas are concentrated. The island is properly known as Tola. Whatever its
name, I soon began to see evidence of its careless exploitation. Scattered along the trail were hundreds of pottery
shards. We came to a tola, half of which had been excavated, and when I asked our guide if he knew what had

A tola (burial mound) on Tolita Island.

been found there, he said, "Oh, nothing much. Just pottery pieces." He dug around in the earth a little, hit something, and said, "This stuff." He showed us a small, globular vase. I recognized it as the type of vessel that was often part of the *cocina de brujo*, the special ware in which a shaman kept the potions he used in his ceremonies.

"How about all the gold I've heard is found here?" I asked our guide.

Small globular jug. Tolita.

"Oh, that's an old story," the man said. "A lot of people have found gold pieces, sometimes inside little pots like that one. But you never hear about it, because whoever finds gold is afraid the government will take it away."

Something caught my eye when I peered into the partially excavated tola. I looked closely and saw that the wall of the tola was of two distinct layers. The texture of the upper and lower strata was visibly different, and there was a thin layer separating the two, which had been the densely packed surface of the older, lower tola. The roots of plants and small trees that had been cut off at the surface when construction of the new, upper tola started were clearly visible in the lower strata. Also in the upper strata, a great number of fragments of pottery of different textures and colors were visible, which indicated the possibility that the earth used to build the tola had been part of a refuse pit of an earlier age.

Facial mask amulet. Tolita.

All this was something completely new. I hadn't found any reference before—in Ribadeneira's book, from Yannuzzelli or any other source—to the existence of two cultural stages at Tolita. Yet the two distinct strata in a single tola seemed to offer just such evidence. I wondered if there were other tolas on the island that had not yet been excavated. They, too, might show evidence of separate cultural stages; and if they were excavated carefully, and the artifacts and other remains preserved and studied, important new information about the cultural development of the island might be found.

Priest with jaguar features and feathered raiment. Tolita.

Our guide offered to show us a few artifacts he had excavated on the island. Still another piece was a small pottery whistle with the features of the Amazon rain forest Capuchin monkey. This piece was from the lower strata of the tola, which seemed to indicate a very early origin for the use of the whistles, also used in the Esmeraldas, Jama-Coaque, Manteño, and other coastal cultures.

Then the old fisherman showed me a number of pieces he had dug out, he said, from the upper layer of a tola, among them a tender little representation of a small animal holding a ball in its paw, and an amulet showing a couple embracing. We returned to the shore and approached one of the houses on stilts. "Come up," he said. We climbed the small ladder and followed him into his house. Among the several pieces he showed us was a strange, triangular face amulet with vacant atavistic features that was probably worn as a talisman to protect the wearer against evil spirits, or as a representation of a trophy acquired in the tradition of the headhunters. Another piece showed a priest with jaguar features, indicating the existence of a jaguar cult in this culture; he wore elaborate pendant earrings, a trait seen in many other coastal cultures, and a feathered raiment whose significance did not become clear to me until much later.

Head with fish headdress. Tolita.

My attention was particularly drawn to a piece showing the head of a priest with headdress in the form of a fish, whose stylized nose was reminiscent of the architectural motif of the gable on the pottery shrine I had seen in Yannuzzelli's collection. The tonguelike shape protruding over the fish's lower jaw probably represented the spirit of

Whistle with monkey features. Tolita.

Small animal playing with ball. Tolita.

the fish-god speaking to the priest in answer to his appeal to provide bounty from the sea to a people living along the coast who subsisted on a fishing economy. The warmth and humanity with which these little figures were rendered contrasted quite strongly with the more primeval, apprehensive quality of what appeared to be earlier Tolita pieces. Further, these did not seem to be priestly figures. Rather, they appeared to be average members of the tribe, considered by the artisan (and therefore by the culture) to be worthy in themselves to serve as subjects for art. This, as well as the more sophisticated style and technology of these and other pieces in the fisherman's collection, confirmed my belief that two distinct cultural stages had indeed existed on Tolita, separated perhaps by hundreds of years.

We spent the night on Tolita, and as darkness came, a heavy fog enveloped the island, giving it an aura of mystery. My thoughts drifted backward in time for more than 2000 years when the Tolita culture had flourished. I now had evidence that it had gone through two distinct stages, but where had it originated? Representations of the jaguar and the Capuchin monkey again pointed to the interior, but so far my answer to that important question was still only conjecture. Perhaps there was evidence in tolas on both the island and the mainland of even earlier stages of development of the coastal cultures, stages that would reveal a positive link to the interior. It was a provocative thought.

The next morning, it took us less than forty-five minutes to reach Limones in Juan's boat. Señora Natalia received us with a broad smile, offered us a drink and a chair on her front porch, and wanted to hear all about our adventures. We talked until it was time to climb back into Juan's boat and then board the old *San Antonio* for our return trip to Esmeraldas.

The voyage was calm and I talked with Democrito about future plans. I told him I would very much like to come back and undertake a more thorough exploration of

Embracing couple. Tolita.

the Cayapas area. We agreed that the best thing to do was look for a place in the village of Piñan to serve as our base, find horses to use, then venture out from there into the paramo in the direction of the three great volcanoes that were so important in Cayapas legends. We might even explore the Cordillera de Lachas, north of the paramo of Piñan. I thought there might be burial grounds in any of these areas. Philip listened to our plans attentively and I knew that he had enjoyed our expedition immensely. But when Democrito turned to him to ask if he would be coming with us on this new expedition, he said, "In the future I think I'd rather hear about your adventures than live them."

Philip and I parted company in Quito. He flew back to Miami and I went to Manta, where I was joined by my friend Jorge Moncayo for another brief expedition to study the coastal cultures of the area. This time we headed south from Manta to Jipijapa, veering, after reaching Procel, into the Cerro de Colonche, a range of semi-dry hills that runs generally parallel to the coast with altitudes ranging between 500 and 600 meters. The southeast arm of this range, called the Cerro de Chongon, extends almost to Guayaquil.

Our destination was the Finca Alvarez. When we reached it, the owner, Alejandro Alvarez, an ex-teacher who had decided to go back to the land and become a farmer, proved to be very talkative. He told us about his explorations, and said he had done most of his work within the Colonche and the Cerro de Chongon. He took us into his house and pulled out some things that, judging by his attitude, he seemed to regard as rather special: two stone axheads. Along with these two stone pieces, he laid out several metal axheads that I recognized immediately as being quite similar to the one I had obtained from Pepe Azueta in the area of Bahía. Alvarez didn't attach too much importance to the metal pieces; in his mind, they had most likely been made by Indians in recent times. But he said he had recovered all the pieces in the same burial

Hard copper axhead. Milagro.

Torteros. *Bahía.*

and I really pricked up my ears when I heard that; stone and metal axheads found together, from the same culture, struck me as particularly significant.

It was quite dark in his house, so I took the metal axheads out on the porch and studied them. When I scratched the underside of one of them with my pocket knife, I saw the characteristic reddish-orange color of copper. My original impression was confirmed. Alvarez's axheads were very similar to the Azueta axhead—and yet they came from completely different cultural areas. I knew that other investigators had reported that such pieces were used as currency, thus explaining their appearance in widely divergent areas. But now I began to wonder, for the pieces I was examining appeared to be too large and heavy for such a medium of exchange. Moreover, their scarcity could not justify such an explanation. Only more research could clarify this puzzle.

Alvarez also had an incredible collection of *torteros* (spindle whorls), headlike ceramic artifacts with a variety of imaginative designs engraved on their surfaces. These vary in size from 1.5 to 3 centimeters and one or two of them, perhaps three, are often found in a burial. Apparently *torteros* were worn as amulets and conferred protection, good fortune, or health upon the wearer. I would see many of them on future expeditions, and observed numerous geometric patterns on their surfaces, as well as figures of the pelican, jaguar, monkey and snake, and of lovemaking couples. The motifs were potent symbols of natural and spiritual forces, and they suggest the importance these little amulets had for the ancient people who wore them.

I was fascinated by these tiny pieces. The skill that it took to do such fine work, on such a miniature scale, was impressive. And somehow, a culture that has developed the expertise to produce, use, and appreciate these miniature objects seems to have reached a finer level of aesthetic development than a culture that focuses on big, monolithic things.

Alvarez then opened another box and took out a

charming figure of a seated woman with a water jar on
her shoulder, very domestic in style. It related closely to a
figure of a woman with a domesticated bird that I unearthed later from a burial ground east of Bahía de
Caráquez. But at that moment I was reminded of the
gentle, human handling of the pieces I had seen in the
fisherman's hut on Tolita Island.

Pottery is, of course, an easier medium to work with,
and much more expressive than stone. Its fabrication and
use reflect a more domesticated, family-oriented culture,
in which great numbers of people have become artisans,
rather than leaving that activity to a few highly trained
specialists, as is necessary with stone. The scenes and con-
cerns depicted in pottery—in fact, the very choice of the
medium itself—indicate that the culture feels the importance of satisfying daily needs, and accommodating the
comfort and well-being of each individual. The focus is on
everyday human activities, as well as on household items
and articles for domestic use.

*Domestic figurines.
Bahía.*

Further, the innumerable figures of gods, priests, and
mythic animals that can be fabricated in pottery mean that
every family, or clan, can have articles of worship within
their own house, or in a little shrine within their own compound. Thus religion is put on a more individual basis
than with stone, where it is likely that one awesome, powerful piece, the object of worship of the whole tribe, remains within the care of the most powerful priest, or shaman, so maintaining his status at a level far above that of
the average member of the tribe.

During my return flight from Quito to Miami, I had
time to reflect on how little is known and understood
about these refined coastal cultures, and even less about
pre-Columbian cultures in the sierra or the Oriente. In
addition to the indifference of so many Ecuadorians and
the rampant destruction of important archaeological sites,
I realized that I faced another problem if I was ever to
find the information I sought: It was very difficult, I had
discovered, to establish precisely the locations of these

pre-Columbian cultures. Among the people in the universities and the government ministries who were involved in any way with archaeology, it seemed that very few had done their own excavations. All they had to work with in their museums or departmental collections were pieces excavated by campesinos. And the campesinos, generally speaking, did not like to reveal the provenance of their findings because it would then be only a matter of time before somebody else intruded upon their digs, which are a good source of income for them. Tremendous confusion has arisen, even around those artifacts of relatively familiar style, as to where the cultures that produced them were located, and therefore what the interrelationships between these cultures might be. Even in the best of what had been published I found that there were some cultural locations reported, and conclusions as to cultural relationships derived from those locations, that were wrong.

I kept hearing the voices of Moncayo, Salvador, and a score of others telling me the same thing: "You're going to learn that the hardest thing in this country is to find out exactly where anything comes from." The obvious solution to that problem was also the most difficult one: I had to continue searching for artifacts myself.

Months later, I again had an insight into how meager knowledge about pre-Columbian cultures is, even among experts. I was in New York at the Museum of the American Indian talking with the director, and at one point in our conversation, as he was expounding the extraordinary value of his collection, he said: "Come with me. I want to show you something." He led me to an anteroom, went to a safe, dialed the combination, and opened it to reveal a series of locked drawers. He then pulled out a key and opened one of the drawers, withdrew an object wrapped in cloth, and with a hushed, tense air, opened the cloth to reveal—one copper axhead. The care with which he kept this piece was a clear indication of the importance he attached to it. I didn't have the heart to tell him that at that very moment at least seven similar axheads were lying in old boxes on the shelf of a cane house in Ecuador.

PART II

The Venezuelan Venture

CHAPTER 5

The Diamond Seekers

The night was balmy and warm, and the reflection of the moon over Biscayne Bay added a touch of romance to the surroundings. I was sitting on my neighbor's terrace on Palm Island, facing the Miami skyline, the sounds of laughter and music from a party mingling with my thoughts. It was a very different setting from the flat, rain-drenched paramo of Piñan. Yet my thoughts returned to that evening in Ecuador many months before when Philip Brooks and I were sitting on the porch of Pinuna's hut, and he urged me to accept an offer to search for diamonds in Venezuela as a means of supporting my future archaeological expeditions.

I knew from my early readings of South American lore that Venezuela—especially the Guiana region in the southeastern corner of that nation—had always held a compelling fascination for early explorers. Sir Walter Raleigh, in his book *Discoverie of the Large, Rich and Bevvtiful Empyre of Gviana,* published in 1596, had detailed his adventures in pursuit of the fabled riches of Guiana. He had learned, from Spanish reports captured at sea (England and Spain were then at war), that the Indians of South America had described the existence of a fabulous stone city known as Manoa, which the Spaniards had renamed El Dorado. Raleigh became convinced that Manoa was to be found in Guiana, but he failed in his efforts to find it, having sailed only from the Atlantic coast up the Orinoco to the cataract of the Caroni, where the two rivers meet.

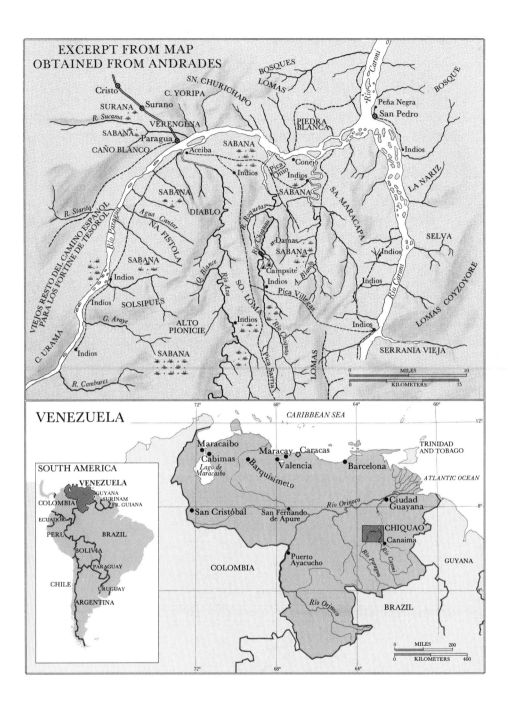

In the following centuries, there were countless expeditions in search of this legendary city. A French archaeologist, Marcel Homet, described in his book *Sons of the Sun,* published in 1963, his search for the sacred stone city in the savage area of the Roraima mountain range, which borders the Venezuelan Guiana Highlands and Brazil. He also described glyphic rock paintings, cave burials, and figurines of stone and pottery that he had seen in this area, but, like hundreds of others before, the legendary Manoa had also eluded him. By an extraordinary coincidence, the diamond concession that I had been asked to investigate was located in this same vast, remote, and practically unknown region of the Guiana Highlands.

The request had been made several months ago by my old friend Virgilio Quinones. An ex-naval officer and former staff member of the Cuban Naval Academy, he had left Cuba following the Castro revolution, and for several years had been the captain of a commercial freighter that sailed from Venezuela to the States and points in between. In Venezuela, his boat routinely picked up goods from the business of Pablo Corrales; the two men became good friends, and Quinones learned that Corrales had a land concession, about 100 kilometers square, from the Venezuelan government to exploit minerals, principally diamonds, in the rugged and mountainous jungle territory near the headwaters of the Rio Chiquao in the uplands of the Guiana.

Corrales had commissioned a general geological survey of the area, which concluded that underwater mining of the many small rivers and streams that crisscrossed his concession would, in all probability, be the most economical and easiest method of recovering the rough diamonds. Over the millennia, torrential rainfall had caused heavy erosion of the mountainous land surrounding his concession, and whatever diamonds there were had probably been washed down into these rivers and streams where they lay trapped on the bottom in the sediment. Corrales told Quinones of this report, and Quinones, knowing of my underwater expertise, contacted me to ask if I would undertake a preliminary investigation. I had refused at first, but I knew that Corrales was still interested in my services. And now I was beginning to think that an expedition to Venezuela might be a very good way to pay for future trips to Ecuador.

The voice of my host, Bill Pollard, interrupted my thoughts. "I want you to meet a near neighbor of ours," he said. "Carl Holm. I think you two have a lot of mutual interests." Carl was an executive of North American Rockwell, and as we began to talk, we discovered that we did indeed have many interests in common. When I told him of my experiences as a diver in World War II, he said that he had developed detection and defense countermeasures against German U-boats and was the co-editor of the *Handbook of Ocean and Underwater Engineering*. I mentioned that I was considering an offer to use my diving experience to search for diamonds in Venezuela, and he said that he was also quite familiar with diamonds, having been involved in a study of recovery operations off the coast of Africa using diving techniques. Moreover, he had spent some time in the Guiana region of Venezuela. And he shared my interest in archaeology. He told me that in the Guiana he had seen what appeared to be canals connecting a network of rivers that seemed clearly to be of ancient origin, although he did not know whether they had been built for transportation purposes, protection from flood waters, or for some other reason.

I was intrigued by his story and told Carl of my hypothesis that the very early cultures of the New World had originated in a belt along the equator. The Guiana, as well as the areas of Homet's activity and the legendary location of Manoa, were all within five or six degrees of the equator, and it occurred to me that if ancient cultures had originated somewhere in the Amazon, then it would be plausible that these early people later moved not only westward into Ecuador but also north into the Venezuelan Guiana. The great tributaries of the Amazon Basin converge radially, like the spokes of a wheel, and river corridors, the most likely routes for migration, extend from the Amazon heartland to the north, west, and the south.

Carl listened to my theories with great interest, and even as I spoke I realized that an expedition into the Guiana might not only be financially rewarding for me but would also provide an opportunity to search for further archaeological proof of my theories. Carl had another thought. He said that if I was able to put a Venezuelan expedition together and establish a solid potential for diamonds in that area, one of the divisions of Rockwell might be interested in supporting the exploitation of Corrales' concession. We agreed to meet again and discuss the project further. And when we did, a few days later, he was most encouraging about the prospect of Rockwell's support. With that the Venezuelan venture looked even more promising to me and I called my friend Virgilio Quinones. He was pleased to learn of my decision to accept Pablo Corrales's invitation.

Arrangements were completed for an expedition into the Guiana by February of 1968, and Captain Quinones and I flew to Caracas, the capital of Venezuela. There we were met by Pablo Corrales, a stocky, dark-haired, energetic man of about fifty, who told me that he had arranged for one of the best guides in the interior, a Zape Indian named Antonio, to meet me near the river town of Paragua, lead me over the trail into the Chiquao area, and work with me throughout the entire expedition. When it was time to come out, Antonio would take me to a small landing strip which was several hours' hike from the Chiquao, where a bush pilot would pick me up and bring me back to Ciudad Bolívar. These plans sounded very workable and we all felt the flush of enthusiasm.

We spent the next few days in Caracas, searching out what little information was available on the geology and topography of the Guiana. Then Pablo and I loaded my gear into a jeep and started south for Ciudad Bolívar, the provincial capital of its namesake state, Bolívar, and the first stop on the journey to Paragua. The trip took two days of hard driving on a badly potholed road. When we first saw the city, built on the bank of the Orinoco River, its pink-colored Spanish colonial architecture seemed to contrast vividly with the sober square structures of its modern buildings; with the construction of the largest suspension bridge in South America across the Orinoco, the city has been transformed from a charming old colonial town into a brisk, commercial center, a gateway for the industrial development of the Orinoco coastal basin. In fact, internationally the area is already called the "Pittsburgh of South America," due to the discovery of huge, high-grade iron ore deposits and the consequent building of Venezuela's first large-scale steel mill in Ciudad Guayana, 70 miles downstream from Ciudad Bolívar. By comparison, the Guiana, which is also part of the state of Bolívar covering its southern region, is the most unexplored and sparsely populated area not only of this state but of the whole country.

I was particularly interested in learning more about diamonds, and in Ciudad Bolívar, Pablo and I visited a laboratory specializing in the appraisal and study of uncut stones. The laboratory is supported by the federal government to help miners establish the value of their diamonds and the service is free, but as the director said, "Not many come to us for appraisal; they are always suspicious of our good intentions." For me, however, it was an enlightening visit. I learned of the complexities involved in grading industrial diamonds into three distinct varieties: *ballas, bort,* and *carbonado*—too irregular, too flawed, or too small to be valued as gems. I was also introduced to the art of recognizing and selecting stones of gem quality by their color, transparency, and light dispersion. A "fancy" diamond has a very distinct color, I was told; red, blue, and green are very rare, but orange, violet, and yellow are more common. To my surprise, I learned that 55 percent of the stones found in La Gran Sabaña—the heart of Guiana—are of gem quality, compared to only 25 percent of the stones found in South Africa, one of the leading diamond producers in the world.

Pablo and I parted company in Ciudad Bolívar, and a young mestizo, Jesus, drove me the rest of the way to Paragua, about 150 kilometers to the south. The ride was uneventful, even though the poorly graded curves of the long, dusty road were dotted with the rusting wrecks of cars and trucks. When we passed one of them, Jesus slowed down and blessed himself. Paragua serves as the center for the diamond-mining operations up and down the river of the same name, and it reminded me of a town of the old Gold Rush days. There was a saloon with swinging doors, banjo music, and a huge mirror behind the bar; young women wearing short black satin dresses and net stockings sold drinks, and pool and card tables were busy with lucky and unlucky players. The general store sold not only provisions but also diving gear, old and new machinery, and cowboy hats.

I wanted to see how the *mineros* (miners) of the region recovered diamonds from the Paragua River and its affluents, and an old miner, Raul, agreed to take me upriver in his motor-canoe. After a three-hour trip from the town, the sound of diving compressors in operation broke the stillness of the surrounding jungle. We rounded a bend in the river, and there, stretching from bank to bank, I saw floating rafts on which men, women, and children were all busily at work. It was a human dredging operation. Using the old-type metal diving helmets, some with hoses at-

Diving for diamonds on the Rio Paragua.

tached to air compressors and others to hand-operated pumps, men jumped overboard, went down to the bottom of the river, and filled up a few baskets with sediment. The sediment was then hauled up topside, where it was panned with *saruccas*—the conventional shallow trays—to flush out the diamonds.

For the next several days, Raul and I visited other mining operations on the river. Some miners work the sandbanks of the rivers, or alluvial gravel beds inland, with *saruccas*. Others work on dredges anchored in the swift and treacherous currents of the river, where sediment from the bottom is sucked up by mechanical devices and then washed and sifted in the endless search for diamonds. I spoke with a number of the *marachuchos* (divers) who worked on these dredges—a polyglot mixture of native and international adventurers with only one thing in common, the hope of striking it rich. Thatched-roof huts and canoes along the riverbanks marked the locations of their colonies, where they have their own laws and system of justice, and a thief caught has no appeal to the mandatory death sentence. The frequent sight of a man in a black suit with a briefcase, the diamond buyer, was proof that these dredging operations produced gem-quality stones. I heard as many tales of fortunes found in the treacherous waters of the river as I did of fortunes lost at the poker tables in Paragua. But rarely did anyone speak about specific diving spots, accidents, or loss of life. Very few complained of the hard work and the sacrifices of a lifetime spent along the river in a quest for the shiny stones.

Raul took me to the spot along the riverbank where I was to meet my Indian guide, Antonio. Two men were waiting for us when we arrived. As I stepped ashore from the canoe, the older of the two stood and we shook hands. It was Antonio. He told me that the younger Indian, Ramirez, wanted to learn the country, and would travel with us into the interior. Communication with them was no problem as we all spoke Spanish.

We unloaded my gear from the canoe and spent the

night there on the riverbank in a small shelter that Antonio and Ramirez had built. We would start out early the
following morning, and Antonio described the trail to me.
It curved inland, then headed generally south, skirting
rapids on the river until it turned up into a number of
savannas and foothills between mountain ranges. Antonio
thought that if the weather remained good, we would be
able to reach the plateau of the Chiquao in four days. He
said the trail was very rough and not often used, but there
was no other way to reach our destination.

That evening, as we squatted around the campfire, the
three of us talked and got acquainted. Antonio was a descendant of the Zape Indians whose ancestral home was in
the valley of the Rio Orinoco, far to the west. But
members of his family had been killed regularly in tribal
warfare for many generations, and finally he had had
enough of it. So not many years ago he had moved to an
area of the Chiquao that he knew to be quite unsettled,
and once there, he sent back word to the other members
of his clan who, one by one, joined him. It had not been
an easy move for an Indian to make, and when Antonio
told me this story, I realized that I was in the presence of
an unusual man.

As the evening progressed, our conversation turned to
my interest in the ancient people who had once lived in
this area and what they left behind. Antonio knew of
these people. He told me that in the region of the Caripo,
in a place called Uruana, there was a huge cave that he
had seen himself. The cave was like a chapel, he said, and
inside there was an altar built of huge stones and covered
with sculptured markings (petroglyphs), some of which
looked like representations of the sun and the moon. In
the center of one of the walls there was also a sculpture in
the form of a huge serpent. The Indians who lived in the
area called this place *La Cueva Pintada* ("The Decorated
Cave"), but they were very much afraid of it because they
believed that the gods lived there—the deities of the rain
and the forest who controlled their destiny. Antonio said
that some Indians knew of other caves in this territory

that had carvings inside. And in another area, he said, there was a very long, old stone wall with a doorway. But no one had ever dared go through the doorway, again because they thought that the gods lived within.

Antonio's stories seemed to confirm what I had been told by a man in one of the governmental offices in Caracas who had surveyed parts of the Guiana region and said that he had seen caves with fragments of stone inside shaped and worked by hand. If these caves did, in fact, exist and fragments of carved stone could be found, they would provide strong proof that there had been an ancient culture in the Guiana, a culture that never had been studied or reported. And if this culture had existed, I wondered if there could be a connection between these ancient Venezuelan megalithic stoneworkers and the cultures of the western Amazon in Ecuador.

In Ecuador, the Andes Mountains consist of three parallel ranges. The central and the western ranges continue northerly into Colombia, and become continuous with the highlands of Central America and the mountains of Mexico. But the easternmost range curves eastward and bends over to the Caribbean coast of Venezuela, becoming continuous with highlands that run eastward all along the coast, and then curve southward, forming an arc, terminating in the mountains of this territory, the Guiana. I had observed in Ecuador that it was easier, and safer, to traverse the highlands and mesas within the mountains than to hack through dense growth and risk the dangers of traveling through the lowland jungles. Certainly the same would have been true in ancient times, and I wondered if the peoples of the Amazon might have followed the river upstream to this highland arc, and then used it as a corridor for migration through Ecuador, Colombia, and the Venezuelan Guiana. The questions to be answered were mounting.

Antonio, Ramirez, and I started out on the trail at sunrise and I realized almost immediately that we had a difficult journey ahead. From time to time the trail simply disappeared under the thick jungle vegetation, and only by working with machetes were we able to clear our way. We also had to cross turbulent streams of water where one false step on the rocky bottom would have meant disaster. Even so, the jungle was very beautiful and everything around me seemed incredibly large—the towering trees, the hanging lianas, the foliage, and flowers, the birds, the crawling animals and insects, the black monkeys swinging high in the branches, the huge spider webs that occasionally hung across our path. I had never seen such an extravagant natural display.

We struggled along this trail for three days—three days of hard work, sweat, and mud, passing through little places with names like La Caritad, Languana, Panguey, and Kalaguesca, gaining altitude steadily. We forded the Rio Cotoluno and then the Rio Tres Puentes. My body was beginning to ache all over. It was close to sunset when we crossed this last river and Antonio finally said, "Now we have entered the Chiquao. We will spend the night here."

The following day we had another river to cross, the Chiquao, before we reached the high, broad savanna that was our destination. It was late afternoon and the fading light of the day illuminated the entire plateau in a wondrous way. Grass moving slowly in the breeze took on the color of gold, and only the sound of the thousands of birds that live in the grass interrupted the stillness of this large empty space. Far away, on the border of the savanna, two ranges of small mountains appeared through the mist, and from time to time we heard the groans of a jaguar in the distance. We built a fire and very quickly prepared our shelter for the night. During supper we exchanged few words; exhaustion from our long journey finally took its toll, and one by one we crawled into the shelter and drifted off to sleep.

The glow of the dawning sun was just tinting the peaks of the far-off hills when we woke the next morning. The savanna was covered with a fading mist left behind by the light rain that had fallen during the night. A new soft sound was in the air, the sound of the diurnal birds that were also beginning their new day. For a moment, not far away, we heard the galloping hooves of a band of peccaries mixed with the hue and cry of the birds fleeing their path, The crackling noise of our fire and the smell of fresh-brewing coffee permeated the air.

Our first day on the plateau passed quietly and productively. Using a corrugated tin sheet that had been dropped earlier by parachute, Antonio and Ramirez worked on building a shelter adequate for several days' stay. I immediately went to work exploring and logging the topography of the plateau and its surroundings, and began gathering samples from the most promising strata of the streambanks in the area. I found a few small diamonds in this process, and as we settled down around the fire that night, I told Antonio that I thought this area had great potential. He nodded, and told me about a white man further up in the mountains who was also prospecting for diamonds. He spoke of him as "El Turco," a man from "the other side of the ocean," and when he described where he lived, I realized that it was within the area of my investigation. I told Antonio that I wanted to meet this man, and he agreed to take me there tomorrow.

Early the next morning we set out on the trail to El Turco's, and for the first hour we followed the path on the open savanna. From the tops of the trees scattered throughout the plain, the ever-present black vultures screeched their message as we trekked by. High above, like a painting against the blue of the sky, soaring eagles scouted their own prey. When we reached the edge of the savanna, the darkness of the mysterious, primeval forest enveloped us and the trail became only a spongy track with rocks and dead branches covered with slippery moss, and hanging lianas continuously barring our way. The dense green canopy above allowed only flashes of sunlight to reach us, and as it played on the leaves, tree trunks, and the ground, strange creatures of the forest suddenly came in focus like actors on a spotlit stage. Two hours later, once we had climbed the last hill, the forest ended at a flat, sandy plateau that looked like a land on which

The shelter on the savanna of the Chiquao.

dozens of meteorites had crashed. Antonio pointed to the pits and said, "This is where El Turco digs for the stones."

"El Turco" turned out to be an Israeli. His name was David, and he had come into this area five or six years before, had married an Indian woman, and now had several children running around the place. When Antonio first mentioned his name to me, I thought that perhaps he was indeed a Turk who had immigrated to Venezuela, then heard stories of *"brilliante"* in the interior and moved in to check it out. But now—just from his manner of speaking—I guessed that he had come here from Israel for the sole purpose of searching for diamonds. He obviously was an educated man.

I think I was the first white man he had talked to for years, and he seemed very glad of it. I asked him if he had found diamonds in the area, and he said, "Sure." He reached into his shirt, pulled out a little pouch that he was wearing on a lanyard around his neck, opened it, and took out two diamonds about the size of almonds. "With these stones," he said, "I can buy my farm when I go back to Israel."

David took me over to a large pit and showed me his operation. He had tapped a source of water and, with pipes made of bamboo, fed it into the pit where he was working. There he dug off the topsoil to get down to the layer of gravel mixed with clay that bore the diamonds. Then, standing in the pit, he worked with his *sarucca,* scooping up sediment and, under the water running from the bamboo pipe, washing away the clay and fine gravel so he could spot the diamonds. The main pit he was working was about 25 feet deep. It was not an elaborate operation, but he seemed to know what he was doing. And he told me that all his wife's relatives were also working for him, digging for stones on the plateau above. I asked him how many diamonds he had gotten out of his operation. He looked at me and said, "Come into the house."

His wife was there. She couldn't have been more than 5 feet 2 inches tall, and must have weighed at least 250 pounds. Their king-size bed was covered with at least ten huge jaguar skins. David went over to one corner of the cabin, pulled back a straw mat that was spread across the floor, and removed a little cover. He reached down into the hole and pulled out his receptacles—four Coke bottles. They were full of uncut diamonds.

When it was time to return to our camp, I shook David's hand and said goodbye. "If you come back through this area again," he said, "I'd appreciate it if you'd bring me two or three hunting knives." I said I would be glad to, and Antonio, Ramirez, and I started back along the trail with the image of those four Coke bottles filled with diamonds dancing in our heads. Now I was certain that this area was indeed rich in shiny stones.

I never met David again. I learned later that he had finally filled a fifth Coke bottle. Then one day he left and no one has seen or heard from him since.

The next day was our last on the savanna. I spent the entire time completing my survey of the area. Antonio, Ramirez, and I hiked to several streams that flowed off the edge of the plateau into the jungle valleys below and took samples from the exposed strata in the streambanks. Panning with *saruccas,* we found several more of the small, precious stones.

The following morning I woke up at the first light of day to find that Antonio and Ramirez had already started a good fire. A fog covered the mountains that surrounded the savanna and the clouds were low overhead, but there was no rain. "Today is going to be a good day," Antonio said. "We might be able to walk further than we planned." After breakfast we packed our gear, and by seven o'clock we were on our way, on the trail that would eventually bring us to Marirupa Salto (Marirupa Falls), a spot that I believed would be worth surveying underwater.

We trekked for hours on a narrow path that curved like a serpent upward from the savanna toward the southeastern slopes of the surrounding mountains. The trail was heavy with mud, the incline made the going even more difficult, and finally I said, "Antonio, let's stop here and take a break."

"No, señor," he said. "Better we go away from here, out of this area. This is *el Mono* area." Seeing the puzzled look on my face, he added, *"Si, señor, el Mono Grande."*

"A big monkey," I said. "How big?"

"Señor, *el Mono Grande* is big like you."

"A monkey my size?" I said in amazement. "Six feet tall?"

"Si, señor. Si!"

"Oh, come on, Antonio. Don't tell me such stories. How can there be a monkey that size?"

"Señor, I saw him. My son was killed by one of these monos. They are big. They are strong. They defend themselves and attack you with a club."

I looked at Antonio, and perhaps he saw the disbelief in my eyes. But his expression was dead serious, and I knew him well enough by this time to know that if he was not sure of what he said he would not mention such things. If there were big monkeys in this area, I wondered if they could be something similar to what has been reported in North America, the animal known as "Bigfoot." I tried to reassure Antonio. "I have the rifle," I said. "If anything happens, we can defend ourselves. Don't worry." But Antonio insisted that we move quickly.

Late that day, after we had passed the first range of mountains, we were out of the terrain in which Antonio had seen the mono. The sun was low on the horizon when we stopped and made camp for the night. Each of us went about our chores; Ramirez collected wood for the fire, Antonio fetched water from a nearby stream, and I opened the pack to put together the evening meal. But for some reason the atmosphere was tense and my companions were not in a talkative mood. Were they still frightened about *el Mono Grande?* I was burning with impatience to ask Antonio further questions about the animal, but I sensed a certain reluctance on his part to discuss it. So I decided to open a bottle of trago, and as we drank and the tension slowly eased, I steered the conversation to Antonio's encounter with the big mono.

In bursts of words punctuated by long pauses, he told me an incredible story. A few years before, he and his two sons were hunting on the slopes of the mountain range through which we had just passed. As they entered a heavily wooded gorge, three huge furry creatures came into their field of view, set up a horrible howl when their territory was invaded, and grabbed heavy branches, which they began swinging like clubs. The creatures came toward them and Antonio discharged the shotgun he was carrying in their direction. But that didn't stop them. Antonio and his sons turned and fled down the trail, but his younger son fell. Antonio ran back to help him, but one of the creatures was already over the boy with a club, and before he was able to reload his old muzzle-loader shotgun, it had disappeared into the forest leaving behind his battered son. Staring into the fire, Antonio said in a soft voice, "The boy died a few hours later as we were carrying him down the trail."

Now I understood his fear, and that night I turned and twisted in my sleeping bag for hours. Antonio's words kept reverberating in my head and every nocturnal sound was magnified. When daybreak came at last, the sky was gray and overcast. It took most of the day, trekking through mud and rain with only an occasional ray of sunshine piercing through the clouds to warm us up, before we finally reached the Marirupa Salto. Only eight hours

away, across the mountain to the west, was the small plateau with a landing strip where in three days I was to
meet Captain Vaseo, the bush pilot who was scheduled to
fly me back to Ciudad Bolívar.

I was a little disappointed when I saw Marirupa Salto. I
had expected the falls to be something quite imposing,
with a lot of water crashing over rocks into the river
below. They were small, but they fell deep within a
rugged canyon. We camped just above the falls on a small
hill, and that night I asked Antonio if he ever had panned
for diamonds in this location. He said that he and the
other Indians sometimes looked for stones on the land,
but never in the water—they didn't like the water. When I
asked him if diving in this area would be dangerous, he
said, "Nobody can tell."

The following morning I got ready to skin-dive in the
small brackish lagoon under the falls to collect some sediment and check the possibility that it contained precious
stones washed down from the canyon and mountain
above the falls. The morning was clear and the sun was
shining, perfect for what I intended to do, and around
ten o'clock I was ready to go into the water. I dove once,
twice, three times, taking every possible precaution and
filling my small pail with sediment. Then I decided to
move to the southern part of the small lagoon. And there,
during my first dive, I had the shattering, fateful encounter with the aimara.

After I tore my hand and foot free from the jaws of the
two fishes and was thrashing toward the shore, I had a
moment of despair when I saw that Antonio and Ramirez
sat there immobile, and were not going to help me get out
of the water. In that split second, I might have believed
anything: that they didn't care, that they had brought me
to this lagoon for some malevolent purpose and wanted
this to happen—anything. But later, when I got to know
them and other Indians of the interior well, I better understood their behavior. The Indians are very fatalistic
and believe that any terrible event happens because it is
supposed to happen. It has been caused by the forces that

move life in the jungle and no one can interfere, not so
much because he would incur the wrath of jungle spirits,
but simply because it would be pointless.

The situation was different once I had beaten off the
attack and fought my way to shore. Then the attack was
past. I had contended with the forces that were bearing
on me, and my own force had triumphed. Events were
once again in the hands of the individuals involved, and
Antonio and Ramirez could offer their help. Indeed, by
using mysterious healing powers and taking me to the
landing strip to await the plane that would fly me out of
the jungle, they had saved my life. Antonio's feelings in
this situation, however, were complex, and I could tell in
my later contacts with him that he felt responsible for the
attack; he should have known that there were aimara in
the lagoon. He did what he could for my hand, and I
know that he had confidence his healing powers were
going to be effective. But I am certain he felt that, in a
larger sense, he had failed me, and he was probably sure,
as I flew away, that he would never see me again.

In the days following my return to Miami, and the startling realization that my hand had healed in such an incredible fashion, I was hardly aware of anything else.
They were days of agitation and restlessness, and of a
gnawing apprehension that there had been forces at work
inside me—and might still be—of which I had no understanding or control. Night after night I dreamed of the
huge green eyes of that fish boring into me and woke up
yelling out of my sleep. The strange, other-worldly images
that had filled my mind while I lay waiting for the plane
to take me out of the jungle kept coming back in flashes.
But as the days went by, my mind slowly began to
reorganize itself to some degree, and more normal con-
cerns started to come back to me. The sediment samples
that I had left in Caracas with Quinones were my primary
concern. He had said that he would bring them to Miami
in about two weeks' time.

I was immensely relieved when I finally heard from him
and he came to my house with all the gear that I had left

behind in Caracas. He looked intently at my hand, asked me about it, and was very cheered to see that it was healing so well. We shook our heads again in wonderment at Antonio's healing prowess. Then we began to go through my gear—and were aghast to see that there was only one bag of sample jars: the specimens from underwater. I had put the specimens that I gathered from the land, from all over the savanna and up into the mountain ranges, into another small bag. And that bag was missing. Quinones said that he was almost sure he had left nothing behind when we flew out of the interior. But I knew that, as nerve-racking as it must have been for him and Vaseo to find me in that condition and then fly me quickly to the hospital, anything could have happened.

There was no getting around it; the samples were gone, and without them to compare with the underwater samples, I could not possibly determine the feasibility of any operation to recover diamonds in the area. Most of our efforts and suffering had been wasted. "There's no avoiding it," I told Quinones sadly. "I have to go back and gather more samples from the savanna and the mountains." We agreed that as soon as I was able, we would return to Venezuela. "But no more underwater diving," Quinones muttered softly.

The series of inner disturbances and distress that had been triggered by the attack, and the visions that I experienced during the healing process, stayed with me for weeks. It was not until much later that I learned that the milky substance that Antonio had given me was not milk at all. It was *ayahuasca:* a hallucinogenic drink prepared from the leaves and vine of a tree which, in some places, is also called *yage.* The shamans and brujos use this drug to stay in contact with the spiritual forces of the jungle, and to aid their healing powers. The word *ayahuasca* means "vine of the soul," and the shaman believes that it transforms an individual's physical being into a spiritual state, so that the body—left behind, so to speak—can devote all of its energies to repairing itself from the effects of disease or injury.

Now I knew why I had experienced such strange, un-worldly hallucinations: those jaguar shapes with elongated, undulating, liquid bodies, the snakes with smiling expressions on their faces that appeared as if they could tell me great, universal secrets. All those phantoms which I at first believed had been caused by my delirium and fever had actually been due to the *ayahuasca*. But even though the visions eventually receded in my mind, I believe that the drug permanently altered my spiritual awareness. How else, on my subsequent trips to the jungle, could I have come to understand the spiritual forces at work there, an understanding that helped me develop a depth of relationship and an influence with some of the Indian tribes that no white man has ever had before? It was *ayahuasca* that released that power within me.

All the people familiar with jungle medicine, including the missionaries I have talked to about it, are aware that when a person drinks *ayahuasca*, whether in an initiation rite or for some other reason, the effect of this "vine of the soul" is to produce a deep change in his psychological processes. That, apparently, is what had happened to me. And I was to discover that it would not only affect me personally, it would also affect my relationships with persons intimately connected with me.

That discovery itself, when it came, had its own agitation. But as I began to plan my second trip to Venezuela, a question occurred to me, almost as a challenge: What would happen if I took *ayahuasca* again? Intuitively, I think I knew that it would not be so totally revolutionary. I had the feeling that if, through this one experience, I had achieved a new level of awareness, that was where I would remain. My concern now was how this experience would affect my future life. And that, I knew, only time would tell.

CHAPTER 6

El Mono Grande

When I returned to Venezuela for my second trip to the Chiquao, I had decided to look for something more than diamonds. In my research I had discovered that this region, including all of the southern and eastern parts of Venezuela, was almost unknown archaeologically, apart from findings reported from a few sites near the great waterway of the Orinoco River. Yet I had been intrigued to note that a few clay artifacts recovered from Trujillo, a truly Venezuelan Andean state, showed an elaboration of facial and anatomic features, and body painting strikingly similar to that of the Chorrera period of Ecuador. Conversely, even though the artifacts from near Venezuela's Lake Valencia had the so-called coffee-bean-shaped eye style of the Chorrera and Milagro periods of Ecuador, the head and body treatment were unique. I wondered, once again, if there was a relationship between these early cultures, and it was my intention, along with my quest for diamonds, to do some field research.

Antonio would again be my guide. We were to meet at the same airstrip in the Chiquao where we had parted several weeks before. Antonio had already been advised of my arrival by Vaseo, the bush pilot, who had dropped him a message in a tin can attached to a flare-sized parachute. I marveled at the efficiency of these jungle modes of communication.

After a brief reunion in Ciudad Bolívar with Pablo Corrales, Vaseo and I took off for the Chiquao. The flight

Pottery figurines from Venezuela which show striking similarities to artifacts from the early cultures in Ecuador. Lake Valencia/Aragua.

Pottery figurines: (top),
Chorrera; (bottom),
Milagro.

was much more serene than the last one I had taken with him, and when we reached our destination, I saw Antonio, Ramirez, and another figure waiting for us at the small airstrip. Vaseo made the kind of expert landing I had routinely come to expect from him, and we taxied up to them. I climbed out of the plane and walked over to greet Antonio. Ramirez, and a boy of about seventeen or eighteen whom I did not know, were standing slightly behind him. Antonio did not once glance at my hand. He may have seen all he needed to see as I first got out of the plane, but as I walked over to him to say hello, his eyes never left my face. I noticed, however, that Ramirez was looking at my hand with an expression of tense anticipation.

"How are things with you?" I said, as Antonio and I clapped each other on the back.

"Fine, fine. What brings you here again?"

I told him about the loss of the samples, and that I would need his help again. We looked thoroughly around the little shelter where I had lain waiting for the plane a few months before but found nothing. I knew then that Antonio and I would have to retrace our steps to collect new samples from the flatland and the streambanks of the savanna.

"Your medicine worked very well," I told Antonio. "My hand is fine."

"I expected so," he said. Still his eyes did not drop to my hand. It was as if he had no need to look at it at all.

After a few more minutes Vaseo took off in the plane, and Antonio walked away to do something. Then, and not before, Ramirez stepped up to me, took my hand, and excitedly turned it over and back, pulling at the fingers and watching them move. "Oh, *bueno!*" he said. "*Muy bueno, señor!*" The young boy, Chancho ("Little Pig"), looked at my hand too, and Ramirez described the accident with much animation, explaining to him what Antonio had done. They spoke in their own Indian tongue; Chancho understood very little Spanish. I saw much more clearly than I had on our first expedition the tremendous respect

Captain Vaseo and his plane.

that other Indians had for Antonio. Whenever he spoke they held back, never interjected a word, and would not even step forward. Ramirez often interrupted me; I was an outsider, and that was permissible. But he never interrupted Antonio—he was the medicine man, the supreme authority. I would receive further proof of that in the days ahead.

I was burning to ask Antonio about his healing powers, but I was never able to. It was as if it was something over and done with in his mind, and he didn't want to discuss it. It was past, that was all. I attempted to bring the subject up several times. There might be a pause in our conversation and I would say, "By the way, Antonio. You can tell me now. What happens during the healing ritual that you performed?" But when he spoke again it would be of something else, as if he had not even heard me. He answered my questions about the herbs used in the healing ceremonies, showed me the plants, and explained how the potions are prepared, among them the practical use of the *"burundi,"* a herb to maintain sexual potency, and the *"ruda,"* which was used to avoid pregnancy. But he would not discuss the healing of my hand. That was finished and was something he wanted simply to dismiss. It was not important any more.

Antonio with Ramirez and his youngest son.

Still I soon began to sense a change, a closer rapport between Antonio and myself. During my previous trip, our relationship had been very detached. Antonio had been more than helpful and did everything that was needed, but there was always the sense that I was an outsider. Now, however, I felt a bond between us that was deeper and more complex than just friendship, a bond that had been forged by my experience with the mind-expanding drug he had administered to me. Perhaps in his mind I had been initiated into one of the Indian healing rituals, and having survived it and come back, I was now accepted.

There was another mystery from my first trip that I hoped I would be able to investigate. But I did not bring the subject up until after we had reached our old base camp on the savanna and I had presented Antonio and Ramirez with the gifts I had brought for them and their families. Then I said, "Antonio, I want to go back to the area where you saw *el Mono Grande.*" He just looked at me.

I had been fascinated by Antonio's story of his encounter with the big mono, and when I returned to Miami after the first trip, I had decided to pursue it further. A big-game hunter named Ralph Scott, the donor of a famous white tiger to the Miami Zoo, was a good friend of mine, and one evening I mentioned Antonio's encounter to him.

"There may be some truth to the story," he said. Then he pulled out a book and showed me a photograph of a large primate that had been shot in 1920 by François de Loys, a Swiss geologist, in the Sierra de Perijaá of the Venezuelan highlands. The animal in the picture seemed to fit Antonio's description. It was not as massively built as a gorilla; its general proportions and facial appearance were closer to the gibbon. But it was much larger in size than any gibbon; it stood over 5 feet tall, and could clearly be seen to have been quite strong.

Intrigued, I did some further research and learned that Alexander von Humboldt, the famous German scientist and explorer, during his exploration of the upper Orinoco River in the Guiana Highlands in 1800 had heard of and reported the reputed existence of a large hairy primate in that area. It was said to be able to build shelters and steal Indian women. But reports of the existence of such primates in the virgin forests of South America did not come only from the Guiana Highlands. Cieza de León, in his *Crónicas del Peru,* mentioned reports of large hairy creatures in remote areas of that country. The Indians, he wrote, mated with the female, and their offspring grew tall and hairy, with monkey features. They could not speak a language, but they wailed and howled.

I placed little faith in such reports, but I had brought a copy of the photograph Scott had showed me and, reaching into my pack, I pulled it out and showed it to Antonio. He looked at the picture and an expression of complete incredulity came over his face. He couldn't believe his eyes. "Where did you get this?" he asked. Ramirez looked at the photograph over Antonio's shoulder and his eyes grew big.

"From a book," I replied. "The animal was shot forty-eight years ago by a Swiss geologist. His account of the incident says that the creature was as big as a human. Do you think this is the kind of animal you saw?"

"Yes," Antonio said. "It looks very similar. I've never heard of this incident, but if you have this picture, it must be so."

Nothing more was said on the subject for the next three

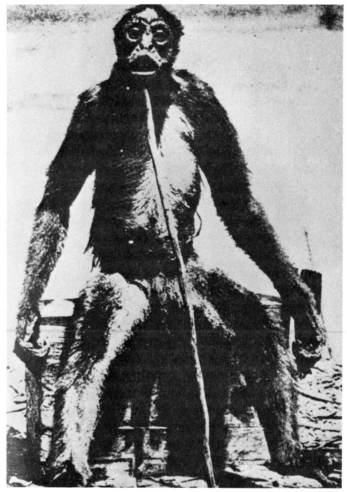

El Mono Grande.

days while I collected new sediment specimens from various sites on the plateau, from the riverbanks around its perimeter, and from the surrounding mountains. With the help of Ramirez and Chancho, I also recovered several fine stones. Meanwhile, Antonio busied himself with another project. Pablo Corrales had suggested that we build an airstrip on the savanna, which would be much more convenient than the location we had used before. He planned to send in a few of his own workmen to clear the strip. All we had to do was some preliminary clearing and rolling; so Antonio went in search of a tall, straight tree that could be cut down, trimmed, and used as a roller to smooth the strip after it was cleared.

Finally all our work was done, and I spoke again of my determination to be taken to the canyon where Antonio had seen the big mono. I explained to him that in North America some people had claimed to have spotted creatures that were similar to the description of what he saw, but no one as yet had been able to bring back irrefutable proof of their existence. Perhaps if the creatures he had seen were still in the area, I might be able to confirm it and, in the future, mount an expedition to try to make contact with them. I was finally able to convince Antonio that no harm would come to us as we had the protection of much more powerful and efficient firearms that he had carried.

When we set out from the camp, we began hiking southeast across the savanna and after a few hours entered the forest, where we followed a narrow track through undergrowth so thick that it reduced our vision to only a few feet on either side. Only now and then did a small clearing enable us to have a field of view of 6 to 10 meters ahead. When we entered the canyon where Antonio had seen the big mono, the Indians became very alert and apprehensive, stepping carefully, and sensing every sound and movement in the brush around them. I was carrying a 3.5 Winchester automatic and kept it at the ready. Tension was mounting as we slowly made our way along the trail. The subdued light created lurking shadows and a mood of mystery. It was getting toward late afternoon when suddenly we heard a howl, very loud, coming from somewhere in the thick vegetation. The Indians froze. The howl was as loud as the roar of a jaguar, but it was higher and more shrill in pitch. It reverberated through the forest, encircling us as if it came from all directions. Something was moving, crashing powerfully through the underbrush.

The Indians turned abruptly and raced back along the trail, yelling at me to follow. But I was frozen in my tracks, my heart beating so hard that I could hear it. Then, suddenly, the howling stopped. I waited, and when I had regained control of my movements, I advanced slowly along the trail, my finger on the trigger of the gun. Then, as I reached a small clearing, the howling started again, in one crescendo after another. But again, as suddenly as it had started, it stopped. It was then that I saw two furry patches running away from me with a leaping sort of step through the foliage that bordered the clearing. As they bounded across the surface of a group of boulders at the far end of the clearing, I was able to catch a fleeting glimpse of them. They clearly were erect, hairy, apelike creatures, and appeared to be over 5 feet tall. Then they disappeared around the rocks into the jungle, and I heard the cracking sounds of dry twigs and branches as they hastily forged their way through the thick underbrush.

I waited for what seemed an eternity for something else to happen, trying to impress on my mind what I had just glimpsed. I opened my mouth to yell to my companions, but no sound came out. Finally I turned and retraced my steps, and encountered them advancing cautiously back up the trail. "They're gone," I said. No one uttered a word. We continued on up the trail, this time with me, rather than Antonio, at the head, with the Winchester in readiness. We crossed the clearing and climbed the summit of a hill, then hiked down heading toward a remote jungle trading post, Casa Eureda, some four hours away where we would spend the night. We did not see or hear the creatures again.

The owner of the Casa Eureda invited us to share a meal of fried cod fish and boiled potatoes, and when the meal ended, the Indians went off to a common house that was maintained for them, to stretch out on a platform for the night. It was raining and I looked around to see what sort of shelter I could crawl into. The owner cut short my dilemma by saying, "Señor, the best I can offer you is my stock room." I laid myself out on four bags of rice, with about fifty flanks of salted cod hanging overhead. The stench of the fish was pungent, but as I lay there on my rice mattress, what I had seen and heard that afternoon passed through my mind again and again. All night long every minute detail kept reappearing before my eyes like an endless nightmare. I was sure that the encounter had really occurred, but something deep within my consciousness was not ready to accept it. Not until two years later in Ecuador would this extraordinary experience come into sharp focus.

In the morning, smelling like a fishmonger, I am sure, I rejoined Antonio, Ramirez, and Chancho, and we started back to our camp on the savanna. Antonio took his natural position at the head of the file, and by mid-morning we were approaching the place where we had encountered the monos the day before. Antonio beckoned us to stop, and he listened for a few moments. He detected nothing and said, "It's all right. We can go ahead." I had my hand on the Winchester and said, "Why don't I go first now?" He nodded, I took the lead, and we proceeded along the trail.

We saw nothing, and within three hours or so we were out of danger and Antonio had resumed his place in the lead. Had he not done so, I would have suggested it. The Indians living in the interior have extraordinarily well-developed senses. No amount of experience on the part of an outsider can equal the natural awareness the Indians have of the dangers that may be present around them. They can hear a snake moving across the ground many meters away, or a jaguar grumbling far in the distance. As I watched the back of that small man walking in front of me, I thought again of what he had done with my hand several weeks before. The rational, objective side of me, the side that was familiar with the realities of twentieth-century medicine, still refused to accept what had happened. Now, just as Antonio sensed so keenly what was going on around him in the jungle, I realized that his mind worked in ways that were beyond my comprehension. There were forces in the jungle—forces that affected me—which he understood and I didn't. And that left me

The author with diamonds recovered on the Chiquao.

feeling uneasy, unsettled, vulnerable. I felt that there might be much more for me to learn in the jungle than I had originally set out for, and I began to wonder where my search would ultimately lead.

I made a startling discovery soon after we returned to our camp. Working my way down to the southeastern edge of the plateau collecting more sediment samples, I noticed an area where the land had been undercut by a small stream, and had broken away and slid into the stream bed. I crawled over the edge and down the side to examine the freshly exposed strata. Several layers were visible, all of them sedimentary, and the third or fourth of these layers was a mixture of clay, gravel, and small rock. I dug out a sample of this material and found a number of small diamonds. That meant that the entire plateau, or certainly a good part of it, was underlain by this diamond-bearing material. All the time we had been moving around on the savanna, we were walking on diamonds. With that realization, any lingering regrets that I may have had about making this second trip dissolved completely. This one find alone justified the entire trip and, I thought, would make a very big impression when I returned to Miami.

When the day came for Vaseo to pick me up, I said goodbye to my good friend Antonio, and told him that I would probably be coming back in a few months with more people. I also told him to expect the crew that was to begin work on the airstrip, probably within a few weeks. "Good, we'll be waiting," he said, and he and Chancho started down the trail for their home. Ramirez and I set out in the direction of the airstrip on the trail that by now had become very familiar. It formerly had no name, but the Zapes were beginning to call it the *"pica del Pino."* How nice, I thought. Maybe one day I'll see my name on a map.

I met Vaseo as planned, he flew me to Ciudad Bolívar, and the following day I was back in Caracas, where I met Pablo Corrales and told him of my extraordinary finds in the Chiquao. We finalized a general agreement regarding the future exploitation of his concession and discussed what we would need to mount future expeditions. Better maps of the interior were high on the list of our priorities. The ones I had been working with included only the important rivers and a few trails and settlements. Topographical and geological information was completely lacking over broad areas, including the Chiquao. Pablo gave me the name of a gentleman who had been working for the Venezuelan government for thirty years and could probably help me.

When I arrived for my appointment with Marcos Andrades, a young secretary showed me into his office, offered me a cup of coffee, and said that Señor Andrades would be there shortly. As I drank the coffee, comfortably seated in a brown leather chair and taking in my surroundings, I noticed on a shelf behind the desk two small effigies that appeared to be in the typical style of the ancient Venezuelan cultures. As I stood up to have a closer look at them, a voice behind me said, "They are intriguing, aren't they?" I turned and shook the hand that was being offered. Señor Andrades was a pleasant-looking man in his early sixties, with broad shoulders, a dark complexion, and the easy manner of a gentleman of the old school.

"They are beautiful," I said. "What area do they come from?"

"Near Lake Valencia," he replied, "but I cannot tell you the exact site."

We began an animated discussion of the archaeological study of his country which, in his opinion, was being sadly neglected. "Very few people know the true potential of Venezuela," he said. But soon our conversation turned to the reason I had called on him: the availability of maps of the Guiana Highlands. Señor Andrades didn't immediately respond to my question, but then, with a sudden joyful burst, he exclaimed: "Yes, yes, there is a rare map! It is very old. It was done in the nineteenth century by a German explorer. He spent years in the hinterlands and he mapped some areas completely. His map is not official; we almost never release copies of it. So not too many people, even in the cartography department, know about it. I myself had almost forgotten it."

He left the room, and when he returned he spread out a large paper negative of a hand-drawn map for me to look at. I was very surprised at the number of topographical details; it was almost impossible to imagine that one man could have covered and single-handedly drawn up so much of the territory of the interior. I was even more excited at the great number of sites marked simply "Ruins." I thought immediately of what Antonio had told me about the *Cueva Pintada* and other sites where he said there were strange petroglyphs carved in stone.

Señor Andrades gave me two prints of the map and wished me well on my next expedition into the interior. We would meet again two years later when I visited his office and, conscious of the importance of this irreplaceable map, asked if he could give me two more prints. Sadly, he told me that, a short time before, he had discovered that the map, along with all the negatives that had been made of it, had completely vanished. He didn't know how or when. I could hardly believe him when he said, "For all I know, your prints may be the only ones in existence today."

I flew back to Miami with a certain sense of *déjà vu:* the

situation in Venezuela seemed the same as in Ecuador. I was certain that the interior was rich with archaeological evidence that might shed considerable light on the genesis of South American cultures in the equatorial belt. Yet there was no effort by the Venezuelan government to investigate these areas and very little information about them was available. As for the geological information that I had hoped to find about the Chiquao, what I already had seemed to be all there was. And that was practically nothing. I was more encouraged by the specimens I had found there. A geologist in Miami reported that the sediment samples looked very promising and the rough diamond stones I had collected totaled 143 carats. Of these, 70 percent were of gem grade and 30 percent were industrial. I immediately called on Carl Holm, and we discussed in detail the preparation of the proposal to Rockwell for a possible joint venture in the Chiquao.

A few weeks later, Carl reported that Rockwell was interested and had authorized him to organize an expedition into the Chiquao for a first-hand report. I went back to Venezuela with him and his party, and again we explored the region with promising results. But after we returned, six months passed by during which the only news from Rockwell was that our proposal and geological reports were being studied. Finally the company's interest in the diamond venture simply faded away. Its eastern division, of which Carl was the head, was closed due to a reorganization of the corporation, and Carl formed his own company, Global Oceanics, to pursue his work.

To me, the venture in Venezuela never represented anything more than a potential means of pursuing my archaeological quests. And fortunately, there was the possibility of financial support from a Canadian foundation that would eventually become an important factor in the continuation of my research in Ecuador. But Pablo and my other friends in Venezuela were extremely disappointed, although they were convinced I would return to their country someday. Perhaps they are right. The many unresolved mysteries of that land are too intriguing to be ignored or forgotten.

PART III

Strange Tales and Puzzles

CHAPTER 7

The Jaramillo Incident

In archaeological research, accumulation of data alone is not sufficient for the process of understanding an ancient culture if it is not accompanied by intuition, insight, and a good deal of imagination. Legends and tales, ignored by many investigators as figments of the primitive mind, have always stimulated my imagination, for I believe that they are born from a fundamental truth. One might easily discount such legends as the fabled city of Manoa or stories of buried Inca gold, but there was one tale I had heard on a previous visit to Ecuador that had never left my mind entirely: Major Petronio Jaramillo's account of the Cueva de los Tayos. Back in Quito in the summer of 1968, I decided, on a hunch, to get in touch with Major Jaramillo. I called him on the phone and we made arrangements to meet at his home.

On the appointed evening, a cab dropped me off before a modest apartment house in one of Quito's middle-class districts known as El Dorado. The sound of the doorbell had not yet faded away when the door flew open and an imposing, matronly-looking woman in a yellow dress announced, "I am Señora Jaramillo." She ushered me through a long corridor to the sitting room, where the major was waiting for me. The light was low, and a strong smell of onions pervaded the apartment, a smell that obviously had not come from one recent meal but hung in the air permanently. The overstuffed furniture was covered with red corduroy, well worn and ragged in a few places. As I entered the room, a thin man, not more than 5 feet 10 inches tall, wearing tweed pants with a black jacket and tie, came toward me and introduced himself: "I am Májor Petronio Jaramillo-Abarca, at your service." He offered me a chair and we sat facing each other, while his wife took a seat across the room.

I began our conversation by telling Major Jaramillo that his account of the Cueva de los Tayos to my friend Andrea Salvador had interested me greatly. "Yes," he replied, "my cave may prove to be one of the most important discoveries ever made in South America. I was taken there by a Jivaro Indian chieftain, a great cacique named Samakache, and his son Mashutaka. These two are very powerful Indians, and they are the only ones in the Amazon who know the location of this incredible cave. They were my guides. They led me throughout the caverns of the Cueva de los Tayos, and I tell you, Señor Turolla, it was an experience that has changed my whole life."

Major Jaramillo warmed to his subject and we talked at some length. But always, he skirted mention of the contents of the cave and carefully avoided revealing its exact location. At one point Señora Jaramillo broke into the discussion to clarify the location of the home territory of Mashutaka's clan. She let drop the name "Pescado," and I remembered it carefully. But throughout our conversation it was clear that Major Jaramillo had had considerable practice in protecting the details of his secret.

During a lull in the conversation, my eyes wandered to the fireplace. Hanging over the mantel was a crudely done painting, a primitive, showing the flag of Ecuador on one side, the flag of the United Nations on the other, and in the middle, in an oval panel, a portrait, barely recognizable, of my host, with his name written underneath. Major Jaramillo noticed my interest in the painting and said, "Yes, that is how I see myself. I feel it is my duty to bring forth the truth that will help unify all peoples, to be a bridge, so to speak, between the people of Ecuador and those of the rest of the world."

As the evening wore on, I realized that Major Jaramillo had told me all he intended me to know about the Cueva de los Tayos. Finally I said that the cave sounded very interesting, but that I couldn't undertake any cooperative venture with him to explore it without more specific information. "Yes," he said, "I understand that. I have been thinking of writing an account of my journey through the caves with the two Indians. I will do this, and the next time you are in Quito I will have it ready for you." With that we said goodnight.

On my way back to the hotel, I began to doubt the wisdom of my visit. The image of Jaramillo's self-portrait between the Ecuadorian flag and the flag of the United Nations hung before my mind as a perfect crystallization of the man's grandiose ideas, ideas that exceeded all bounds of plausibility. Yet he had spent years in the Oriente, and the discussion between him and his wife concerning the Indians, Samakache and Mashutaka, had a definite ring of credibility.

During the next six months I spoke with Jaramillo several times on the telephone. Always the story was the same. He hadn't been able to put his mind to the narrative; he had had other things to do. But he would try to get it out shortly.

Finally, I suggested that we sit down together with a tape recorder and he could simply narrate his story just as he had experienced it. He agreed readily, and the head of the publicity department of Ecuadoriana, the Ecuadorian airline, offered me recording facilities and the president's office for our recording session.

As soon as we entered the office, Jaramillo's eyes fell on the president's chair. He walked over and assumed it like a king taking his throne, chin high, looking around the room, one arm straight out with his hand on the desk, the other hand tucked in between the buttons of his coat *à la* Napoleon. He watched as I set up the microphone and turned on the tape recorder. Then, when I told him everything was ready, he took the microphone and rose, paced as far away from the desk as the cable would allow, threw back his shoulders, inhaled, and began in a firm, robust tone:

"I am Major Petronio Jaramillo-Abarca. I am an Ecuadorian citizen, and for some years have been retired as an officer of the Ecuadorian armed forces. I am a man of scant intellectual resources. I have not studied ancient civilizations. During my army career, I studied only artillery; upon my retirement, five years ago, I went to the university and obtained my degree in International Affairs. I obtained this degree because I wanted to make diplomatic contact with other countries and obtain scientific support to investigate and bring to the world the great secret I am now going to tell you about. . . ."

At this moment he looked inquiringly at me to see if he was doing all right. I nodded approvingly and gestured for him to go on. He resumed pacing, and continued:

"The background of this story begins in 1941, when I was barely twelve years old. I lived with my uncle, a captain in the Ecuadorian army, in Loja, the capital of Loja Province in the south of Ecuador. One day my uncle brought into our home a Jivaro Indian boy, about my age. The boy was given by his father to my uncle to be educated. The little one's father was Samakache, who was a cacique—or chief—of a large number of clans of the Jivaro tribe. This tribe lives in the south Oriente, and they are very savage, uncivilized Indians. The little boy's name was Mashutaka. Later he acquired the name of my uncle, Gilberto, so that he was then called Gilberto Mashutaka. That is a custom among the Indians of this area, giving a godchild the name of the godparent.

"Mashutaka and I established that very cordial and sincere friendship which comes naturally to the young, and he once told me that in the eastern jungles of his homeland there was an enormous cave inhabited by big birds. That is just how he described them—big birds with large eyes called 'tayos.' He said it was a very deep, dark cave, and only a few of the most powerful leaders of his tribe knew where it was. That is all I can tell you about the start of my story, in 1941. But the memory of this cave, this description, has stayed with me all my life.

"Many years later, in 1956, I was an artillery lieutenant stationed in the Oriente. In that part of the country it was ʊur practice to go out on routine patrols, and on one of these patrols I had a very strange experience—very dangerous and very impressive. My patrol and I were on the eastern side of the mountains, in the eastern jungles, and we woke one morning to find ourselves surrounded by fifty Jivaros—fifty menacing men, threatening my soldiers and me. . . .”

At this point in his narrative, the major was no longer in the room with me. He had a look of reverie on his face, and his eyes were focused far beyond the walls of the office. He was back in the jungle, many years before.

“. . . I looked at the man who was leading this group, and I saw a face that had not changed a great deal. It had only grown older with time. It was Gilberto, my friend of former days. He recognized me, and it was this recognition that saved my whole group from being killed.

“Gilberto explained that he would have to take us prisoners and lead us back to his compound to request permission from his father, Samakache, to spare our lives. This was something that could only be granted by the cacique. When we reached the compound, there was one more requirement. Gilberto demanded of me that I repeat his Indian name, so that he could be fully convinced that I was really his boyhood friend. I can assure you that, in other circumstances, to retrieve that Indian’s name from my memory would have been very difficult. But standing before him and seeing his face, it came back automatically, and I could call out his name, Mashutaka. Then Mashutaka came over and embraced me, and was reconciled with me. . . .”

Jaramillo glowed as he relived this memory. His face showed the flush of relief that he felt when Mashutaka recognized him, and the gratification that must have flooded through him as this powerful Jivaro, an object of fear for other white men, warmly accepted him, Jaramillo, in the middle of the Indian compound.

“When we were released and left his compound, Mashutaka invited me to come back some day. I did so later, and that is where this story really begins.

"After I returned to my garrison, I applied for permission to visit the compound of Samakache again. This was granted and, shortly afterwards, I made the necessary arrangements. With me I had the badge of army captain to present to the great cacique, Samakache. By tradition we, the military, bestow the insignia of rank of captain on the chiefs or caciques of high authority in the jungle. This enormously pleased Mashutaka. We spent the next few days discussing the customs, myths, and legends of his tribe—a tribe that in the past, Mashutaka believed, was descended from the fearsome nation known as the Auchiris.

"Slowly I guided the conversation to that large cave he had told me about in his youth, with the big black birds. After much discussion with his father, Mashutaka told me he would take me to see the cave. We started out, Samakache, Mashutaka, and myself, on a two-day walk to reach this cave, far in the interior. No one else but my two guides knows the secret of the cave, and even today I cannot reveal its exact location. I will not do so until the proper time comes, when an organization will appear which, under God's protection, may support the full investigation of this secret, not only for the benefit of my own country but for all humanity. Until then, the location of this cave must be deeply guarded, in the depths of my innermost being."

At this point Jaramillo stopped, thought for a moment, then turned to me and said, "Is it all right?" I said it was just fine and asked him if he was tired and would like to sit down. "Oh, no," he said, "it is better for me when I am on my feet." I gestured for him to go on, and he continued:

"As we walked, my guides told me more of this cave, and in my mind it became transformed from a rustic black hole into an immense underground cavern. They said that it had many entrances, some of them separated by a distance of a two-day hike, or even three, four, or five. It was an immense cavern, with chambers fashioned by the hand of man, possibly in an epoch long before the

Christian era. From what they told me, I calculated that it must have been approximately sixty-four square miles in area. If we gathered together a hundred basilicas of the Roman Catholic world, even then you would not have an idea of the immensity of what I later saw.

"This cave was just one of hundreds that honeycomb the eastern mountain range of Ecuador where the Andes meets with the lowlands of the Amazon Basin. They are enormously large caverns, very deep, very long, with a great number of hillocks and peaks inside, a great number of levels, and many mysteries. All of this awes the spirit, much more so when one enters suddenly—as I did when, late in the second day, we reached our destination, and Samakache and Mashutaka led me into one of these caves.

"For two days we had hiked and climbed for many kilometers into the interior. We crossed deep ravines and gorges, and then a plateau surrounded by high peaks known as 'peñas blancas'—white peaks. Finally we climbed over the top of another small plateau and looked down and saw at our feet a good-sized stream. We jumped into it from a considerable height—something I had never done before in my life—and crossed it. Then we came to what looked like the entrance to a small cave. But as we entered it, leaving the water behind us, I realized I was treading on steps made in perfect symmetry. Now we found ourselves in a great vault, a basilica, hewn with architectural lines. On the right side of the entrance were several torches standing against the wall, left there previously by the Indians. We each lit one and walked toward a large round platform, which in turn led to a great number of levels. We walked ahead and came to a canal through which water was flowing at a depth of three to four feet. We lowered ourselves into the water, forded this canal, then moved up onto the other side of the cave. We had been climbing steadily through a series of caves that apparently followed the crest of one of the ranges of the Andes. We came to a great vaulted chamber that was quite light, as the sun shone through many crystal rocks.

These were not natural rocks forming this chamber. They had been worked and formed by hand—shiny rocks, white rocks, greenish rocks, some of them black—perfectly arranged as if the result of some architectural design. This vault was wider than any of the others we had seen, and had the dimensions of the largest of the cathedrals in the city of Quito. Right in the center of the vault was a large curved seat, big enough to accommodate twelve slender persons, or seven stouter ones.

"We continued along the left side of this vault, up some steps, and then found ourselves on a higher level until we finally came to a plateau, from which there were several different ranks of steps leading in different directions to other rooms. We followed one of these and came to the door of a large room. Samakache and Mashutaka told me not to enter, but to look inside.

"The room showed all the colors of the rainbow—yellow rock, white, pale pink, sky blue, red, and purple rock. On the floor were many *bolitas,* or balls, known in this country as *'jorutos'* or *'pildas,'* which are said by the Auchiris to have been a traditional toy of their ancestors. They were scattered on the floor, and clustered on the side of the room—some of them were of yellow metal, and others yellow-green. I looked closely and saw that all had inscriptions on them in a strange script, something like modern shorthand.

"Then Samakache told me to step back to a safe place, and he threw a rock at the threshold of this room. As the rock hit, a great stone slab rolled down—a rush of black stone which splintered Samakache's rock. Samakache told me that this stone door would roll back to its raised position overnight. As they explained it, it used light and darkness to close and then open again. I have no other way to explain it."

Jaramillo paused for a moment, then glanced at the clock. It was noon, and he had been talking for a long time. I asked him if he was hungry and would like to take a break for lunch. "Yes," he said, "I was thinking of that."

Thus far, Jaramillo's account was so graphic that I

could almost see the colorful vaults of the cave and the great stone door that, triggered by a touch on the threshold, came crashing down and then rose again mysteriously. But I was becoming aware of the same feelings that I often had when listening to stories of ancestral times told by the Indians—a sense that I was listening to a beautiful legend.

During lunch Jaramillo expostulated further on the great significance of the cave and the benefits that would befall all mankind from its secrets, the most profound of which I had not yet heard. After a nourishing meal, we returned to the office, and he picked up the microphone and resumed where he had left off:

"We went back down the steps, then up to a second room. We walked in—there was no stone door in this room to fall on us—and there we found ourselves surrounded by a great number of carved stone animals. I touched them with my hands. There were representations of elephants, mastodons, reptiles, snakes, coyotes, jaguars, horses, birds. Some of these statues stood on small stands, others were placed on the floor. Nearly all were about thirty centimeters high. But there was one animal that impressed me exceptionally, due to the purity of its form. It was a brown cat standing on a triangular pedestal, and it had brilliant red eyes.

"Strangest of all, lying in the center of this room was a large crystal coffin, its sides about 2.5 centimeters thick. Inside was a human skeleton fashioned in gold. It was quite large—2.8 meters long; I measured it with the spread of my hand. It was complete with all of the bones of the human skeleton, and each bone was fashioned of gold, as if to preserve the form of human beings who lived in another time. These large men would be like the Achuyanos, a tribe living in the deep Amazon today, slaves of the Auchiris. The Achuyanos have white skin, yellow hair, and blue eyes, and they are all more than 2.5 meters in height, very strong and high in spirit. So I imagine that the Achuyanos are the descendants of the people who made this skeleton in the crystal coffin."

Jaramillo paused momentarily, lost in his reverie. Then he looked at me and asked, "Would it be possible to listen to what I have just said?"

"Of course," I said, and backed up the tape to where we had begun following lunch. Jaramillo took a seat, and we listened again to the description of the room with the stone animals, the crystal coffin, and the gold skeleton. It was the first time that Jaramillo had ever heard his recorded voice, and he sat, rapt and smiling, as his words filled the room. When the recorded passage came to the end, he said, "Yes, that is very good. Very good!" Then he rose and picked up the microphone, and with new determination resumed:

"We went back to the central room, then took another rank of steps, even a greater number, to a third room. This room was something to terrorize any spirit. There were perhaps eighty figures—half human and half animal. Some had the upper half of a hawk and the lower half of a horse. There were figures of men who had wings instead of arms, and elephants' feet, pigs' hocks, or large fowls' feet. In a corner of this room was a large cauldron on a stand, both made of a yellow metal that must have been gold, or very like gold. Behind it was the figure of a man with a head like a monster, and gold teeth. His mouth was open, his hair hung down, his ears and feet were very large. He was sitting behind the cauldron, staring into it. I looked inside, and saw in the pot some ten or twelve figures of children. I was deeply shocked and my mind raced to those strange times when children may have been cooked and eaten.

"We left this frightening room and went back to the central chamber. It was becoming dark. Night was falling, and the light that normally came in through cracks and openings in the rock, refracting and multiplying as it spread from one crystal rock to another, was fading. Here we spent the night, and slept. . . ."

It seemed to me that something about the character of Jaramillo's narrative was now beginning to seem too smooth, too rehearsed. It was as if he had worked it out very carefully beforehand, and was reciting details he had already gone through many times before.

"The next day we got up very early and spent all the morning, into the early afternoon, examining another hall. This hall was not made of pink, yellow, blue, and red rock as the others had been. The new chamber had an arch completely made of crystal of a very special color. The arch was supported by about fifteen cylindrical columns, between twenty and twenty-five meters high, some of which were reddish crystal, some yellow, some blue— but all similar in that they had at the center a core of completely white crystal, like the steel frame within a reinforced concrete structure.

"We walked through this vaulted chamber, and my guides led me into a wide room, some twenty by twenty meters square. I looked around and felt fortunate indeed. The room was filled with shelves, as in a library. There were shelves on all the walls, and also standing in the middle. And all the shelves were made of yellow metal.

"On these shelves were books of yellow metal with deep red backs. The books measured about two feet square, and were about six inches thick. The pages were sheets of very, very thin greenish-yellow metal, with inscriptions impressed or engraved into the metal. On some of these sheets there was writing in the same strange script, resembling shorthand, that we saw on the balls in the first room. Other sheets had symbols—curved and straight lines, broken lines, geometric figures, triangles, trapezoids, circles and half circles, tangent lines. In other words, they resembled books of geometry.

"In all, there were about two hundred of these books. I took some down from the highest shelves, but could not put them back up again. They were very heavy; they seemed to weigh about fifty kilos [110 pounds], and it was quite impossible to heave them back into place. Samakache said it was quite all right to leave them on the floor. I wanted to uncouple one of the sheets, but my guides said that I could not possibly take anything with me. Everything was sacred. . . ."

By now there was something very familiar about Jaramillo's narrative. Then it hit me. He was working in every essential element of the legends of Atlantis, the mythic ancient civilization: the great benefit that would be bestowed upon mankind when its secrets are again revealed; the tall, blond, blue-eyed people, strong and intelligent; the great numbers of golden books containing secret writing. Every important feature of the legends of the "record room" of Atlantis was here.

"They told me there were other such libraries, far away, and that it would take a long hike to reach them. This was impossible; my leave was coming to an end, and I had to get back to my garrison.

"Our departure from the cave was as extraordinary, frightening, and dangerous as our arrival. We had to retrace our steps through all those strange chambers and again ford the canal in order to get out. I returned to the village, to my garrison, and this was the end of my experience in the Cueva de los Tayos. But among all the hundreds of caves that exist in the area of the tayos, this cave is a very special one. This cave I believe is El Dorado. Francisco de Orellana, the great Spanish discoverer of the Amazon, heard this legend and left Quito with four hundred Indians in 1542, traveling east, to find it. He was unsuccessful, but he did discover the Amazon River, and took this information back to Spain. Later, he returned to the New World to look for El Dorado again. On his last expedition he vanished in the jungles of the Amazon.

"We all have read about El Dorado, believing that it is a city. Now I can say, yes, El Dorado is a city, but a city that is deeply buried. . . ."

Jaramillo paused, and I took this opportunity to tell him that although El Dorado was originally thought by the Spaniards to have been a golden city, it was actually a legend born from the Chibcha Indian nation in the area of Lake Guatavita in Colombia. There, in ancient times, their great ruler, on the most important ceremonial days, had himself covered first with a layer of grease and then with a layer of gold dust. And once coated with gold, he became *El Dorado*—"the golden one." Later, the name El Dorado came to be applied to the religious center where

A representation in gold of the ceremonial balsawood raft carrying El Dorado on Lake Guatavita, Colombia.

these ceremonies had taken place, and eventually it came to signify a great sacred city.

Jaramillo said that was very interesting. Then he turned, gazed at the floor thoughtfully for a moment and, entirely ignoring what I had said, resumed his narrative.

"And now I would like to investigate the great ancient culture that inhabited this cave, in a scientific manner, without offending the interests of my country, and above all without offending those Jivaros I love and respect, especially Mashutaka, my boyhood friend, who will some-day be the tribal cacique of his clan.

"The first son of Mashutaka was born when the night sky was tinted with red flashes, and the tribal legends said that this was to be the omen that he was to be named Yucalchiri—*'Yu-'* meaning God, and *'-chiri'* meaning son. He is the son of God. When Yucalchiri grows up, not only will he be cacique of his tribe but he will also acquire the knowledge to decipher all those hieroglyphs, all those passages written in the strange script I have seen in the Cueva de los Tayos.

"Mashutaka, following in the tradition of his own father, brought his son, Yucalchiri, to me to educate as Mashutaka himself had been educated by my uncle many years before. To pay for the education of his son, Mashutaka gave me a large golden piece shaped like a pear, and many other gold pieces through the years. I sold them, and with this money I was able not only to educate Yucalchiri but also to travel to many countries in South America to increase my knowledge. I know Peru, Chile, the Argentine, Uruguay, Brazil, and Colombia. . . ."

Jaramillo's mention of a golden piece shaped like a fruit immediately brought to mind the historical description of Pizarro's arrival by ship at the mouth of the Rio Tumbez in 1527, which today marks the official demarcation line between Peru and Ecuador. An emissary, Pedro de Candia, was sent ashore to verify an earlier account of the incredible wealth of the Inca town and fortress of Tumbez. Candia reported back to Pizarro that Tumbez was indeed a magnificent place. Among its other splendors, he described a complex of structures surrounded by walls that included a temple emblazoned with gold and silver decorations, a residence for the virgin brides of the Peruvian nobility, and a garden resplendent with fascsimiles of vegetables, flowers, animals, and fruits—all made of pure gold and silver.

The tone of Jaramillo's voice changed and my attention was drawn back again to his narrative.

"It was in 1966, ten years after he brought his son to me, that Mashutaka came out of the Oriente to my town, snatched Yucalchiri away from me, and took him without giving me any explanation."

Jaramillo stopped. I thought he was through, but before I could say anything he turned, faced me squarely, and continued with great emotion:

"I have kept the secret of the Cuevo de los Tayos for many, many years on account of my boyhood friendship with Mashutaka. Yet now he has taken his son away from me with no explanation, and he has threatened to kill me. But I do not think the Jivaros are the sole proprietors of that great archaeological museum. They are only the guardians, because they do not know just what it means. I am very resentful about Mashutaka taking his son away from me. I protected that boy morally and intellectually, and I received financial support from Mashutaka for us both. It was this support that allowed me to travel in many countries. And now I am unable to travel and this secret, which belongs not only to Ecuador but to the world, remains unknown. I have thought long and deep on this, and I believe there should be an organization of international scope which can provide the scientific support to achieve this discovery. The secret must be told, and in you I sense a man I can trust. Yes, I am determined to take you to the cave, although I understand that it will involve great and imminent danger for me. I am not afraid; this is simply a fact. But we must go forward and overcome these difficulties."

As the reverberations of his last words faded away, a vague uneasiness crept over me. The room was silent except for the hum from the tape recorder. I moved to the desk and switched it off, my mind racing for a moment as I pondered how to proceed. Putting aside all thoughts and decisions, I told Jaramillo that his story was indeed an extraordinary one, and that when I had had time to think about it carefully, I would be in touch with him again.

I left him that afternoon feeling that the whole of life had suddenly become unreal. I returned to my hotel room and there I sat, lit a cigarette, and settled down to try to separate the rational from the irrational in Jaramillo's narrative. His years of military service in the Oriente I knew to be true. And the details of his association with the Indian, Mashutaka, could have happened. Andrea Salvador, and many others, had told me of the existence of numerous caves in the Oriente and throughout the east Andean range. But it was Jaramillo's description of the artifacts he said he had seen inside the Cueva de los Tayos that seemed to me to be totally incredible.

On the other hand, such a cave might actually contain archaeological remains of extinct civilizations, and only Jaramillo's imagination changed them into a crystal coffin, a library full of gold books, rooms filled with strange-looking animals, and a slab of stone that operated from the forces of light and darkness. Jaramillo was educated enough to have read the tales of the Arabian Nights, and the many versions of the legends of Atlantis. He certainly possessed enough imagination to have put all this into a hodge-podge of fable. But what were his motives? Fame, money? He had mentioned that he had lost his financial support from the Indians. Could that have any bearing on his story? Was he, perhaps, not quite sane?

I was in no position to mount an expedition into the Oriente to explore the Cueva de los Tayos, even on the assumption that it existed and Jaramillo could find it. Proof of my archaeological ideas would have to rest on facts, not on fables. Still, I could not help but wonder if Jaramillo's narrative was, at least in part, true, or whether he was just a wonderful spinner of yarns.

CHAPTER 8

The Good Padre

It had been two years ago, while having lunch with Father Julio Herrera in the small village of Guapulo near Quito, that he had mentioned the name of Father Crespi to me. He was the old priest who in his earlier years had founded La Misíon de Maria Auxiliadora in one of the oldest towns in southern Ecuador, Cuenca, the beautiful capital of Azuay Province. Father Crespi, Father Herrera had said, was an inveterate collector who, during his more than forty years of missionary work, had amassed an incredible number of "old things" unlike anything else known in Ecuador. Looking intently through the sparkling glass of white wine he was holding in his right hand, Father Herrera said he didn't want to go into much detail about the collection. I should go to Cuenca and see it for myself, and then when we met again, I could tell him what I thought of it.

I had decided to follow his suggestion, and a few days later when I arrived in Cuenca, a cold wind drifted across the town, tossing the rain against the stained-glass windows of the Maria Auxiliadora Mission. I found the father superior, Father Pedro Lova, and introduced myself; he told me that Father Crespi was too ill to see anyone, but that he would be glad to take me into the barn where the collection was kept. We walked together to a long, tin-roofed structure with windows built along only one wall, and Father Lova unlocked a rusty old padlock that looked as if it wouldn't be able to withstand two blows of a hammer. He turned on the light switch, but no light came on. "Probably the storm is responsible," he said. "But I hope you'll find there is enough light to see something. Unfortunately, I can't tell you much about the collection."

We stepped inside, I looked around, and was overwhelmed. Built along both of the long walls of the barn were benches that were completely buried under heaps of artifacts. Shelves had been built between the benches and the ceiling, and in the darkness I could discern that they, too, were loaded with artifacts. A row of tablets and plates was hung immediately under the ceiling, slanted down so that they could be seen in the dim light below. At first glance, I had the impression of an incredible treasure. But the great mass of material looked very odd, totally unlike anything I had seen before. The amalgamation of clay, stone, and metal artifacts all seemed to be in a strange and undefinable style. If they were authentic, I wondered, why have no pieces in this style shown up anywhere else? Instinctively, I felt that something was out of order, but I couldn't put my finger on it. "Where did all these artifacts come from?" I asked Father Lova in puzzlement.

The author examining the Crespi collection.

He shrugged his shoulders a little and said, "You'll have to talk to Father Crespi about that."

We walked out of the barn, Father Lova closed and locked the door, and before I left the mission he said, "I hope you will come back when Father Crespi is well because there is another room full of more pieces, but only he has the key." Thanking him for his trouble, I wondered what the other room contained, and made a mental note to query Father Crespi himself about his collection when I was able to return to Cuenca.

Now, two years later, I had almost forgotten about Father Crespi, but soon after my meeting with Major Jaramillo, I thought of him again. If there was any truth in Jaramillo's tale—if there had ever been a civilization in the southern Oriente capable of producing such objects as he had described—then the possibility had to be considered that some of the pieces in Father Crespi's collection came from, or were at least influenced by, this culture. That might account for their strange and unique style. I decided to try to see Father Crespi again.

I returned to Cuenca to find that the church at La Misión de Maria Auxiliadora had been almost completely destroyed by fire a year before, but the generous hearts of the citizens of Cuenca had supplied the means to rebuild it. Fortunately the building that housed Father Crespi's collection was untouched, and Father Crespi himself was well and able to meet me.

From everything I had heard about the extraordinary work that he had done—his establishment of a mission that by now included a school and a body of twelve or fourteen priests, his well-known impact on the Indians—I had expected to find Father Crespi a very pious and well-organized, methodical man, who was fluent in the Indian tongues. I was presented with quite a contrast when he finally stood before me. His frock was so old that it had faded from black to a sort of grayish-green and looked as if it hadn't been washed for months; spots of oil and food ran all the way down the front, only partially covered by his long, scraggly beard. After I had talked with him for a few moments, I noticed that he kept repeatedly spitting, not expectorating saliva but expelling the hairs of his mustache from his mouth. He said a few words, then, pouf, the hairs of his mustache would flutter out in the air for a moment, then settle back into his mouth as he continued talking.

His age was indeterminate; he must have been at least seventy. And I was amazed to find that after all his years in Ecuador, his Spanish was still very poor. When I suggested that we speak in Italian, his native tongue, he said, "Oh, of course. That's the best way to do things." I wondered how he was able to deal effectively with the Indians without a fluent command of Spanish, let alone their own tongues. But then, as the minutes went by, it became clear: he didn't have to deal too closely with them at all. We were standing in the courtyard before the church and a stream of Indians passed us continually, asking his blessing as they entered the church. He spoke with all of them with hardly a break in his train of thought: "Oh yes, Señor Turolla—*benedice domini*—I am delighted. First—*benedice domini*—I want to show you our . . ." Evidently a few words of Latin, spoken automatically, maintained his relationship with the Indians.

Father Crespi led me to the same long, barnlike structure that I had previously visited with Father Lova, and took out the same rusty key to open it. We entered and he began to show me his collection. He pointed first to a shelf containing several large urns with distinctive geometric designs. "They come from the Ingapirca area," he said, "from a culture that existed before the Inca arrived."

I examined the urns, which appeared to be authentic pre-Columbian pieces, but then with a gesture toward the hundreds of other artifacts in his collection, I asked how he had amassed such an enormous quantity of objects.

"When my father passed away in Italy," he replied, "he left me a legacy, and I could think of no better way to use it than by salvaging these ancient treasures from greedy traders and black marketeers." Then he launched into a long diatribe on the histories of the Mesopotamian and Egyptian civilizations, the Phoenician maritime expansion, the Mesoamerican and Inca cultures of the New World, and even a smattering of present-day history. As he talked and we walked the length of the big barn, he pointed out many objects to illustrate and emphasize the significance of what he was saying: small, ceramic, pyramid-shaped depictions of Phoenician royal crematories topped by the effigy of the God of Eternity; crudely carved stone tablets with images of the sun, pyramids, snakes, and humans; a complete collection of ceramic musical instruments (saxophone, flutes, clarinets) held by lifelike pottery figures; a winged centaur made of metal lying next to a clay figurine of a woman on her knees with hands clasped together in an attitude of prayer; Sumerian-like winged lions along with Greek-looking pottery; hammered copper figures and grotesque stone-carved objects of no discernible style or period: a bishop's mitre complete with a cross and Christian symbols, diadems and crowns; a helmet with extended horns reminiscent of the headgear of Viking warriors. Thousands more of these weird objects unfolded before my eyes in a chaotic display, among them, here and there, artifacts from known Ecuadorian cultures. I began to feel a little uneasy as I looked at all of this.

Father Crespi then turned to me and said, "I want to show you the treasure room." Apparently this was the room to which, as Father Lova had told me on my previous visit, only Father Crespi had the key. He opened the door, flicked on the light, and the impact of what I saw was staggering. The entire room was paneled with sheets of plywood on which were hanging thousands of metal objects. Rough-hewn cabinets built along the walls housed even more objects of every description. There were dozens of boxes, each containing from four to six gold-colored metal sheets on which had been hammered in relief dragons, camels, elephants, palm trees, pyramids, half-moons, stars, the sun symbol, gods and deities, warriors and stylized boats. "These are my gold and silver treasures," Father Crespi proudly announced, rubbing his hands together.

My attention was drawn toward a heavy yellow metal

The author with Father Crespi, who is holding a tablet he believes to be gold, containing the commandments of the Egyptian pharaohs.

sheet, approximately 51 centimeters high by 13 wide, which was divided into fifty-six squares, and in each square, depicted in relief, were different symbols. Father Crespi solemnly declared that this tablet contained the commandments of the Egyptian Pharaohs. Then from one of the boxes he retrieved a greenish metal object, which depicted an Egyptian-looking bird balancing a disc on its head framed by a snake. "A very ancient calendar," he said. Lying on the floor in the center of the room was some kind of boat or canoe with what seemed to be elaborate gold carvings. Pointing to the object, Father Crespi said: "This was the 'bark' that the ancient sun god used when he was traveling on the waterways." He then explained that he was convinced the ancient tribes of Ecuador were the descendants of a great and very old civilization. The objects in his collection were the treasure, the patrimony, of this civilization brought here to Ecuador for safekeeping.

Father Crespi rambled on as I walked back and forth in the barn, examining his strange collection. Apart from a few pottery pieces, everything was of dubious authenticity. Why, then, did some of the pieces seem familiar to me? Suddenly I knew why. Many of the objects that Major Jaramillo had described in his fantastic narrative of the

Cueva de los Tayos stood before my eyes on Father Crespi's shelves. Of course, Jaramillo had been here and seen the collection. He had spent many years in this area, was fascinated with anything that was said to be ancient, and the fame of Father Crespi's collection was certain to have attracted his attention. I had come to Cuenca hoping to find corroboration for Jaramillo's tales in Father Crespi's collection. I found, instead, just the opposite.

If I needed any further proof of the doubtful origins of the collection, it came when, with a rather hushed reverence, Father Crespi removed a yellowish metal orb from a concave plate, extended it toward me, and said: "Very ancient, my son, very ancient—with glyphics." I looked closely at this mysterious orb and it proved to be a float from a toilet mechanism, bearing the legend "RF" (République française). I chuckled and looked at Father Crespi, thinking he was playing a joke on me. But his face was very serious as he said, "Very old, my son, probably three thousand years before the birth of our Lord."

Father Crespi went on to point out other pieces, and the inconsistencies between historical facts and his bizarre interpretations of the objects he had collected began to

Metal objects from Father Crespi's "Treasure Room," including (center) the hammered figure said by him to represent the Sun God.

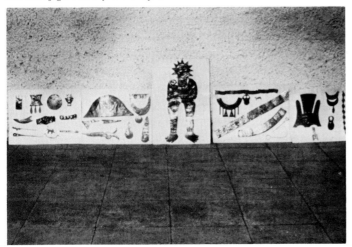

reach a disturbing level of absurdity. I had seen enough of the collection; but Father Crespi was not through yet. "Come with me," he said. "I have something else I want to show you now." He led me out of the barn, locked it, then took me to his spartanly furnished room in the priest's dormitory. There he unlocked a box, pulled out a large sheet of parchment, and handed it to me. "This," he said, "is a drawing by Leonardo da Vinci." Though my credulity had been severely stretched by now, I looked at it and saw an anatomical drawing of the human hand, in a style very much like da Vinci's. Perhaps it was authentic. But then Father Crespi pulled out a painted canvas and said, "This is by Raphael." Then another and another: "This is by Cimabue . . . and this is a Botticelli Madonna . . . and this is a Tintoretto." Forty or fifty Renaissance masters, lying unprotected in a fragile box in one corner of a priest's room—that was beyond belief.

Still, I tried to conceal my doubts and asked him confidentially how all those wonderful paintings had come to be in his possession. "My order," he said, "the Salesian Order, is one of the oldest in Italy. Many of our founders were sons of great Italian families—families that go back to the Renaissance and before. Their families had these paintings. But times were very troubled in Italy then, and they were gathered together by our order and brought here for safekeeping."

When Father Crespi and I parted that day, I went in search of Father Lova. I wanted to ask him about Father Crespi's collection; but one has to start very softly, very tactfully, with such questions, so I said: "Father Lova, if everything Father Crespi says is true, why are such priceless artifacts kept in an old barn behind thin glass windows with no protection?"

Father Lova gave a sort of knowing smile and said, "Well, actually, we don't have money to build the kind of place Father Crespi ought to have for his things." Not until many months later, when Father Lova and I had become better acquainted, would he confess that Father Crespi's voluminous and ever-growing collection, and his strange ideas, were an embarrassment both to him and to the order.

"Do you know where they came from?" I asked him then.

He looked at me and said, "We don't know. Father Crespi is very secretive. Perhaps you, if you have time, could find out. Would you do that for me?"

At first, I found myself confronted with a wall of silence as I checked around, talking to oldtimers in the area about Father Crespi. There was a definite reticence on their part; but gradually the story emerged. Decades ago, Father Crespi's mind began to change and he became fascinated with the idea that the ancient Ecuadorian civilizations had sprung from Egypt. He believed that one of the Pharaohs had left Egypt and sailed across the Atlantic Ocean to the mouth of the Amazon. Then he navigated this great river, crossed the east Andean range, and established himself with his court in the southern part of what today is known as Ecuador. Father Crespi gathered together books and pictures of Egyptian, Phoenician, and other Old World cultures, gave them to the natives, and said: "If you ever find anything like this, bring it to me, and I will reward you."

The Indians and mestizos, being only too glad to oblige, took the pictures and made artifacts according to the designs they had been given. Then they brought them to Father Crespi, telling him they had been found in tolas, tombs, landslides, or whatever. This exchange had been going on for many decades; Father Crespi's collection continued to grow and some of the native craftsmen had become quite expert in the fabrication and decoration of "ancient" objects made from very modern bronze, brass, copper, and tin.

It hardly took an expert to discover that Father Crespi was living in a dream world of his own creation. I knew that the day he showed me his collection. But what of Jaramillo? Was he equally convinced that every word he uttered about the Cueva de los Tayos was true? I began to doubt it when I returned to Quito and we spoke again of mounting an expedition to explore the cave. Jaramillo had now become curiously reticent about sharing his great secret with the rest of the world. Yet, apart from his fanciful descriptions of crystal coffins and golden skeletons, at least one part of his tale might be true: I felt instinctively that the two Indians who had guided him to the cave, Samakache and Mashutaka, actually existed. And the name "Pescado," that Señora Jaramillo had inadvertently dropped, kept ringing in my ears. Legends always have some basic truth; had not Heinrich Schliemann discovered the golden treasures of Troy because of this belief? Samakache and Mashutaka were the key to the puzzle. I must try to find them.

CHAPTER 9

The Cueva de los Tayos

How was I to find two Jivaro Indians who lived, sup-posedly, somewhere in the jungles of the mighty Amazon? Father Herrera was, as always, ready to be of assistance. He made no comment when I told him of my visit to Fa-ther Crespi's collection. But when I related Jaramillo's description of the Cueva de los Tayos and told him of my determination to seek the two Indians, Samakache and Mashutaka, who I believed really existed, he became fascinated by the story and asked, "What clues do you have to their whereabouts?"

"The name 'Pescado' that Señora Jaramillo dropped during her conversation," I said, "and the names of two towns: Loja, the birthplace of Major Jaramillo, and Za-mora, where he was based during his military service."

Father Herrera brightened. "If you plan to travel to Zamora," he said, "my good friend Monsignor Maschera is the head of the Franciscan mission there. I'm sure he'll be happy to assist you. I'll contact him by radio and tell him you're coming."

A trip to Zamora necessitated a return to Cuenca, and there at the airport I was met by Oswaldo Mora, a young man in his late twenties to whom Father Lova had in-troduced me on one of my previous trips. As I arrived and was walking toward the terminal, I spotted him stand-ing squarely in the doorway, indifferent to the passengers and airport personnel who were struggling to pass through. But that was Oswaldo, handsome, short of stat-

Oswaldo Mora.

ure, resourceful, always self-assured, and in a certain sense, a modern reincarnation of his lineage—the Spanish conquistadors. He had agreed to accompany me on the journey to Zamora.

He had already found a Jeep for the journey, and we left early the next morning en route to our first stop, Loja, about 215 kilometers from Cuenca. The road twisted up and over several mountain ranges, at times reaching an altitude of 3000 meters. The weather was clear and our view ranged across valleys, ridges, and peaks looming up into the sky all around us. Broad slopes covered with flowers swept down away from us into valleys far below. Patches of reclaimed land were being worked by native peasants dressed in heavy ponchos to protect themselves from the chilling wind. From time to time a lonely traveler followed by his faithful burro crossed our path. Sporadically, signs would remind us that we were driving on a segment of the ancient Imperial Road built by the Inca, hundreds of years before, to connect their empire with its capital city, Cuzco, in Peru. We reached Loja before noon, and passed through the entrance gates of the old colonial town that had been founded in 1536 as a settlement on the slopes of one of the highest massifs of the Andean mountain range, the Villonaco.

From the window of the small café where we stopped
for lunch, I could see dozens of Saraguro Indians dressed
in ponchos and broad-brimmed hats passing by on horseback or on foot, coming to the weekly market. The
women wore their hair in ponytails and were resplendent
in trinkets of shiny gold or silver. The men carried machetes in scabbards hanging from their colorful high belts.
On a festive day they gather in groups, rope a young calf,
cut its jugular vein, and collect its blood in a pan. They
then mix the warm blood with *aguardiente,* a strong homemade alcohol brew, and drink it as part of their ancient
rituals.

More than 4000 years before, I reflected, this same land
had seen the beginnings of a flourishing culture known
today as Chorrera, named after a small settlement where
one of its important sites was discovered on the banks of
the Rio Babahojo in the foothills of the Western Cordillera. When first uncovered, this culture was believed by
many authorities to have originated and developed on the
coastal plain. In 1943, however, Donald Collier, curator of
the Field Museum of Natural History in Chicago, together
with John Murra, described the discovery of potsherds in
the Andean highlands that were strikingly similar in some
of their characteristics to those of the Chorrera.

Whistling bottles
representing a monkey
(top) and a macaw
(bottom). Chorrera.

Such evidence suggested that the ancient Chorreras
might have descended from the southern highlands—
between the Eastern and Central Cordilleras—in places
named Alausi, Cerro Narrio, and Descanzo. But what intrigued me the most were the Chorrera sites discovered in
the area of Loja near the banks of the Rio Zamora, a river
with direct access to the lowlands of the Amazon Basin.
Moreover, Chorrera ceramics display elements traditionally associated with the tropical Amazon forest:
human figurines with ear spools, a tradition of some of
the Indian tribes still seen today; prehensile tailed monkeys; tropical forest birds; and jaguar effigies. The artifacts of the Chorrera culture, in particular, seemed to
offer substantiation of my theories that early Ecuadorian
cultures may have originated in the Amazon.

If such a cultural migration took place, no doubt the

Hollow ceramic figurines displaying striking similarities in style: (top), Correra; (bottom), Ajalpan/Tehuacan Valley, Mexico.

natural topography of the country through the millennia played an important role. There is a complex interrelationship between the multiplicity of rivers found in Ecuador and much of its terrain. Most of the country is composed of volcanic or sedimentary rock that retains water very poorly, and since so much of the country is mountainous, most of the voluminous rainfall runs off the land rather than soaking into the ground. Because of this, swift-flowing rivers have carved great passes and canyons through the Andes, between the massives of the highlands, the Amazon to the east, and the coastal plain to the west. Could these passes have provided natural routes of access from the Amazon to the Mesa, and from the Mesa to the coastal plain? Such routes, I reasoned, could have been provided through the Central Cordillera by the Rios Aguarico and Coca in the north, which are affluents of the great Rio Napo; by the Rio Pastaza in the center, affluent of the Marañon (the Peruvian trunk of the Amazon River); and in the south by the Rio Zamora, affluent of the Rio Santiago, which, like the Rios Napo and Marañon, becomes part of the great Amazon River. Thus there are three great corridors from the Oriente into the Mesa, and other lesser ones, formed by the ubiquitous rivers.

The first appearance of pottery making on the South American continent was associated with the beginnings of the Valdivia culture, which flourished in the lowlands of the Pacific coast of southern Ecuador. It was, however, from the Chorrera that there emerged a very complex and spectacular ceramic tradition. Ornate pottery vessels, whistling bottles, stirrup bottles, and far advanced techniques of iridescent pottery painting appeared in the Chorrera culture far earlier than in the cultures of Peru, Colombia, Guatemala, and Mexico. The Chorrera culture spread from the foothills of the western range of the Andes to the coastal plain, both to the south and north. And stylistic traits of Chorrera figurines and ware can be seen in artifacts from cultures that flourished in Colombia and in Mesoamerica to the north, and in Peru to the south, at least 1000 years later. But again the question arose: Where had the Chorrera originated? And how had such a highly developed, expansionist society supported itself? The only crop capable of sustaining such a culture is the high-yield staple, corn, but as yet investigators have found no evidence that the Chorrera cultivated corn. Perhaps, I thought, somewhere in the Cordillera, or further east into the Amazon, the answer to both questions could be found.

After lunch, Oswaldo and I took a brief look around Loja, Jaramillo's birthplace, and then set out on the road to Zamora, 54 kilometers away. As a provincial capital, Zamora, on the map, is indicated with a prominent geographical symbol; in reality it is a frontier town with a total population of 1300, including the cats and dogs, where the largest building is the Franciscan mission. What distinguishes Zamora is its location near the headwaters of the Rio Zamora—one of the major waterways to the Amazon Basin—which makes the town the southern gateway to the Oriente.

Oswaldo and I went directly to the mission where Father Herrera's friend, Monsignor Maschera, made us welcome. When I explained, as succinctly as possible, that I was searching for two Jivaro Indians named Samakache

Zamora.

and Mashutaka and asked him if he had ever heard of them and a place called Pescado, he replied that he hadn't. But he referred me to Emmanuel Garbo, the young doctor at the mission hospital, who confirmed that in about 1956 an officer named Jaramillo had been with the military in Zamora, and then mentioned that there was a Jivaro woman patient who spoke Spanish in one of the wards. I questioned her, and she told me that there was a settlement named Pescado (in Spanish, "fishing place") 30 kilometers northeast of Zamora on the shore of the Rio Cumburatza. She also said that she had heard of a Jivaro man named Samakache who supposedly lived in Los Enquontros, halfway between Zamora and Gualaquiza, a small settlement across the Rio Bombaiza.

I was elated by her answers, and early the next morning, with a Jivaro guide supplied by Monsignor Maschera, Oswaldo and I set out for Los Enquontros. It was a difficult and frustrating journey that took us, finally, up a steep and muddy trail to a Jivaro compound. Just before we reached it, our guide told us to stop for a moment while he whistled a series of modulated signals. A few seconds later an answering whistle was heard from the bushes, and that indicated we could proceed. It is essential to make your presence known at some distance from the settlements to avoid any possible misunderstanding of your intentions.

Samakache was not living in this settlement. We learned that he had moved only a week before to Ansasa, a small settlement about 20 or 25 kilometers back in the direction of Zamora. We also learned that he was a young man, too young to have a full-grown son like Mashutaka. That disturbed me, but I thought perhaps that he might be a member of the old Samakache's family, and still hoped he would be able to tell me something about the Cueva de los Tayos.

Our spirits dampened, Oswaldo and I started back down the same muddy trail, and tired and disappointed, reached Zamora as the sun was settling behind the high peak of the Sabanilla range.

The following morning we drove to Ansasa, impatient to resolve the Samakache question one way or the other. From there we were directed to the banks of the Rio Zamora, which we crossed with two Indians in a canoe, and then began another hike up a narrow trail that led to high ground where Samakache was said to live. After half an hour we approached a clearing with a Jivaro hut, but Samakache was not there either. We were told that he lived in another settlement, and so we followed a different trail, crossed a turbulent mountain stream, and climbed up to a small hill on which we saw another Jivaro hut. We approached it, and there, standing before the hut, was Samakache.

It was the wrong Samakache. He had never heard of Mashutaka, and he knew of no other man named Samakache who had a son by that name. He told us that Samakache means, simply, "deadly snake"; Mashutaka means "wise one" or "strong one," and both were commonly used by Jivaro warriors as battle names. He said that he had once lived in Pescado, but I also learned that Pescado is a very common name for any place along a river where fish are abundant.

It was a great disappointment. Oswaldo and I wearily returned to Zamora. My hopes of finding some confirmation of Major Jaramillo's story of the Cueva de los Tayos were completely dashed. To all appearances my journey had been a failure. Everything about it seemed to prove that there was no tangible reason to pursue my search for the cave further. But fate, unknown to me, had already set in motion events that, by their very nature, would compel me to resume my search.

It was months later, in September of 1969, that I was startled back into the realm of the mysterious and unknown. I had received an unexpected phone call from Oswaldo, and flew immediately from Miami to Quito, and thence to Cuenca where he was waiting for me at the airport. The reason for my trip was a report that had appeared in the Cuenca newspaper, reprinted a day later in the Quito press, about the discovery of a great series of caverns called "Las Cuevas de los Tayos," located in the third range of the Andes in the Oriente region. The man who announced the discovery was Juan Moricz, and I recognized his name immediately. When Andrea Salvador first told me of Jaramillo, he had mentioned that Moricz, an Argentinian (originally Hungarian) who was interested in tracking down the legends of the Indians in the interior, had also heard the major's story. I thought now that, perhaps, he had received more information and clues from Jaramillo, which had enabled him to discover the caves after all.

The report went on to say that the Cuevas de los Tayos were situated in a very inhospitable region on the slopes of the Eastern Cordillera of the Andes. They were part of a multi-level stone city, it was claimed, each level interconnected with passages and tunnels, and the existing stone walls were built of perfectly made blocks covered with mysterious inscriptions. The place was inhabited by a rare species of birds called by the Jivaro Indians "tayos," and the ruins were said to extend deep into the surrounding jungle. In his announcement Moricz offered a theory about the significance of the discovery: he believed that this lost city was once inhabited by a mysterious people known as the Vela, who were said to be the ancestors of the lamas now inhabiting Tibet. That struck me as somewhat fanciful, but if the descriptions of the caves were true, they would certainly be as momentous and significant a discovery as the mountain stone city of Machu Picchu in the Peruvian Andes by Hiram Bingham in 1911.

Sitting in the café "El Correo" in downtown Cuenca, Oswaldo filled me in on the rumors, speculation, and excitement triggered by Moricz's announcement. Government officials were skeptical, he said, but discussions were in progress at the various ministries, and it was possible that an official investigation would be opened. That was the reason for his urgent call. He knew that if I wished to make any determination of the significance of the caves in my own research, we would have to move quickly. Once the government had initiated its investigation, the caves would surely be cordoned off to prevent outsiders from entering.

We decided to make the journey immediately, although we knew how difficult it would be. But first I had to see the chief of the South Military Zone, Colonel Antonio Moral, to obtain a permit for travel in the Oriente. According to the reports, the caves were located close to the border with Peru, and no travel was allowed in this area without a special permit. Colonel Moral also gave me a note of introduction to the commanding officer of the military post at Teniente Ortiz, which would provide a good jumping-off point for our expedition to the area of the caves.

Then preparations had to be made. All the food, equipment, and supplies we would need had to be carried in, because Teniente Ortiz was a very small and remote military outpost. The best way to reach it, we decided, was to rent a small Cessna and land on an airstrip that had been cut in the jungle near the post. There was one other route—by land and water, taking trails and dugout canoe. But that was at least a ten-day journey and time was too pressing.

It was a very difficult task to find a pilot with a small plane who would fly us to the Ortiz airstrip. The flight is perilous. It is not possible for a small plane to fly over the Central Cordillera of the Andes that separates Cuenca and Teniente Ortiz. The plane must fly *through* the mountains, using passes between the mountain peaks that at this time of year were usually cloud-covered, with zero visibility. Over the years many planes have miscalculated and smashed against the mountainside; on a clear day one can still see their twisted wrecks strewn over the bare rock.

We finally found a pilot, Julio Ortega, who was very familiar with the route to Teniente Ortiz and agreed to fly Oswaldo and me there as soon as the weather cleared. When at last we were airborne and rose over the floor of the mesa, the spectacle below was overwhelming. The savage beauty of the Andes, in the clear morning light, was stupendous. Huge peaks rose ahead of us, and then, suddenly, they surrounded us from all directions as Ortega maneuvered through passes and canyons where cloud cover at any point would spell disaster, and only the most experienced pilots can stay alive. When we saw the Ortiz landing strip below us, it looked like a small garden plot surrounded by tall, dense trees. I could not imagine how Ortega could put the plane down on such a short strip. But he skirted over the tops of the trees on the near side, dropped like a rock to within a few meters of the ground, pulled back and touched down, then brought the Cessna to a stop within 5 meters of the trees at the far end of the strip.

The officer in charge of the military post at Ortiz was not very interested in our arrival. In spite of the letter of introduction from Colonel Moral of Cuenca, he had no time to help strangers. Perhaps, he suggested, we could walk with all our gear a few kilometers north to the Santiago Mission where the Salesian brothers, surely, would offer hospitality to two stranded gringos. We decided to take his suggestion, and happily, we received a very different reception there. Juan Arcos, the brother in charge, welcomed us with a big smile, immediately offered us accommodations for our stay, and said he would like to do whatever he could to help us. Brother Arcos, we learned, was a *laico*—a Catholic who had at one time trained for the priesthood, but hadn't finished and was now serving the church in another capacity. A mestizo, he spoke Jivaro perfectly and had served missions in the interior for around twenty-five years. He had built this mission on the banks of the Rio Santiago with the help of young Jivaros.

Brother Arcos was almost as familiar with the surrounding terrain as the Jivaros themselves, and we decided that the best way to reach the area in which the caves were supposed to be located was to travel down the Rio Santiago by canoe to the place where it meets with the Rio Coango, a small torrent that flows from the Cordillera Cutucu to the south. From there we would have to continue on foot, hiking up to a pass in the Cordillera Cutucu where on one of its western slopes the Cuevas de los

Tayos were said to be located. Brother Arcos offered to provide us with a canoe and two Jivaro guides who would take us downriver and pick us up again when we returned from the caves. But we would not be able to have an Indian guide for the hike from the river into the Cordillera. For some reason the military had issued a proscription against Indians traveling in that direction.

We spent the rest of that day learning as much as we could about our intended route from Brother Arcos and the Indians, and getting our gear ready for the trail. The following morning the sky was clear, the canoe was loaded, and we hurried into it to take advantage of the good weather. The Indians pushed the canoe away from the mission pier into the current and by mid-morning we reached the junction of the Coango. The Indians leaned on their paddles and our canoe glided to the left bank of the river, where we landed and unloaded our gear. We said goodbye to our guides, placed our packs on our backs, and began to look for the trail that was supposed to go from this point up into the Cordillera. But there was no trail in sight. Finally, I discovered a faint animal track that went almost vertically up the side of the mountain through the trees and dense vegetation. We decided to follow it, and the ascent proved to be formidable. The mud was so slippery that our feet slid out from under us with every step. In order to make any progress, we had to grab trees and heavy plants and pull ourselves up. We had hoped to reach the pass later that day, but we were forced to spend the night on the mountainside, and did not reach the pass until the following afternoon.

It is very difficult to describe the physical pain we felt as we hoisted our bodies hour after hour and only a few feet at a time up this muddy animal track. It was more than the ache of weary muscles; after the first strain and fatigue set in, it became a brutal, throbbing pain that grew steadily worse with every wrenching beat of our hearts. We kept going on spirit alone, only our will to find the caves sustaining us as we climbed. When we finally reached the pass, we collapsed for a few moments to allow our bodies to recover, and considered what direction to take next. We didn't know exactly where the caves were, and we had to make a choice. I decided that we should continue following the animal track; intuition told me that it led into terrain where caves were most likely to be found.

After another hour or so on the trail, there was very little light left and we started to look for a place to spend the night when, suddenly, against the dark silhouette of the mountain on our left, I saw the light of a fire. An Indian camp? A military patrol? And if so, was it Ecuadorian or Peruvian? We didn't know, but to our tired minds and bodies the light was too inviting to ignore. We decided to take our chances and began to walk toward it.

"Ola!" came a stern voice as we approached the fire. "Ola!" I called back. And with that exchange we found ourselves standing in front of three members of the Policia Civil from Gualaquiza. Oswaldo and I were astonished, and so were they. They asked us what we were doing in this remote section of Ecuador, and after explaining, we asked them the same question. They said that they were there on orders from the Commandante General of the police to guard—the Cueva de los Tayos! As hard as we had worked to locate this cave, I could scarcely believe that we had actually found it.

The soldiers invited us to join them around their campfire and told us that they had been sent here to work with an Indian party that would arrive the next morning to prepare a landing place for a helicopter. It was due to fly in about a week later with government officials and a military party to inspect the caves. Oswaldo and I looked at each other, and at that moment we realized how fortunate we were to get there ahead of them.

I asked Sergeant Spinoza, the leader of the patrol, about the caves and learned that, as far as he knew, there was only one. There were no stone walls with mysterious inscriptions, no ruins in the surrounding jungle. Apparently Juan Moricz had greatly exaggerated the description of his discovery. Still, I couldn't resist the urge to have a look at the entrance of the cave. Spinoza offered to take me there, so we lit our torches and started down a freshly hacked trail. A few minutes later there it was, the entrance of this famous cave. It was not impressive. The cave is deep underground, and the opening, against the wall of the mountain, looked like an odd-shaped well, a deep hole or shaft into the earth, partially covered by a rocky overhang and surrounded by brush, trees, and vines.

I beamed my light into the opening, but I could see nothing. The shaft disappeared into darkness. The only things visible were rocks protruding from its sides. A rudimentary platform had already been built by Spinoza and his men near the opening; ropes and cables were hanging from it down into the shaft.

When we returned to the campfire, Spinoza mentioned that he had orders to prevent anyone from entering the cave without a written permit from the Minister of the Interior. We showed him our permit and asked to be allowed to make the descent, but he was still reluctant because the permit didn't specifically say we could *enter* the cave. Nothing further was said for the moment. From our packs Oswaldo and I took out some coffee and condensed milk, tins of sardines and tuna, and a bottle of trago, and invited Spinoza and his men to share our dinner with us. As we ate, Oswaldo struck up a conversation with Spinoza and quickly found out that he had relatives in Cuenca. They began trading stories and comparing observations on their mutual acquaintances until, finally, Oswaldo gained Spinoza's trust and friendship. By the end of the evening we had reached an understanding. We would be allowed to enter the cave, but we would receive no help from Spinoza and his men, and we had to leave our cameras behind.

Rain delayed our descent the following day, but Oswaldo and I were able to assess what faced us. We saw that the cables and ropes hanging in the mouth of the cave were connected to a series of pulleys to facilitate descent and ascent, and as we peered into the shaft, we heard a muffled murmuring that came from the very depths of the cave. It was the cooing sound of thousands of tayo birds, the inhabitants of this mysterious subterranean world.

Early the next morning we stood again at the entrance to the cave. I shook hands with Oswaldo, tied the safety rope around my waist, crouched at the edge of the opening, grabbed the cable in my hands, and started to lower myself into the shaft. When I was no more than 50 feet down, the light of day was only a small halo above me and I descended into darkness. I felt a shiver down my back. Who knew what lay below? My hands were wound around the cable so tightly that I could feel the pain all the way up my arms. The shaft, narrow at the opening, grew to at least 50 or 60 feet in diameter as I continued to lower myself. I had a light hanging from my belt and turned it on, but I couldn't direct it around the shaft. I didn't dare release my grip from the cable.

Slowly I continued down. Over me, making the cable shake and move within my hands, was Oswaldo. Every few seconds he shouted: "Have you reached the bottom?" And the answer was always: "No." I was sure that I had descended about 200 feet when finally, down below, my light flashed on something. I looked down, and in horror I saw that it was water. If it was a deep underground river, I knew it would be impossible to land. Praying, I put my feet in the water, let myself down a little more, and hit the bottom. The water reached just below my knees. I heaved an immense sigh of relief, released the cable, and flexed my hands to get the blood circulating again. Looking up, I yelled at Oswaldo: "I'm on the bottom now!"

Oswaldo didn't lose any time joining me on the bottom. After attaching two homing blinking lights to the cable, we followed our light beams out of the water and up a slope for a few meters. Then we stopped and looked around to see where we were. We were both breathing as deeply as possible, and perspiring as if we had run for miles.

During our descent the hundreds of tayo birds that inhabited the cave had squealed and flown all around us, their phosphorescent eyes gleaming in the dark. They objected to having their domain invaded by strangers. Now, as we sat on the rocks and looked up, their darting shadows crossed the faint light that penetrated the cave from the mouth of the shaft. I knew that, for the Jivaros of this region, the tayo is far more than a simple bird; from time immemorial Jivaros have descended twice a year into the darkness of this cave to capture them. The fat of the bird is a very important part of their diet and, in time, this twice-yearly harvest evolved into a sacred ritual with chanting, drum-beating, and invocations to the cave and jungle spirits by the tribal brujo. It was clear to me why this cave came to be regarded as sacred ground by the Indians.

Oswaldo and I directed our lights around the cave. Large stalagmites, blocks of stone, and thick tayo droppings came into view. On one side a crude ladder bore witness to man's presence in this dark world; the Jivaros apparently used it to reach the tayos that dwelled in the cracks of the cave wall. Cautiously, we moved ahead between the rubble. Somehow we sensed that we were entering an enormous chamber, but our lights were not strong enough to define its size. The entrance to this chamber was a phenomenal sight: it seemed to be a huge portal built with massive square stones. It looked like the entrance to a stadium, and here the squealing of the tayos became more and more intense.

The floor of the chamber was uneven and covered with all sizes of stones and rocks that had fallen from above. Then the sound of a waterfall reached us, revealing the source of the water we had encountered at the bottom of the shaft. It also explained the air movement we felt inside the chamber. Warily we moved toward it and, unexpectedly, found our way obstructed by a sheer wall. The sound now came from above. Pointing our lights toward it, we saw high above us the entrance to a tunnel. It was then that we realized that this huge cavern had many entrances at different levels. Where did they all lead—to other chambers and caverns? At the mission, Brother Arcos had told me that the Indians believed the cave continued for 20 to 30 kilometers underground.

We followed our lights through passageways into other underground chambers and I looked intently for any sign of human habitation: hieroglyphics, drawings on the rocks, charcoal, signs of carving or construction. There was nothing. But in a corner of one of the chambers there was a pile of granite stones, perhaps several tons each, that appeared to have been cut. Some were square, some rectangular, and to one side of them was a rocky outcropping that bore some resemblance to an altar. These great stones struck me as remarkable; it seemed impossible that their square corners and perfectly flat sides could have occurred naturally. But I was puzzled because there was absolutely nothing else in any of the chambers that looked manmade.

I thought again of Juan Moricz's account of his discovery of the cave and marveled at the power of his imagination. There were no signs of human construction here, or

An underground passageway inside the Cueva de los Tayos.

dwellings that indicated a fabulous underground stone city, no discernible evidence that this underground world had once been inhabited by a mysterious ancient civilization. It was impossible for Oswaldo and me to explore all the many tunnels and chambers, but I had a strong feeling that they would not disclose anything more than we had already seen. I was convinced that the cave was a completely natural occurrence. It was a subterranean lair of incredible magnitude, but its mystique had probably been created by the reverence of the Jivaro Indians for the tayo birds.

We retraced our steps to the blinking homing lights on the cable. First Oswaldo, and then I, made the ascent. Foot by foot, straining and sweating, we climbed up into the arch of daylight and finally reached the top of the shaft. Sergeant Spinoza was relieved to see our faces. Exhausted by our adventure, we returned to the camp, lay down around the fire, and told the sergeant and his men what we had seen. I said that there seemed to be no reliable signs of any ancient inhabitants of the cave; it was simply an outstanding example of what nature can do. Spinoza mentioned that in an area called La Esperanza, about 20 kilometers away, there was a large boulder with petroglyphs that were believed by the Indians to illustrate the exact location of the entrance to the Cueva de los Tayos, and that the Jivaro brujo of the area, Zukma, had the same glyphics tattooed on his face. The thought came immediately to my mind that perhaps these were the "mysterious inscriptions" reported in the newspapers as having been seen inside the cave. A small error, no doubt.

Oswaldo and I spent the night at the camp. The following day we began retracing our steps up to the pass, and from the pass down to the Rio Santiago. Our descent was remarkably swift; we could hardly believe that this was the same mountain that had offered such incredible difficulty three days before. It was simply a question of balance; with all the mud on the trail, it was like going downhill on skis. We reached the mission after dusk, and after a cold bath in the river and a good meal offered by our friend

Brother Arcos, we felt rejuvenated and in good spirits. Two days later when the weather was clear, Julio Ortega made another skillful landing at the small Ortiz airstrip and we boarded the Cessna for the return flight to Cuenca. Clouds were forming in some of the canyons and passes of the Central Cordillera and the trip was hair-raising. It was raining when we finally reached Cuenca, and we felt very fortunate to be back on the ground safely. There, parked in front of the maintenance building at the airport, we saw the helicopter that in about a week's time would fly government officials into the Oriente to investigate the Cueva de los Tayos. For us the adventure was over, at least for now; for others, it hadn't yet begun.

I later learned that the extended government expedition, which included geologists with equipment for exploration and rock sampling, reported that the Cueva de los Tayos was nothing more than an extraordinary geological formation; the great stones and the portal to the central chamber had been carved by water and earthquakes, not by man. The official exploration of the cave, like ours, produced no evidence of any human construction or habitation.

Had my search for Samakache and Mashutaka, and my expedition to the Cueva de los Tayos, been entirely fruitless? I did not think so. If nothing else, the Cueva de los Tayos proved the existence of hidden subterranean caves in the Andean mountain jungles. Certainly, I had learned to be suspicious of the fantasies of men like Major Jaramillo, Father Crespi, and Juan Moricz. But I remained convinced that among the myths and legends of the Indians themselves there were fragments of truth. And I was still certain that the Oriente bore rich evidence of ancient cultural development. My investigation there had to be pursued.

PART IV

In the World of the Unknown

CHAPTER 10

The Rainbow of Intihuatana

During my travels in southeastern Ecuador, I had listened with fascination to the legends told by Indian elders around burning campfires, legends of the ancient heroes like Duma, the great leader of the Cañari Indians, whose long-lived culture had existed up to the time of the conquest and beyond, and whose descendants can still be encountered today on the slopes of the Andean massif of Piedra Blanca, their ancestral home. At its peak, the Cañar culture occupied a very large territory in the Mesa, extending as far north as Nudo de Azuay, and south as far as modern-day Azogues. But it was the ancient culture said to be underlying the Cañar—the Fasayñan—that particularly held my interest.

The Cañari had been a powerful tribe. It was recorded by chroniclers that they, almost alone among the tribes of the Ecuadorian sierra or coastal plain, had had the strength to resist the incursion of the Inca. As the Inca moved north, there was open warfare between them and the Cañari for perhaps 100 years. Then, unable to subdue them, the Inca worked out a political settlement that apparently was enforced for another 100 years or more. Surely the strength of the Cañari political organization had evolved from the customs and traditions of the ancient, mysterious Fasayñan.

Where, I wondered, had this long-lived culture come from? And what, in turn, were the early influences on the Fasayñan people? Might there have been a relationship between the Fasayñan and an earlier ancient culture moving into the sierra from the Amazon? Geographically, the area of Cañar is drained by a number of rivers that eventually become part of the Rio Santiago, which then flows southeast through the easternmost chain of the Andes to provide ready access from the Amazon. Cultural finds are rich along these rivers and their tributaries; and remains of stone constructions, practically unknown and unstudied, dot the surrounding mountain ranges at places bearing such names as Cotitambo, Chobshi, Shabaluca, and Intinaui. Were the Fasayñan their ancient builders? Was it significant, I wondered, that Fasayñan legends related that during the Great Deluge a huge serpent from the Amazon led their ancestors to safety to the sacred mountain of Huasayñan (known today as Piedra Blanca) where they waited for the flood waters to subside? The serpent then disappeared into a lagoon, but it became a symbol both of life and fertility, and was venerated as a deity by their descendants. In many artifacts recovered from the ancient tombs and burial grounds of the Cañar region the snake is always very prominent.

In my search for ancient cultural development in the sierras, I decided it was important to investigate the Cañar region and, particularly, the ruins of Ingapirca, from which I had learned that ancient artifacts had been recovered during recent excavations. I called Oswaldo in Cuenca, and once we had decided on an itinerary, I told him to hire a Jeep and start making preparations. When I arrived in Cuenca in October 1969, I found arrangements virtually complete. The first stop on our expedition was the small town of Azogues north of Cuenca. After hours of a bouncing ride on an only partially cobblestoned road, we arrived in a hot, dazzling sun. There we searched out Father Antonio Santos, who had a well-known collection of artifacts from the area. We found him in a small, sparsely furnished room behind a Spanish-built mission church counseling a young mestizo couple. After sending them on their way with a paternal benediction, he turned his attention to us and was quite pleased to grant my request to see his collection. With a feeling of anticipation, we followed him around to the rear of the mission.

To my surprise he led us to a dilapidated chicken coop. Inside, in a broken-down old cabinet covered with chicken droppings, he showed us a collection of clay plates, cups, and mugs, some plain and some decorated with geometric designs and appliqués, that had been unearthed by campesinos from burial grounds in the surrounding area and presented to the padre. Father Santos said that he believed they were royal ware used by Inca rulers; but to me their style indicated that they were probably much older, perhaps centuries prior to A.D. 1400, the peak period of the Inca Empire in this region.

Father Santos then called our attention to a wooden box in a corner of the chicken coop. Opening it, he said: "You'll be interested to see these pieces. They come from burial grounds on the Fasayñan range, the *Pacarina* [Holy Ground] of the ancient people." I bent down to look and what I saw aroused a deep sense of excitement. The box was half full of stone artifacts: anthropomorphic amulets, axes, and small rocks carved with markings and circular

Father Santos's cabinet.

Three stone pieces. Fasayñan.

holes that seemed to represent dots. Some of the artifacts, notably the axes and unshaped stones with carvings, immediately brought to mind those objects that Indian brujos dig out of ancient graves to use in their rituals. The Cayapa Indian, Pinuna, and his magic stones also flashed through my mind; and when Father Santos mentioned that the Cañari also believed those stones held magic powers, I felt strongly that these seemingly different cultures, separated by hundreds of kilometers of formidable terrain, must have had some common heritage in the distant past.

We left Azogues early the next day and headed north for the town of Cañar. The air felt brisk and very cold, and the smoke of fires from the Indian dwellings that dotted the mountainside mingled with the white clouds still covering the valley below. Cañari Indian horsemen in their colorful furred chaparajos waved to us from the trail above. Finally we entered Cañar, then doubled back a few kilometers southwest to Chorocupte, a small settlement in the heart of a Cañar burial area. There we spent several days digging and investigating burial sites and the artifacts recovered from them.

The typical Cañar or Fasayñan burial is a shaft dug into the earth in the shape of a truncated cone that suggests a representation, underground, and in negative space, of a pyramid. The shaft is ordinarily 2 to 3 meters deep, and the floor ranges from 2 to 2.5 meters in diameter. The shaft is usually capped by stone or wooden planks and covered with earth. A semicircular niche (or more than one) is often found in the tomb wall, bearing a sacred artifact that is sometimes a statue.

The skeleton in a typical burial (usually only one) is ordinarily found in a sitting position with the head pointing east—the direction of the rising sun. Above and on both sides of the skull, artifacts are arranged so that together with the body they form a cross. These artifacts are often pottery, but may include objects of gold or stone. I found that those of stone were more abundant in the burial grounds situated in the *eastern* slope of the Cañar region. I also found carved bone amulets in the form of large fangs, perhaps representing the fangs of a serpent, regarded by the ancients as one of the most important deities. Among the stone objects I uncovered were *metates,* sacred mortars, bowls, small amulets, and mythic figures. Interestingly, some of their characteristics were strikingly similar to artifacts I was to come across later in my investigations in the Oriente and the eastern slopes of the Andean range.

The widespread use of stone suggested that it was once an important medium of expression in the Cañar region,

Stone sculpture of Pacha-Mama, the earth goddess worshipped as the protector of fertility of the land and of man. Fasaynan (?).

and that it must have played an important role in its development. But this whole area had undergone many geological changes. Shaken by constant earthquakes and volcanic eruptions, the land had been subjected to severe upheavals over the millennia, which would make it difficult to establish a chronological pattern of cultural development. Nevertheless, the widespread use of stone and the variety of cultural traits and styles of the artifacts found in this region made clear that it had probably wit-

Stone statue.

Metate *with flat mano.*

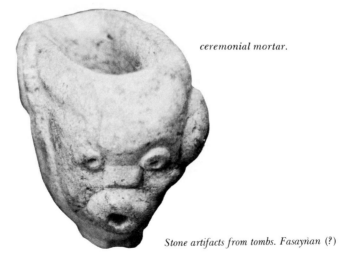

ceremonial mortar.

Stone artifacts from tombs. Fasayñan (?)

Anthropoid amulets from fossilized and natural bone. Cañar.

nessed the rise and development of very ancient cultures—much older than the Cañar.

As the days passed by, the weather worsened and the inevitable early afternoon showers became all-day affairs. It was time to start on our way to the Ingapirca ruins. Just outside Cañar, we turned the Jeep onto a steep trail heading down the mountain. The trail is normally open only two months a year and we very quickly saw why: it carried down immense amounts of rainwater from the slopes behind and above us, and at times we were driving in a tide of mud. Finally the Jeep got hopelessly stuck. A campesino with two oxen pulled us out. We left the Jeep in his care, shouldered our packs, and started down the trail on foot in the direction of a settlement with the academic name of El Colegio. Then, after crossing a roaring, muddy torrent at Puenta San Pedro, the trail rose steeply. Another few kilometers struggling through the mud eastward and we were at Ingapirca.

Ingapirca lies at an altitude of 3160 meters in a triangular area between two rivers, the Silante in the north and the Huayrapungo in the south, and covers an area of about 3 hectares (approximately 6 acres). Built in 1497 by order of the Inca ruler Huayna-Capac, the complex was abandoned after the Spanish conquest and fell into ruin. The northwest section of the site contains a temple of the sun, courtyards, and buildings that were probably the dwellings of the Inca ruler and his court. When I arrived at the site, I was immediately struck by the grandeur, and the state of preservation, of some of the original structures in the central part of the complex. Others were in the process of being reconstructed by the Ecuadorian Department of Antiquity, and it was during this work that artifacts had come to light that did not appear to be of the Inca period. That was why I was particularly interested in exploring the site.

Examining the construction of the complex, I could see that much of it was done with the same type of greenish stone used by the ancient Cañari elsewhere in this area in building their ceremonial centers. This stone, which was also used to fashion small amulets and mythic statues, is called by the campesinos *huaca* stone (gravestone) because such artifacts are so often discovered in burial sites. Found in quarries north of Ingapirca that are venerated by the present-day Cañari Indians as sacred grounds, this same type of stone was later to show up in my archaeological search in a most significant way. Obviously, it was considered something very special by the ancient people in this area, and seemed to be as important as the emerald to the Manabí and Atacames cultures of the northern coastal plain, and as jade to the Olmec and Mayans of Mesoamerica.

The excavation of the site had been carried to a low enough level so that the foundations were partially visible, and I noticed that the styles of the upper and lower levels were markedly different. Above, the stone was finely cut and carefully fitted together, in a fashion very characteristic of the Inca mason builder; but the lower levels were of rougher stone, assembled in a less precise manner. During the next few days as I studied the main complex and its surrounding area, I began to suspect that Ingapirca had been built by the Inca on the ruins of a ceremonial complex constructed by an older culture, possibly the ancient Cañari or the mysterious Fasayñan before them. This practice was characteristic of the Inca, as well as of Mesoamerican cultures. Machu Picchu, which until recently was thought to have been entirely Inca in origin, is now beginning to be thought to have been constructed on the infrastructure of a great complex built much earlier, by a pre-Inca people.

There are probably many reasons for the practice of overbuilding. For one, it is easier to take advantage of the clearing and the leveling of land, and the construction of foundations that has already been done, than to start somewhere else and do all that work over again. Another reason might be the religious or the astronomical importance of a specific site. An early culture may have chosen or created that site, for example, so that at the equinox, or on some holy day, the rays of the sun fall on it in a certain way. In that case a subsequent culture that also worships the sun may be forced to use the same site to achieve the same astronomical effect. There is also probably a question of cultural ego involved in overbuilding. A new culture has an impulse to establish its own identity, to show the world—once it has arrived at a level of power—that it is now paramount over its predecessors. It does this architecturally, by obliterating the manifestations of the previous culture and putting its own construction, its own surface, over what was there before.

One day as Oswaldo and I were pursuing our investigations of Ingapirca, two campesinos came up to me and asked if I wanted to see something they had unearthed nearby. One of them was carrying an object wrapped in his poncho. He opened it and showed me a small pottery obelisk, about 22 centimeters long, that was very well preserved. I saw that it was quite similar to obelisks I had seen associated with the cultures of the coastal plain, and later was to see in the area of Pisco in the northern Mesa. It was apparently a funerary representation of larger stone monoliths that once stood in ceremonial centers such as Ingapirca in the middle of a stone platform or terrace. Sometimes, the platform or terrace was marked off into halves or quarters with radial lines, thus probably serving as a sundial. As the earth changed position throughout the year in relation to the sun, the shadow of the obelisk falling across a certain point on the marked platform may have indicated the equinox, the time to plant crops, or a sacred day. In addition, the obelisk may have had a phallic significance. The bulbous contour of the base of the small pottery representation was particularly suggestive of this.

The great obelisks were venerated by the ancient cultures as the central point of religious authority, and the complexes in which they stood were considered the most sacred sites. The Spaniards recognized their importance as they extended their conquest over South America, and the monolith complexes were always destroyed by them when encountered. One of the few in stone to escape destruction, called *Intiltiwatana* in the Quechua tongue, was

Ruins at Ingapirca.

found in Machu Picchu, because the Spaniards never discovered that remote city high in the Andes. Hence, the
only obelisks remaining in any number are the miniature
funerary representations, placed in a tomb of the priest or
ruler. The stone representation of the obelisk I was to see
later in the eastern region suggested unquestionably a
very ancient origin for this cultural tradition.

Each evening after we had finished our work, Oswaldo
and I headed for the house of the Teniente Politico in
charge of the area. He had insisted that we be his guests.
Over supper one night, as I was commenting on the grandeur of the ruins of Ingapirca and the magnitude of effort represented in their construction, he said sadly: "The
government tried to preserve and rebuild the complex.
Unfortunately, over the years, Indians and campesinos
alike have steadily taken the ready-cut stones from the ancient ruins to build their homes and churches." Such, I
reflected, has been the fate of ancient constructions all
over the world.

After several days investigating Ingapirca, Oswaldo and
I set out to explore an area east of the ruins, at the foot of
the mountains, where there was a spring of crystal water
which, it was said, had been used by the ancient people to
supply the complex through a canal system. After an hour
of hacking through the brush, we found the spring but no

*Pottery obelisk seen at
Ingapirca. Cañar (?).*

sign of canal construction. From there we followed a narrow trail that led up to the Quinnaloma mountain ridge to gain a better view of our surroundings. We were on the trail skirting the ridge when my attention was drawn southward to a mountain peak below us. It seemed to appear too smooth, too regular, and too flat to be natural. "We have to see if we can get down there," I said to Oswaldo.

It was a difficult climb, first down a dry creek bed that served as a trail, then up again toward the peak that had caught my eye. There had apparently been showers the night before, and water was still draining down the slope. Near the top, the slope was steaming in the mid-morning sun and small rainbows arched above many of the pools of water that had collected here and there among the rocks. The vapor and the rainbows lent a wonderful, fairyland quality to the terrain. Finally we reached the crest and paused to look at the range of mountains to the north and west that now spread magnificently across our field of view. But then I realized that the crest on which we were standing stretched no more than 10 meters before rising slightly to a promontory. I walked toward it, and as I stepped up onto the promontory and looked at the rock under my feet, I saw that it had been carved in the shape of a dugout canoe, a canoe of stone, dominating the entire valley that stretched far below, the Rio Silante, and the Ingapirca ruins. I cried out in excitement, and yelled at Oswaldo to come up and look.

We examined the stone canoe closely and saw that its gunwales, along their entire length, were carved with a chain-link motif that was both decorative and undoubtedly symbolic. A stone seat was carved in one end of the hull, but I noticed that the other end was oddly truncated. Then I saw that there were, in fact, two boats. Alongside the main hull was another smaller hull, connected in the style of an outrigger on a canoe. It was simply a boat-shaped depression carved into the rock, and the connecting member between the two hulls was carved in the fashion of a trough, so that the interior spaces of the two hulls were in communication. Low in the side of the main hull, opposite the connection to the outrigger, there was a small hole, perfectly perforated from inside the boat to the exterior. I was puzzled about its significance. Was it simply to allow rainwater to drain out of the boat? If that was its only function, it could have been much more easily achieved by cutting a notch somewhere through the wall of the outrigger hull.

The shape of the main hull also puzzled me. Part of it appeared to be missing. As Oswaldo and I were considering what might have happened to it, two campesinos, curious as to what two strangers were doing in their midst, appeared and offered us their services. When we asked if other similar structures were located in the area, they said no. But the younger of the two pointed down the slope and said that a boulder with the same chain-link design was lying there 200 meters below in the bushes. We climbed down to inspect it and the puzzle was solved. The boulder was in the shape of a prow with a stone seat, and carved on its gunwales was the identical chain-link design of the structure above. I estimated its weight at about 5 tons; it measured about 1 meter 87 centimeters in breadth at the cut edge, and 1 meter 63 centimeters in length from the cut edge to the front tip. No doubt the whole structure must have been the representation of a double-ended hull that extended about 1.5 meters beyond the edge of the precipice—as if the boat were about to sail off into space. Somehow, the prow had broken off and fallen.

Darkness began to come down and Oswaldo and I decided to spend the night on the promontory. The air turned colder as the sun gradually declined behind the mountains, but the grandeur of the site impressed us so much that we did not seem affected by it. As we settled into our sleeping bags, it started to rain and we moved down the slope a few hundred meters from the exposed promontory where, under the cover of an overhang, we slept the rest of the night. We woke up very early the next morning, just as the first light was beginning to break in

Views of ceremonial stone boat. Barranco Gulan.

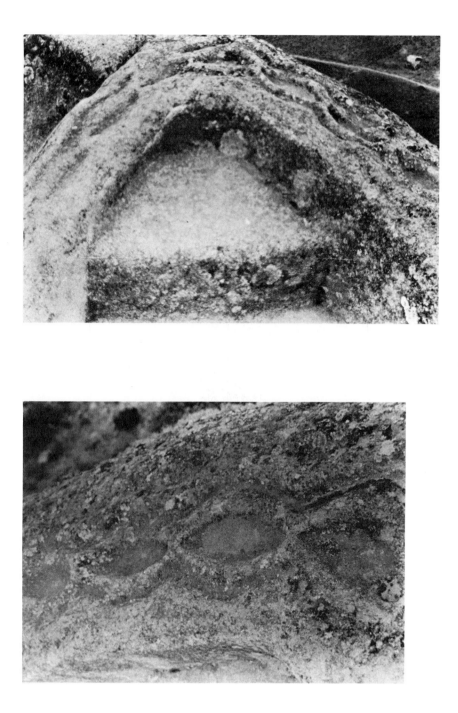

the east, and climbed back to the promontory. I wanted to observe the effect of the sunrise from the boat itself. I sat on the stern seat and waited.

The sky began to brighten behind the center of the three great peaks in the distance, and as the sun itself appeared, its first beams shone down on the promontory. I looked around me as the sun climbed higher into the sky. There was rainwater standing here and there, in hollows in the rocks. Vapor was rising from the water, and a small rainbow hung in the air over each of these little pools, as it had on the slope below the day before. Perhaps, I reflected, that was the significance of this spectacular site, which overlooked both the mountain peaks that the Indians venerated as dwelling places of the gods and the Ingapirca ceremonial complex far below. Was this stone canoe what the Indians called "Intihuatana"—a sacred place where their spiritual leader communicated with the gods, receiving guidance and inspiration? Perhaps the priest of the ancient tribe that constructed this site, as the ceremonial day approached, ordered a plug to be put into the drainhole of the boat so that it would collect rainwater and become a pool. Then the priest seated himself inside the boat before his assembled congregants, and in their eyes, a rainbow produced by the vapor rising from the boat would be a symbol of his powers of communication with the spirits of the sun and the universe. Perhaps, too, the chain-link motif carved along the gunwales of the boat was symbolic of their belief in the close interrelationship of all the physical and spiritual forces that dominated their world. And the boat itself was the vessel that sailed through a river of light, the rainbow, to unite their physical with their spiritual beings.

There was another element of this ceremonial site that merited reflection. Why had these people—mountain dwellers—chosen a canoe for their symbolic vessel? Its position, I realized, with the prow projecting over the precipice out into space, was not only facing eastward in the direction of the rising sun and Ingapirca but also in the direction of the Amazon Basin. Had the ancestors of these mountain dwellers originated there and thus become familiar with the boat and its construction? If so, it seemed quite natural to me that the boat, the chief means of travel through the Amazon waterways, would inevitably become the symbolic representation of their means of spiritual travel.

Oswaldo and I left the "Intihuatana" site with deep emotions. Long after reaching the plain of Ingapirca, my gaze kept returning toward the peak on which it was located. On the trip back to Cuenca I had ample time to sort out my impressions of the last few weeks. I had been looking for evidence that the known ancient cultures of the sierra were related to even earlier stone-carving cultures that had migrated from the Amazon. I had found tantalizing clues among the ruins of Ingapirca. And the stone canoe, in particular, seemed to loom large in this progression. I couldn't be sure, but it seemed likely that the boat fell into the Fasayñan culture, the possible ancestor of the powerful Cañari that later occupied the south Mesa. And it seemed quite plausible that the people who had carved that boat so expertly were descendants of, or at least influenced by, an ancient stone-carving culture.

CHAPTER 11

Meeting at Plan Grande

I returned to Ecuador in the spring of 1970 to begin the next phase of my quest, an investigation of the area south and east of Cuenca, including the valley of the Rio Santiago which, I had surmised from my exploration of the Cañar region to the north, may have served as a corridor of entry for the migration of ancient cultures from the Amazon westward into Ecuador. My plan was to use Limon, a jungle settlement on the slope of the Crusado Mountain, as my base camp. It lies at the head of two important trails: one leads south to the Rio Zamora, and the other east into the valley of the Rio Namangosa, the two major rivers that flow into the Rio Santiago. Oswaldo had again agreed to accompany me on the expedition. But before we set out from Cuenca I went to see Father Aurelio Torres, whom I had met on one of my previous trips. For twenty-five years the padre had been the pastor of a small church immediately northeast of Sigsig, a village in the heart of the Cañar region, and had traveled extensively in the Oriente. He was retired now, living in Cuenca permanently, but he still kept in touch with his flock in the interior. He was said to have a very interesting collection.

I walked up to the front door of the shabby little house where the padre lived with his limping, old *perpetua*—his housekeeper. If she liked you, maintaining contact with the padre was reasonably feasible. If she didn't, you couldn't get into the house. I cranked the ancient, hand-operated bell several times, and finally heard Father Torres's steps inside. He peered through a small grimy window to see who was there, and then, pulling out his ring of keys, undid several locks and bolts on the door to let me in. After the greeting formalities, he led the way up an old, creaky wooden stairway to his second-story "sitting room." In the dim light the impact of the room was jarring; it might have been a warehouse, a museum, or a supply depot. It was packed with spears and fragments of old armor; painted figures, large and small, of the madonna and several saints; flags, banners, and tapestries; old stirrups and domestic implements from the Spanish colonial period; paintings and decorative objects in a bewildering variety of styles. It was the accumulation of a lifetime of wholesale collecting.

When I told the padre of my particular interest in the stone-carving cultures of the interior, he took me over to a wooden cabinet and opened it. To my amazement I saw about thirty pieces of stone sculpture. Reaching down, I picked up one to examine it more closely. Father Torres said that it had come from little-known ruins in a place called Chupianza, immediately south of Mendes, where the trail from Limon ended. Chupianza was on the Rio Paute, one of the major tributaries of the Namangosa, and very much in my area of immediate interest. The padre then showed me three stone artifacts that had come from the area of the Rio Yuganza, another river flowing into the Namangosa. They confirmed my belief that the valleys of the Namangosa and its tributaries, which I intended to explore shortly, would prove to be an important area in the possible progression of an ancient culture—perhaps a "stone-carving" people—that had preceded the highly sophisticated ceramic cultures in this land.

Stone sculptures from Father Torres's collection. Namangosa.

Father Torres also showed me several pieces of black pottery recovered by campesinos in a *huaca* on the banks of the Rio Yuganza. Though it was difficult to determine their age, I was certain they were far older than the pottery I had seen in the Cañar region. As I turned these pieces over in my hand, it occurred to me that the region

Black pottery ware. Rio Yuganza.

drained by the Santiago and its tributaries might have been a transitional area. As the ancients moved from the Amazon into this mesa, they encountered clay suitable for making pottery. And they must have undergone a change in social values, so that artifacts for everyday use, fabricated by more of the members of the tribe, especially the women, gained ascendancy over the elaborate, time-consuming stone pieces probably crafted by a few specialists.

The *perpetua* interrupted our conversation by announcing that coffee was ready, and the smell of the strong brew enveloped the room. As the padre and I drank, our conversation turned to his life in the interior and his adventures among the Jivaro Indians. I mentioned my own search for the two Indians, Samakache and Mashutaka, and surprisingly, the names were familiar to him. He said he had heard of them long ago, and that they lived near Pescado, a small Indian settlement on the banks of the Rio Upano. Needless to say, his words were totally unexpected. The location he described, incredibly, was northeast of Mendes, the settlement where the Limon pica ended, and I knew that when Oswaldo and I reached the area, I would have to try once more to find the two Indians.

When we had finished our coffee, Father Torres said:

"I have something precious to show you." From an old
cabinet in a corner he pulled out a shoe box tied with a
string. "Gold was believed by the ancients to be the tears
of the sun changed into the precious metal when they
reached the earth," he said, as he untied the box. Then,
under the dim light, he removed a gold sun-disk and a
gold mythic frog which, he said, had been recovered in
burial grounds southeast of Piedra Blanca. I knew that
there was evidence that for thousands of years alluvial
gold was panned along the banks of the Rio Gualaceo to
the west, and along the tributaries extending far up into
the Eastern Cordillera.

*Gold frog. Piedra
Blanca.*

Precious metal technology reached a very high level in
ancient cultures, and these pieces were a superb example
of their skill in soldering and brazing. The frog consisted
of two separate halves, the upper and the lower, each of
which was formed and embossed from flat sheet gold.
The two halves were joined by brazing, and the seam was
almost invisible in places. Detail was then created by adding fine gold wire and beads and brazing them to the surface of the artifact, in the fashion of appliqué. The tail of
the frog bore the distinctive shape of the axhead, endow-
ing the artifact, no doubt, with significant mystical powers.

The workmanship of the gold disk was very fine. The
surface was smooth and quite free of irregularities, and it
had been fabricated by the depletion gilding method.
The gold is so thin on such disks that corrosion of the
copper often begins underneath, and the gold flakes
away. Polished, these pieces may have served as reflectors.
A priest wearing a gold disk may have stood before the
sun, reflecting its light, generating the impression that he
was indeed blessed with the sun's powers. To my amazement, when I looked into one side of this disk, I saw my
face was magnified, as in a shaving mirror, while on the
other side it was reflected in its normal size.

*Gold sun-disk. Piedra
Blanca.*

I was examining the disk when Father Torres produced
from his collection two hard metal axheads that seemed
very similar in appearance to axheads I had seen that had

Two hard metal axheads.
Rio Yuganza.

Stone artifact. Rio
Yuganza.

been recovered in the coastal plain. To my knowledge, previous investigators had never reported the recovery of such artifacts on the eastern slopes of the Andean range. Of course, the appearance of these axheads could always be attributed to trade between the inhabitants of the coastal plain and the sierras. However, if the information from Father Torres was correct—that these metal axheads had been recovered from burial tombs similar in type to the Fasayñan culture—then they had to be *older* than the ones recovered on the coastal plain. And if this assumption was correct, the development of metallurgical expertise, dated until now at about 800 B.C. on the South American continent, would have to be revised. I left Father Torres encouraged that the area I was about to investigate would yield valuable information.

Oswaldo and I left Cuenca the following morning for Limon. Rain pursued us during the entire trip and our Jeep sloshed through the muddy road like some amphibious beast. When we finally reached Limon, we went directly to the mission. Searching out the padre of the local settlement had become a standard practice. These gentlemen often prove to be repositories of information about the archaeological finds in the area they serve. Father Raphael Clemente was no exception. During our stay at the mission, he produced a most interesting stone artifact said to have been recovered on the banks of the Rio Yuganza. Its stylistic traits were strikingly similar to some of the pieces from Father Torres's collection.

Limon is a small trading post with a poor and dwindling population, but the villagers we spoke to responded to our enquiries in a friendly and open manner. Some of them were indeed familiar with stone carvings which, for them, were only curiosities unearthed as they worked their land along the river. But I found them of great interest. Many of the artifacts recovered had been carved from ovalized hard river stone, and many bore representations of the serpent, the sun, the moon, and anthropomorphic and mythic animals. Those that had carved human representations had a unique and puzzling trait: a well-defined depiction of a cup held between the hands at chest height. In later explorations, I was to see this trait in findings in other areas.

We struck up a conversation with the local blacksmith, a jovial and talkative man, and as we warmed ourselves around his forge, he related that two years ago some Germans had come through the village carrying large sculptured stones on their mules. Some of these stones, he remembered, were flat pieces carved overall with strange markings, animals and human figures. He also recalled that he had seen this same type of carving on big boulders in the area—often around rivers and on the walls of small caves. Later, at the mission, Father Clemente confirmed the existence of these boulders. They are non-Inca, he stated, for it is known that the Inca never entered this part of the country. He added that some could be seen near the settlement of Plan Grande, halfway between Limon and Mendes.

One afternoon, as Oswaldo and I were walking on the south side of the village, we saw an Indian woman sitting in the rain in front of her adobe-built casa, crying. Walking over, I asked her what was the matter. She replied that her son, Ysma Kuouchi, was sick. He had had some kind of surgery a few weeks before and was suffering terribly from stomach pains. I asked if I could see him. I had some Maalox tablets with me, and thought they might help.

She eagerly bade me enter the casa, and followed us in. In a darkened corner of the one-room dwelling lay a young Indian holding his hands to his stomach and moaning with pain. I gave him three of the Maalox tablets, sat down while he took them, and waited. The old woman stirred the fire that was burning in the center pit and the darkness of the room lifted.

Finally, the Maalox began to take effect. Feeling better, the boy looked at me intensely and said, "No gringo has ever crossed my threshold." He wanted to show his appreciation, but did not know how. He was a Jivaro, educated at the mission, but he said he came from the village of

Pescado. Concealing my astonishment, I asked him if he knew an Indian named Mashutaka who also lived in Pescado. He answered simply, "I am a nephew of Mashutaka's." What unbelievable luck—to have stumbled across a member of Mashutaka's family!

I learned from Kuouchi that Mashutaka was no longer living in Pescado, but near Plan Grande. Then he told me about an Ecuadorian with whom Mashutaka had had a fight a few years before. The man's name was Major Jaramillo, and the fight revolved around the education of a small boy, the son of Mashutaka. Virtually everything Kuouchi told me corresponded with Jaramillo's version of the story—with one important exception. He said that Mashutaka had given his son, Antonio Pinciupa, to Jaramillo to be educated and exposed to the important things in the civilized world. But Jaramillo treated Mashutaka's son like a slave, using him as a domestic servant and preventing him from ever leaving the house. When Mashutaka learned how his son was being treated, he went to his home in anger, reclaimed the boy, and threatened to kill Jaramillo. Now I understood why Jaramillo had been apprehensive about entering the interior, and why he was so reluctant to undertake the expedition to the Cueva de los Tayos.

When Kuouchi learned that I had been looking for Mashutaka for over a year, he immediately described how to get to Plan Grande and wrote a note to his uncle for me. Rain delayed our departure, but finally Oswaldo and I set out for Plan Grande with two hired mules. The first few kilometers east of Limon were not difficult; this was a portion of the new road that some day will run from Limon to Mendes, a distance of about 65 kilometers. Road building with very modern equipment had begun about two years before, but in all that time only 10 kilometers had been built because the land is so savage and the canyons so deep. Bridges spanning the streams keep collapsing under flood waters and have to be continually rebuilt.

Beyond the first 10 kilometers there was no more sign of construction, and the pica became one of the worst trails I have ever encountered. The maximum width available to the mules was about 1.5 meters, and the trail was completely filled with rocks that had fallen from the cliffs above, mixed with the ever-present mud, ranging in depth from 50 to 100 centimeters. In addition, the trail was ominously steep; the Ecuadorians call this part of the Oriente the land *"esta vertical."* All the picas go straight up from the valley floor to the top of a mountain, then from the top of the mountain straight down to the next river. The steepness, and the rocks mixed in with the mud, make it virtually impossible even for a mule to keep a steady footing.

By mid-morning we reached the Rio Janamas. There was no bridge and we had to cross it by lowering ourselves up to our waists in the water and pulling the mules along behind us. It was only the first of three river crossings we were to make that day. I had hoped to reach the Rio Kuntsa by nightfall, but it soon became clear we would never make it. Both mules were completely exhausted, and we could not help them by getting off and walking because the sea of mud was so thick and deep, it would have trapped us. Night was coming on and there was no place to stop. Then Oswaldo fainted and fell off his mule. I had to get down and help him back on. I had not realized it before, but Oswaldo suffered from vertigo; when we crossed a small ridge where the pica narrowed over a 100-meter drop, he became almost paralyzed with fear.

It was now very dark, and the mules refused to move one more step. I reached into my pack, took out my flashlight, and by its light could see that the mules themselves were not sure where the pica was. I tried taking a few steps and found that the mud was a little less deep. So, with me in the lead, we started out again. Struggling, slipping, clawing our way up the slope for another two hours, we finally reached a small plateau, a space where we could stop.

We took the packs off the mules and tied them to some trees nearby. Our shelter was another tree with an opening at its base that had been hollowed out long before by carpenter ants. It was really too small for two men of our size, but at the moment it looked like the best refuge in all of Ecuador. We inspected it carefully—scorpions are a constant threat in this country—then, finding nothing, we crowded ourselves in so that at least our heads and chests were out of the rain. We pulled our packs in with us, and opened a can of sardines for our supper. We ate in silence, then leaned back and listened to the rain and the sounds of the night creatures of the Oriente: the squeaks of running rodents mingled with the screech of an owl, and the wail of a howler monkey in the darkness of the treetops above us. Sleep was impossible.

Several hours later Oswaldo let out a terrible yelp and leaped out of the tree. By the time I got my flashlight beam on him, he was standing in the rain with his shirt pulled up and his pants down, clawing with one hand at his back where a good-sized scorpion had sunk its stinger into his flesh. It must have crawled up Oswaldo's pantleg while he was sleeping. I knocked it off with my hand, reached for my knife and lanced the wound, squeezing out a fair amount of blood and dressing it with some ointment. This time we examined our shelter even more carefully before crawling back in.

Later, I must have been dozing, but suddenly my head snapped up. The mules were hoofing the ground nervously, their tails swishing against their wet thighs. They were jerking at their tethers, trying to free themselves. I was puzzled about what the trouble might be, and my first thought was that a jungle cat, a jaguar or a cougar, or a snake had alarmed them. Then I heard a strange indistinct noise. I crawled out of the shelter and fired my pistol three or four times in the direction it was coming from, but the noise grew louder. At this point the ground began to tremble under my feet and I almost lost my balance. Oswaldo jumped from the shelter and yelled, "We have to get out of here!"

It felt like everything around the tree was breaking loose. I also sensed a motion up beyond it, and when I flashed my light in that direction, my heart froze. A massive sea of mud was moving toward us. The plateau erupted in the sharp sounds of whipping as branches snapped from the falling trees uprooted by the grip of the landslide. Quickly we stepped behind our tree, searching for notches to pull ourselves up by, praying that it would stand. The mud reached it, and divided into two rivers flowing past on either side, carrying rocks, branches, and clumps of foliage down the slope. The tree shook and trembled, but it held.

In a few minutes, it was all over. Then I heard another sound and thought, "My God, the mules!" Beaming my flashlight in their direction, I saw they were all right. The trees we had tied them to were just above the angle of the slope down which the mud had come. What an immense relief! If something had happened to those mules, there's no telling how we would ever have gotten out of our predicament.

The sudden crisis had an eerie and unsettling effect on us both. In the dark, we couldn't see exactly how high we were or, directly behind us, how far the drop was. But we realized that there might be other masses of mud above us waiting to break loose, and we decided we would be safer with the mules. We rescued our gear from the shelter, hiked up to the animals, and spent the rest of the night with them.

At daylight we packed the mules and tried to find where the pica resumed. Every trace of the trail had been wiped away by the mud slide. I checked my compass and found that north lay up the slope, in the direction from which the mud had come. I was glad. That section was clean and the tangling underbrush had been swept away. We started out that way and soon found the pica as it began to head straight down the other side of the slope. At the bottom we had to ford another foaming torrent, but we could find no trace of the pica on the other side.

I was jogging along the bank looking for it when two Jivaros on horseback appeared. I asked them where the new pica began. "Through the swamp," they replied, pointing downstream. "You must first go into the middle of the river, walk for a short while, then you will see the opening into the swamp." They warned us to be careful to bear to the right, otherwise we might be swept away in deep *remolinos*—whirlpools—where the current was very strong. Luckily, they then offered to take us through, perhaps to show that they were masters of the situation. But once inside the swamp, the river simply disappeared. We pushed ahead between the tall grass, unable to see 3 meters in front of our noses, just following the Indians. When we finally got to the far edge of the swamp, they showed us where the trail resumed, then they disappeared.

It was late afternoon when we reached the plateau of Plan Grande. Not much larger than a football field, it was surrounded by thatched-roof huts, a small wooden church, and a thatched enclosure that served both as a classroom for the children and a meeting place for the villagers. We approached what, at first glance, was a fair-sized dwelling built of stones and wooden planks with a corrugated tin slat roof. Zoila Gaiera, a mestizo woman, its owner, lived there with her nine children. She was standing squarely in the doorway and by the look on her face, I could see her surprise and curiosity at two strangers all covered with mud suddenly appearing on her doorstep.

Plan Grande.

Nevertheless, with no questions, she welcomed us warmly and invited us in.

Upon entering Casa Zoila, I could not avoid the feeling that I was entering a brewery—the pungent smell of beer was overpowering. It was the resting place for the travelers and pack-mule trains that transported goods from Limon to Mendes. Bottles of beer, after having been carried for days on the back of a mule over these trails, spurt out everywhere when opened and the scent, over the years, had permanently permeated the place. Rustic tables and benches lined the walls which, in turn, became gaming tables, couches, or whatever else the passing wayfarer was in the mood to use them for.

Señora Gaiera offered us shelter for as long as we needed it. When I asked her if she had heard of a Jivaro named Mashutaka, she said: "Yes, I know him. He lives about four hours by mule from here in El Pigos, on the Cordillera Roguco. He is one of the richest Jivaros in the whole area and is a member of the Shuara Indian Council. He's very well respected. Nobody dares trespass into the territory where he, his three brothers, and their relatives live."

Now, at last, I had no doubt that I would soon meet the Indian I had been pursuing for so long. But Señora Gaiera went on: "Mashutaka is not at home now. He's in Puyo, for the Indian Conference. He left five days ago, and passed through Plan Grande on his way. Surely he'll be back tomorrow or the next day. The Indians don't like to stay away from their territory for long."

Oswaldo and I had a choice of three small, narrow, windowless rooms, but we opted for the roof-covered terrace above the stable. Settling ourselves in our hammocks stretched between the posts supporting the roof, we finally had a decent night's sleep. There was nothing to do but wait in Plan Grande for Mashutaka, but the following morning I decided to send a messenger with a note in Spanish to his compound. I was afraid he might come back into his territory by another trail that did not pass through Plan Grande. The Indians often use personal trails they have established themselves, and avoid the commonly known pica that everyone else uses.

The messenger returned late the next day. He was not alone. A slim man, whose age was difficult to determine, and a young Indian woman, were with him. It was Mashutaka's older brother Homero Kageca, with his youngest wife. I later learned that Kageca was the cacique whose name for decades had been most feared both by his own people, the Jivaro, and the mestizos in the area. When he grew old, he was replaced by Mashutaka. He was said to have a total of 138 children. At one point, he had eighteen wives, all stolen in various wars against other Jivaro clans. There is no prescribed length of time during which a man remains cacique, no predetermined age at which he is retired. When the cacique gets too old or weak to lead a raiding party effectively for revenge against enemies or for kidnapping young maidens, then the clan, by common consensus, replaces him. The strongest, most able man among those whose birth and social standing qualify them as contenders is selected to succeed the outgoing cacique.

The Jivaros as an Indian ethnic group extend from south of the equator on the slopes of the Eastern Cordillera to well into the Amazon. The Jivaro tribes are grouped into loosely organized "nations," held together by language, geographic proximity, intermarriage, and political ties that are fluid, sometimes ephemeral, and depend greatly on the personalities and character of the leaders. The nations normally have little contact with each other. At times of a common threat to the welfare of more than one nation, perhaps posed by natural calamity or by human intrusion (either Indian or Western) into their territory, the leaders might meet to confer on the problem. But it is unlikely that the leaders of all the Jivaro nations have ever met at any one time. Indeed, almost nothing is known of the nations living deep in the Amazon Basin. They speak little or no Spanish, and the tradition of *tsantsa*, or headshrinking, is still practiced by some of these nations.

The Shuara are the westernmost of the Jivaro nations. They occupy the Mesita, in the southern Oriente, and of all the Jivaro nations, the Shuara have been in closest contact with the Western world through the efforts of the Catholic missions. But such contacts created enmity and warfare with many of the surrounding tribes and nations, and consequently their numbers declined steadily. Further, the nation was riven by internecine strife and intratribal conflict. Eventually the Shuara split up into several factions, each of them aligning themselves with a different Jivaro group. Mashutaka was the leader of a clan that controlled one of these factions, and the council meeting he was attending in Puyo had probably convened to discuss a common problem.

Now his brother Kageca stood before me, and I sensed his deep curiosity to know why I was seeking Mashutaka. However, his demeanor remained emotionless as he gazed at me. Then, after a few moments, he said in broken Spanish that Mashutaka would be returning from Puyo the next day. With this he turned and began retracing his steps back to where he had come from, his youngest wife trailing behind.

That same afternoon the sound of whistling and shouting from the hills above announced the arrival of the mule train in Plan Grande. Francisco, Señora Gaiera's brother, was returning with the monthly supply of goods and the mail, which caused quite a commotion in the normally placid settlement. Young and old all came running, anxious to hear news from the outside world.

That evening, as we sat around a large table at Casa Zoila, the loquacious Francisco told us that near the banks of the Rio Tagacay were enormous rocks carved with strange inscriptions and figures. He called them "magic." The Indians believed that any signs found on big boulders were there to protect them as they moved through the territory, hunting or fishing. I asked Francisco where these boulders were, and with the characteristic gesture of anyone in the Oriente, he gave a sweeping wave of his arm toward the east, covering at least half the horizon, and said: *"Para allá."* Then, with little prodding, he offered to guide me there.

Early the next morning Francisco, Oswaldo, and I set

Cross carved in a boulder. Rio Tagacay.

out on the trail leading to the Rio Tagacay, a small stream about an hour away from Plan Grande. After searching its banks, Francisco, machete swinging, cut a path through the tall grass and led us to a group of boulders, roughly 1 to 2 meters in diameter and 1.5 to 2 meters high. Carefully scraping away the moss encrusting them, we discovered glyphic carvings. The stones had eroded badly, and many of the glyphics were almost erased, although some were still clearly visible. One had the outline of a serpent and a crude cross carved on it.

A few feet away another boulder attracted my attention. A cross with a ring at the intersection was carved on it, and the arms of the cross were slightly flared, like the Maltese cross. Examining it, I remembered the facial decorations with the cross motif used by some of the Jivaro Indians, and the ceramic artifacts with the cross that appear in tortero amulets and seal stamps. I was struck by the power, the omnipresence of this symbol in the art of this area and, indeed, of the entire world.

It is believed by many that the appearance of the cross as a symbol in South America was related to the arrival of the Spanish conquistadors and the zealous Christian missionaries who followed them. But for those who have gazed upon the splendor of the Southern Cross constellation high above the Andes, there is no doubt that the ancient people of this land knew and recognized the cross as a heavenly symbol.

Yet there was considerable compatibility between Catholic practices and the primitive religions of this land. The primordial symbol of the Christian faith is the cross, and the cross is also prevalent in the art and ceremonial practices of the interior. Catholic faith embraces a panoply of saints, each with its own supplicants, above which is a supreme God and also the mother of God who, in many observances, may assume preeminence as an object of adoration. The native religions also involve a host of spirits, any one of which may be addressed by members of the tribe, a supreme god-figure or creative spirit, and very often a powerful earth mother who has given birth to other gods. Catholic practices involve a considerable number of ceremonial trappings, ornament, and chant, as do the native religions.

Cross with circular center and dots. Pimampiro.

The Indians, therefore, had little difficulty in adapting much of the Catholic teaching of the padres and incorporating it into their own beliefs and practices. The result is an interesting blend: saints' names mixed in with names of the native spirits, native practices being performed during Catholic holy days, rosaries taken by the Indians and used during supplication to the jungle spirits, and the like. A Catholicized Indian may no longer place daily offerings to the goddess of the garden plot, but the name of the goddess, "Nunui," remains in the native lexicon. The story of Nunui is told from one generation to the next, and the small children believe in her implicitly until they are age seven or eight, as do Western children in Santa Claus.

The significance of the circle in the center of the crosses carved by the pre-Christian cultures cannot be discounted. Particularly with the boulder glyphics, in which the art is created with great difficulty by craftsmen using only the most primitive tools, we have to assume that no element would be incorporated unless it was really important. Undoubtedly the cross came to symbolize the four cardinal points, and the circle, the sun, the giver of all life.

Cylindrical stamp with cross and center circle. Tungurahua.

The cross and circle motif as seen on the headdress of a ceramic statue-brazier of the Old God of Fire. Vera Cruz.

Ceramic depictions of crosses grew to be more elaborate and sophisticated. In a ceramic cross from the Pimampiro area, the center circle is enlarged and elaborated to bear a ring of ten dots. Later, in the Tungurahua area of the middle Mesa, I came across a cylindrical seal stamp with an ornate design in which, significantly, the central motif is a cross with a circle in the center. This motif is also seen in the artifacts of Mesoamerica. In the seal stamp from Tungurahua, the cross is framed by diamond-shaped concentric scalloped lines, termed by some authorities the "meander" motif. Increasingly, I was to encounter this step-spiral design in the artifacts from the upper cordilleras and the lowlands of the Oriente. It is also prevalent in the art of Mesoamerica. Like the depictions of crosses, the significance of this motif surely went beyond that of decorative design.

Francisco, Oswaldo, and I returned to Plan Grande that afternoon. With every step, as we neared our destination, I became more keenly aware of a feeling of expectation. Then, suddenly, there he was standing before me: Mashutaka, a man who seemed ageless, with very black hair, a dark complexion, and a straight and open face. After the introductions and preliminary small talk, I asked him if I could speak with him in private. He nodded, and we drew aside. I began by saying I had been searching for him for the last year and a half. Mashutaka gazed straight into my eyes and said, "You lost much time to find me. I knew you were looking for me." The grapevine had apparently been at work.

I told Mashutaka of my meeting with Major Jaramillo and my interest in his story of the Cueva de los Tayos. Mashutaka listened with a slight, enigmatic smile, neither approving nor disapproving my words. He kept gazing into my eyes, with a straight, intense look that began to seem almost diabolical. Then he started talking. He said that Jaramillo was a thief and a liar; he had never been inside the cueva—Mashutaka had never taken him there. Jaramillo had told me of Mashutaka's own experiences, and related descriptions of the cave that Mashutaka had told to him. Mashutaka said that it was true he had taken many valuable objects to Jaramillo so he could sell them and use the money for the education of his son. However, Jaramillo had used the money only for his own benefit. He had betrayed his promise and word. And for all these reasons, Mashutaka said, it was true that he had told Jaramillo he was going to kill him—and he meant to do so one day.

From Mashutaka's account, I realized that Jaramillo had apparently fabricated many of the details of his story. For example, Mashutaka's father, named Kuguchi Samakache, had died when he was eight years old. The man who knew the location of the cueva, and took Mashutaka to see it, was not his father but his uncle, Vichuncho, who lived in Pangi. Vichuncho had taken the name Samakache at a later time. And he became Mashutaka's father-in-law; Mashutaka married his cousin. Yet despite these discrepancies in Jaramillo's story, I could hardly contain my excitement. Apparently, the Cueva de los Tayos of Jaramillo's account actually existed. I steeled myself to ask Mashutaka the all-important question: "Can you tell me where the cueva is?"

To my surprise, he said with no hesitation: "Above the

boundary of the area of Copa, halfway up the Rio Paute, above the village of Chuplan, before you reach the junction with the Rio Balata." He then added that if I tried to go alone, I would never find it, but he offered to guide me there. He would advise his father-in-law of the expedition and suggest that he join us. He also said that he and his father-in-law would not want any of the contents of the cave. There was an unwritten code handed down to the cacique of the Shuara tribe since ancient times that its contents were sacred, and nothing is to be removed. Mashutaka asked only for some small compensation so that he could establish a new territory for a number of his Jivaro people who had nothing.

I accepted his conditions immediately and asked when we would be able to make the expedition. He thought for a moment, then replied that it would be impossible now because of the weather. I agreed. He decided the best time to go would be the first week of September and we made an appointment to meet in Plan Grande the third week in August. He pointed out that the cueva is a four-day trip by mule, starting from Plan Grande, and the area we would cover was completely unexplored.

Mashutaka left Plan Grande after sealing our agreement in the Jivaro manner; he shook both my hands, with his arms crossed over one another. When a Jivaro gives this handshake, he is making a sacred promise and nothing can break it. I couldn't believe that everything had fallen into place so easily. No complications, nothing. The agreement came about so naturally that it seemed as if Mashutaka and I had known each other for a long, long time.

That night I could not sleep and lay tossing from side to side. For some reason a vague uneasiness persisted in my mind. My meeting with Mashutaka had gone too smoothly, it seemed: no objections to my request, no reticence to describe the location of the cave. Incredibly, instead of elation I felt a bewildering disquiet.

The next morning I wanted to leave Plan Grande immediately. But with the memory of our trek up still vivid in my memory, after talking with the natives I came to the conclusion that if we worked our way southeast, through the settlement of Cingularassa and then on down to Mendes, we might be able to find a better way back to Cuenca.

It was hard to imagine such a thing could be possible, but it soon became clear that this pica was worse than anything we had encountered on our way in. It was not a trail at all, just a river of mud, and one factor alone made it possible for us to make any headway. The mud was flowing in the same direction we were moving—southeast, down the slope to the Rio Paute.

After five hours of sliding and struggling, we reached Cingularassa in darkness. A small wooden church offered our only hope for shelter, but it was locked. We walked up to one of the casas and banged on the door. Instantly, the whole settlement was awake and we prevailed upon the old custodian to open the church. Oswaldo went in and came back out like a shot, covering his head with his hands, just as the custodian advised me to be careful because a clan of bats lived inside the church. I entered, threw my flashlight beam up onto the altar, and I could see he was right: the bats were hanging in clusters from the open arms of Christ, over the altar. Oswaldo was terrified and wanted to sleep outside. I had no energy left for discussion.

We started out again the following morning and after seven more hours on the insufferable, oozing pica, we arrived in Mendes. To our tired eyes, the village looked like an oasis. We headed for the Salesian mission, and there met Father Botazzo, who offered us his hospitality. He told us of the possibility of getting passage on a plane that flew to Cuenca, carrying meat from a small landing strip at Puyomo nearby. He also offered to send our mules back with a mule train that would pass through Mendes tomorrow. But when we talked about my archaeological quest and my hope of finding clues in the interior, I sensed that the padre understood and knew more than he was willing to acknowledge.

Puyomo, a three-hour hike from Mendes, was the most

nauseating place I had ever seen. It was a true *"matadero,"*
as they say in Spanish—a stinking slaughterhouse. The
area was saturated with blood, and the horns from all the
cows killed there lay around in every direction, sticking
up from the ground like some kind of exotic plant. The
men who worked there were covered with blood. They
walked around with their long knives at the ready, killing
the poor animals as they were brought in from the surrounding area. Often, before the animal was completely
dead, the skin was flayed from the carcass. The hides
were laid in the sun by the dozens to dry, like Oriental
carpets, and were covered with millions of big flies. Indian
women argued and fought for the right to open the stomach of each animal—the woman who opened the stomach
had the right to take the intestines, the liver, and all the
other entrails. A thick, heavy smell pervaded the entire
place and covered your skin like a blanket. Once the smell
descended on you, the millions of flies and other insects
followed you anywhere you went.

We made arrangements to fly back to Cuenca, and
while we were waiting for the plane to land, to my surprise, Father Botazzo arrived at the landing strip, breathing heavily from the long hike from Mendes. He had
forgotten, he said, to tell me about Father Raphaele, a

The author with Mashutaka.

Indian women disembowling steer for food.

priest who had been very interested in archaeology and who had died four years ago. He then reached into his bag and, to my amazement, pulled out several stone sculptures. They were carved in the now-familiar Oriente style and included mythic animals and faces with large round eyes and oval mouths. Father Botazzo also showed me a skull. "Padre Raphaele uncovered these pieces," he said hoarsely, "and many others, in an area called Quinta, near the pyramid."

Startled by that remark I said, "What pyramid are you talking about?"

He replied, "In a place called Quinta, across the San Jose Valley, there is a pyramid. It has steps that circle all the way to the top. And there is an underground passage from the pyramid that goes to a cave. I was there many years ago. Not very many people know about this because everything is covered with a very thick jungle."

I thanked the padre very much for this information, and especially for taking the trouble to show me these pieces. Then I remembered that three weeks ago in Quito, I had spent an afternoon with Doña Lola Ponze, the wife of a former President of Ecuador. She had heard of a pyramid somewhere in the interior, southeast of the Cordillera Cutucu. Quinta was southeast of the Cutucu and I wondered if these stories could be referring to the

Stone sculpture in the Oriente style.

same structure. I felt that, no matter if my information was sketchy, Quinta should be explored. The possibility of a pyramid in the Oriente virtually dwarfed everything else.

When the plane arrived, the crew threw open the doors and the slaughtered animals, divided into glistening quarters, were immediately flung in onto the floor. A swarm of big black flies took their cue, and entered the plane along with the carcasses. In ten minutes the plane was loaded and the pilot told us to jump in. I sat down on a box and looked into the face of another passenger, no longer alive: the severed head of one of the butchered steers, its big, sad eyes gazing at me. Moments later, the pilot took off and more intimate contact was established. As the plane tilted, the steer's head slid across the bloody floor and came to rest at my knees.

Immediately after take-off, the pilot yelled at the mechanic, "You have to take care of the flies. I can't see the instruments!" The flies were clustering like a gray haze from the cockpit to the back of the plane. The mechanic, with the familiar air of a man who had been through this many times before, walked to the rear of the plane, took off his jacket, and asked us if we would help. Following his lead, we began swishing our jackets, chasing all the flies toward the cockpit. Then with practiced timing, the pilot opened the starboard window and all the flies swooped out, presumably to return to Puyomo and wait for the next plane.

As we flew on toward Cuenca, I had time to sort out and clarify the profound impressions and images that had assailed me on my journey to Plan Grande. My meeting with Mashutaka and the unknown consequences of our agreed-upon expedition to the cueva still left me uneasy. My earlier visit to the cave reported to be the Cueva de los Tayos had proved a sad disappointment. Yet I could not ignore the possibility that Mashutaka's cueva might hold greater promise.

CHAPTER 12

Journey to San Jose

Anxious to establish if the story about the existence of a pyramid reputed to be near Quinta, in the area of San Jose, was true, I returned to Ecuador in July of 1970. I didn't really expect that the weather would change dramatically from what it had been a month and a half before, but if I had to sit and wait for the weather to be agreeable, I might never make any headway.

I had heard from many sources reports of pyramidal mounds in the uplands of the cordilleras and in the Oriente, and I had searched for verification through all the old literature I could find. In the library of the Universita Catholica in Quito, I came across several handwritten manuscripts, chronicles of Spanish padres of the sixteenth and seventeenth centuries, that described numbers of "mounds with steps." The manuscripts were in old Spanish and very hard to read, yet there was remarkable agreement from one chronicle to the next on the details of these constructions, even though they had been seen and reported in different places and at different times. According to these chronicles, the mounds were made of earth in the shape of a truncated pyramid, with heights ranging from 20 to 50 meters, and on the front face of the pyramids steps had been cut into the earth, leading up to the top. There, on the flat upper surface, were often found earthen or stone remains of buildings that were doubtless shrines, or the dwellings of the priest leaders or shaman.

The chronicles noted the existence of these "mounds with steps" in several areas of western South America, extending as far as modern-day Peru to the south and Colombia to the north. None had ever been found at altitudes higher than 3000 meters (about 10,000 feet). One of the known pyramid-like constructions is that of the Temple of the Sun in the valley of Moche, on the northern coast of Peru. It is a stepped pyramid 41 meters high, and is believed to have been part of an elaborate city complex of the Mochica civilization (ca. 200 B.C.–A.D. 600).

Numbers of these "mounds with steps," in time, eroded away due to climatic conditions, and many were destroyed by the Spaniards, driven either by the hunger for gold presumably buried within, or by the messianic desire to erase all vestiges of preexisting pagan power. But considering the numbers of them that were reported in the chronicles, I felt it was within the realm of possibility that a pyramid existed near Quinta, and that perhaps others, elsewhere, hidden and camouflaged by jungle vegetation, must be lying yet, waiting to be discovered. It was for that reason that the San Jose area seemed the next logical place to explore.

When I landed in Quito, Oswaldo met me at the airport with the news that Mashutaka had been in Cuenca in late June and had contacted him. He had confirmed that he would be ready for the expedition to the cueva during the first week of September, but he said he wanted some kind of guarantee from me, and wished to talk to me as soon as I got back in the country. He had refused to elaborate further to Oswaldo but left an address with him, that of an Indian woman living near Cuenca who could get a message to Mashutaka at any time.

We flew to Cuenca and drove immediately to the address Mashutaka had given Oswaldo. As we approached the small, wooden shack on the outskirts of the city, we saw an aging Indian woman sitting in front of it, spinning wool. I told her who I was and she said she had been waiting for me. I gave her a message and she promised to send it immediately to Mashutaka in El Pigos.

I checked with the airport on the weather conditions in the Oriente and learned that there had been torrential rains and a few earthquakes over the last few weeks, and intense cold. It would be days before Mashutaka could reach Cuenca. He arrived the following day. I was astounded. I had no idea how the message could have gotten to him, and how he could have made the trip to Cuenca so quickly. When I thought of the struggle we went through to reach Plan Grande a few weeks before, it seemed that the Jivaro Indians must have some system of flying from peak to peak, to move through the terrain as rapidly as they do. Perhaps, though, Mashutaka had not been far from Cuenca.

He looked just the same. Nothing had changed. But as we greeted each other, I wondered what new conditions he would ask for, or whether he had some objection to making the expedition to the cueva after all.

Mashutaka gave me the same straight look, direct in the eyes, and said he would be ready, with his father-in-law Vichuncho, to guide me to the site of the cueva in September. He repeated that he expected some compensation for their help. Then he spoke of his new condition: Oswaldo could not accompany us; he would have to remain behind at Mashutaka's compound and wait for our return. I was taken aback by this demand. It was so totally unexpected that the only thing I could think to say was that I would have to speak to Oswaldo about it. Mashutaka again gave me his very direct look and said that I had to make the decision, not Oswaldo.

I looked at him and saw there was no shaking the man. The Jivaros—especially one who has had the strength to become a cacique of Mashutaka's standing—are dead serious when approaching a matter like this, whatever their motive, and there is no arguing with them. I gave Mashutaka my agreement. Now the question was, how to broach the news to Oswaldo.

I did not mention it as we planned our expedition to San Jose. Our aim was to reach the small settlement of Amaluza, northeast of Cuenca, by Jeep. From there, we would engage horses and travel east into the area of San Jose and the Rio Namangosa. However, the road to Amaluza proved to be impassable. Just beyond the recently built bridge over the Rio Negro, a landslide had swept everything—including the roadway—into the valley hundreds of meters below. With no way to get through, we had to abandon the Jeep, shoulder our packs, and make it on foot to Amaluza.

The settlement turned out to be a cluster of thatched-roof adobe casas sitting on the top of a mountain, the center of a population of 150 souls. On the surrounding slopes columns of smoke betrayed the scattered presence of Indian huts. The Teniente Politico, Gilberto Gomez, asked us innumerable questions. He apologized, but said that new regulations required that he enter into his log-book the activities of all strangers in the settlement. Security was apparently being tightened throughout the area.

Satisfied with our answers, he offered us his kitchen for the night and the promise that we would be able to rent horses or mules for the trip to San Jose. The trek there, Gomez said, was fourteen hours for the natives—gringo time was anybody's guess. "I don't know if you can get across the Rio Negro," he said. (To get to San Jose, we had to cross the Negro a second time, back to the south bank.) "We have had terrible downpours the last two weeks," Gomez continued. "Most of the old road has been washed away, and the water will probably be so high it will be impossible for men or horses to cross. There are old trails that you can take, but you will need a guide like José Gonzalez who knows the area better than anyone else."

Gomez brought Gonzalez to the casa that night, and he told us that the day before a road crew had stretched a cable over the Rio Negro. He had doubts that we would be able to cross through the water, but we might be able to get over by using the cable. I asked him to see if he could find some horses anyway, in case we found a crossing at the river level. He returned the next morning with a man and three horses, and we started discussing the price. The man asked a very high figure, so I decided to rent only one. "We'll go on foot," I thought, "and the horse can carry our packs and food." We started out later that morning, but as soon as we reached the Rio Negro, I realized we would never be able to get the horse across. The cable was the only means of crossing. We unloaded the horse and sent it back to Amaluza with one of the men from the road crew who was going in that direction.

José showed us how the system worked. You wound a piece of Manila rope twice around your waist, and attached yourself to a wooden double hook suspended from the cable. Then slowly you pulled yourself across—hoping the cable would hold. José went first, then we hooked our packs to the cable and, with the help of an extra line attached to them, he pulled them across one by one. Then it was our turn. I asked Oswaldo to go ahead, but after a long pause, he turned to me and said, "I think I'll feel more comfortable if you go first. You're heavier than I am!"

I wound the Manila rope around my waist, slung my body under the cable, and slipped the wooden hook over it. Thinking "I hope to hell it will hold my weight," I gave myself a push and started to pull myself to the other bank. The sensation of dangling over the roaring and swirling river below was unnerving, but I made it, and Oswaldo then followed.

The author crossing the Rio Negro.

Our destination, Siete Arroyos, the home of José's brother Marcos, was only 12 kilometers away, but the journey, up a steep and muddy trail, with packs on our backs, became an eternity. We gasped and heaved as the air got thinner, our shoulders and ribs aching from the weight of the packs. Finally we reached Siete Arroyos: three small, crudely built casas, one at the base of the mountain at the river, one halfway up the slope, and one on the small plateau near the summit. Nothing more. We settled in with Marcos and his family, which included four children and a score of domestic animals, cats, dogs, and chickens, all in one big room. Oswaldo and I stretched out near the fire for the night, our eyes smarting from the smoke. Upset by our presence in their usual quarters, the chickens clucked and moved around us all night long.

José left before dawn to look for horses or mules for the next leg of our journey to San Jose. He returned with three pack horses and their owner, an old man whom he had convinced to let us hire his animals. Taking no chances, the old man had come to collect the agreed price. Nothing was known about the condition of the pica we proposed to follow, but José believed that if we could reach Chantilla we would be over the worst. It took nine hours of struggling through mud and angry streams, forging new trails when sections of the pica had been washed away by the continuous rain and landslides, until as if by magic, with a shift of the wind, the clouds scattered, the sun reappeared, and Chantilla lay below us—one lonely casa on a patch of flatland in a narrow valley. From saddles and gaps between the surrounding peaks foaming waterfalls were crashing down, splintering and leaping into the Rio Palmira, a silver ribbon far below in the valley, shining in the last light of the sun. The land looked beautiful—green and serene. But we knew, from experience, that there were many more hardships, discomforts, and dangers ahead if we decided to continue our journey.

From this point on, my chart would be useless. Neither Chantilla nor the trails ahead were marked. There were no settlements or trading posts, and what we carried in our packs would probably be the only supplies available. We would have to ford the treacherous Rio Palmira whose water level, from the steady rain of the last two weeks, would be so high that it would be difficult for us and the animals to cross. But still, after spending the night in Chantilla, we decided to go on.

When we set off the next morning, there was no rain but the clouds were very dark and heavy. The pica was dangerous, dropping steeply along slopes and skirting the edges of creavasses hundreds of meters deep. The mud on the pica was so thick and sticky that the horses found it almost impossible to descend the trail. We had to dismount and walk ahead, leading them.

Suddenly, from behind me, I heard Oswaldo yell: "Pino! *Ayuda* . . . help!" I looked back, and what I saw made my blood run cold. Oswaldo's horse had fallen, pinning Oswaldo under him. They lay right on the edge of a sharp incline that sloped precipitously for 30 or 40 meters, then dropped straight down to the Rio Palmira. I yelled: "Don't try to move! *Don't move!*" I called to José, who was in front of me, quickly tethered my horse, and we ran back together.

José took hold of the bridle of Oswaldo's horse, stroking his head to quiet him down. He seemed to understand and didn't move. But as I untied the cinch to free the saddle and Oswaldo at the same time, the horse suddenly jerked violently and tried to stand. Oswaldo slipped free; but the horse lost his footing and slid down the slope, twisting and twitching, getting closer and closer to the edge of the precipice. Miraculously, his slide was abruptly halted by some stumps and shrubs that were growing out from the side of the mountain. José crawled down very carefully where the slope wasn't quite so steep and saw that we could carve a path through the brush to get to the horse. Oswaldo, too shaken to do anything, stayed with the other animals on the pica, while José and I rescued the frightened horse.

Much delayed by the accident, we finally reached the

Rio Palmira. A swift current raced between steep rocks and there was no evident place to cross. But after searching hard, we came to a point where the river had channeled a narrow passage between high rocky banks; there we managed to stretch two good-sized tree trunks over the swiftly churning waters. We carried our packs and saddles across the improvised bridge, then swam the horses across further down below where the waters, crashing over rock ledges, had formed a pool of subdued green water.

Once on the other side, we discovered that ahead of us the pica suddenly disappeared. A tremendous landslide had cut a swath, at least 30 meters wide and 1000 meters long, from the top of the mountain all the way down to the Rio Palmira, It looked like a broad driveway down the slope, bereft of trees, vegetation, everything. We could have picked our way across the slide, moving very carefully, but it would have been impossible for the horses.

I told José to cross the slide and continue toward San Jose, check the pica ahead, and come back with other horses if possible. In the meantime Oswaldo and I broke our gear down into small, manageable packs, carefully picked our way across the slide, and waited for José to return. Finally, at dusk, he arrived with a new team of horses accompanied by a native who would cross over the slide and take the old team back to Chantilla. We decided to move on immediately, convinced that dangers of more landslides lurked in the darkness of the surrounding mountains.

Just before midnight a dim yellow light appeared ahead in the somber gloom. It was San Jose: four adobe casas perched on the side of the mountain. The bark of dozens of dogs announced our arrival and the door of one of the shacks flew open. The silhouettes of Luis Nieto and his sister Teresa stood out against a burning oil lamp. In the short time it took us to settle ourselves in their loft, the rest of the inhabitants of this tiny settlement had congregated in the room below, curious to see the strangers in their midst.

The next morning a young man, Manolo Espinosa, who had heard of our arrival, came to offer us his help and, at the same time, to satisfy his own curiosity. I explained my interest in the area and inquired if he knew about a pyramid that was said to exist here. His eyes lit up immediately. He had heard something about it, he replied; there were many stories told about the existence of unusual structures. In the eastern mountain range—I took him to mean the Cordillera Cutucu Occidental—he had also heard that there was a dormant volcano, inside which was a circular stairway cut into the inner wall from the top down to the floor of the cavity. On the lower sides were ranks of benches cut into the sidewalls, similar to a Roman stadium. A sidewalk of paving stones, he said, crossed the floor and led into a tunnel. The Indians believed that the god of fire, brother of the sun, lived inside the tunnel. The man who had told Manolo this story said he had walked into the tunnel himself, but could only go about 20 meters or so because it became hard to breathe as the air grew very thin.

While Manolo was talking, my memory slowly focused back on my first impression of this little-known range, which I had first encountered when I crossed the turbulent Upano River that separates the Cutucu from the central Andean range. Savage, densely covered by mountain jungle, with its peaks shrouded in fog most of the time, its slopes had revealed evidence of an ancient stone-carving culture. It was not inconceivable that such a structure might be found there. But Luis Nieto suddenly interrupted my thoughts by saying that if I was interested in old *infieles*, he could take me to see a standing stone with human features that was only a few hours away from San· Jose.

We set out on horseback the next morning, heading east into the Machenga range. A frigid wind was blowing, and squall clouds were drifting through the mountain peaks to the north, showering the earth below. At last we reached the place where we had to leave the horses. The *infiele*, Luis said, was in a small hollow, at least 250 meters

Menhir discovered on a slope of the Machenga range.

down the side of the mountain. Carefully we made our way down, at times sliding and sinking into mud 1 meter deep. Then the ground leveled off and there in the center, on one side of a clump of brush, stood a much-eroded stone carving—a menhir. It measured about 1.5 meters tall, 35 centimeters wide, and 30 centimeters thick, obviously crafted by a people who had in their minds a clear concept of what a menhir represented.

Trying to calm my inner excitement, I went around to the other side of the clump of shrubbery. And there, lying on the ground half-hidden by the mud, was another much larger menhir. We tried to lift it and stand it upright, but it was too heavy and wouldn't budge. After clearing the mud away, I could see that the sculptured features of both menhirs were similar in style.

I knew that this form of small megalithic monument, in many instances, was connected with graves, usually shallow and hidden by stone slabs, or in natural crevices sealed by vertically placed stones. Perhaps the presence of menhirs in this location had a deeper significance other than as mere magical markers. I described to my companions the kind of clues to look for, and we began searching the surrounding mountainside. Hours later, I was just about ready to call it a day when I saw below me a large outcropping situated so that it commended a superb view of the valley beyond. I called the others and asked them to help me cut away the underbrush around the base on the side overlooking the valley. There we discovered a crevice sealed by small, irregular, upright stones.

Stone figure, perhaps a jaguar. Machenga range.

We removed the stones and carefully sifted through the loose earth that practically filled the entire cavity. Remains of bone fragments came to light and two artifacts: an anthropomorphic mythic animal with offspring on its back that seemed to represent a jaguar sculpted in the Oriente style I had become very familiar with; and an intriguing, gracefully carved figure showing three frogs, apparently in sexual union, with tadpoles sculpted on each side of the base of the supporting frog. This symbol of the power of life, of frogs in the position of copulation, is a fertility figure encountered with some frequency in the Oriente and in the cordilleras.

Stone sculpture of three frogs. Machenga range.

The discovery, at a later time, of six ceremonial platforms extending out fron the side of the slope like a high terrace, gave new dimensions and importance to this area. The front face of these platforms varied in height, depending on the angle of the slope, but they were built tall enough to provide a floor area of about 10 by 14 feet.

Stone figures in the round. Raranga range.

They had been completely buried in mud and foliage and I wasn't able to find any clues as to what their use might have been. However, their importance and significance were evident by the stylized manner in which they had been constructed. In a terrain almost devoid of horizontal land surface, these platforms may have been built to facilitate the performance of religious ceremonies; they overlook a vista of awesome magnitude that would be inspiring for people of any religious beliefs. Or they may have served as foundations for ordinary dwellings.

This type of platform construction is encountered not only in the Namangosa Valley but also in the southern range of the Raranga Mountains, as far south as the Picacho range and the Cordilleras Saguerson and Tacuambi. Burials are also found throughout this area in natural crevices formed between exposed strata on cliffs or riverbanks, or at the base of an outcropping. They are all horizontal burials; access to the burial space is lateral, via the side of the crevice. There is no regular geometric arrangement of artifacts around the skeleton as is seen in shaft or pit tombs. The artifacts are generally clustered near the head, their placement dictated by the geometry of the crevice.

Mythic figures with ax-shaped brows. Raranga range.

On later expeditions to this area, as I came across more carved stone artifacts in burial crevices, it became clear to me that this eastern region of the Andean Cordillera showed many evidences of the rise and development of a very ancient stone-carving culture. The pieces were done in a style that by now had become very familiar to me, with an admixture of mythic animals and human forms, often with the typical Oriente face involving a heavy oval mouth, oval eyes, and a blunt or square nose. Frequently, the nose and brow seemed to suggest a crescent-like design that brought to mind the shape of an ax, a trait that in the artifacts of later cultures became very significant. Many of the sculptures were in the round.

Stone axheads were also recovered in the Tacuambi area in burial crevices, some of them reminiscent of styles I had seen in the coastal cultures, an indication that the axhead heritage was widespread. Only a few clay pots were found associated with them, indicating either that the ceramic technology of that society was still in its infancy, or that clay, as a material, was scarce; however, stone vessels of various sizes were uncovered.

But the most extraordinary and momentous find in the Namangosa Valley was the recovery of a mastodon tooth from an ancient riverbed near one of the stone-built platforms where landslides occurred frequently. What was extraordinary was not the find itself, for mastodon bones have been uncovered before in Ecuador—Max Uhle in 1928 reported that he excavated part of a mastodon skeleton in a cave high in the cordilleras—but the results of a carbon-14 analysis by the radiocarbon dating laboratory of the University of Miami that yielded a date of 3530 B.C. ± 120. For it was believed until that time that the mastodon had become extinct in this area by 6000 B.C. This explained the stone artifact of a carved elephantine creature that was recovered from an ancient crevice burial in the Namangosa Valley. It also explained carved elephant-like heads on stone mortars recovered in adjacent areas.

Stone axheads. Tacuambi region.

The mastodons were forest lovers and preferred a temperate climate. Due to the equatorial temperature, it was possible for many species of animal, and man, to survive in Ecuador at the peak of the last glacial period (20,000–11,000 B.C.) when the globe as a whole was at its coldest. In North America as many as 70 percent of the early species known, including the mastodon, became extinct by 8000 B.C. But the new evidence suggested that the mastodon had survived in the equatorial regions of South America for at least another 5000 years. The discovery of a mastodon tooth in the Namangosa Valley also suggested another possibility. For the Santiago/Zamora/Namangosa valleys form a natural corridor from the Amazon into the sierra, and if it provided a migratory path for early animals, might it not have also provided a corridor for the migration of an early people?

Stone vessel. Raranga region.

The vividness with which an elephant-like animal was rendered in the stone pieces discovered in the Namangosa

Mastodon tooth, dated 3530 B.C. ± 120. Namangosa Valley.

Valley strongly suggests that it had to be alive in Ecuador within the memory of the tribes that produced these artifacts. A more stylized form of the mastodon-like features can be seen in the clay artifacts of later cultures recovered in other areas: a standing clay figurine from the Pisco area of the northern Mesa, and a seal stamp from Tungurahua (ca. 400 B.C.). Several species of animals that were thought to have been extinct thousands of years before apparently survived in Ecuador long enough to have been recorded in its ancient art. Moreover, there are striking similarities between findings associated with the last glacial age in Europe and those I encountered in Ecuador, specifically, numerous stone-carving representations of human figurines and animals, including the mammoth, that were uncovered in upper Paleolithic sites, which date as late as 10,500 B.C., in Avdeevo and Eliseevichi, Russia. They led me to the belief that mastery of the art of stone

Carved stone elephantine animal. Namangosa Valley.

carving is not only the forerunner of more sophisticated and complex cultural development but also an important step forward in ancient man's intellectual awareness.

In Central America the tradition of the elephant form can be clearly seen in Mayan art, both in stone and clay, and during the last century this has caused great controversy as to its interpretation. Many authorities have postulated that the representation of the elephant in Mayan art is proof of Asian-American contact. However, it can be shown that the tradition may have been carried north from the equatorial belt. Pottery vessels with the unmistakable depiction of the elephant or mastodon have been recovered from archeological sites in Guatemala, Honduras, and the Yucatan. But without doubt, the mastodon or elephant form played a significant role in the spiritual and religious beliefs of both South American and Mesoamerican cultures.

Stone mortar with elephant heads. Orejones.

Pottery figurine with elephant features. Pisco.

Seal stamp with stylized elephant features. Tungurahua.

Even today, around the campfire, jungle-dwelling Indians recount ancient legends of a huge creature with a serpent-like nose and wings for ears that once walked the land. According to their tales, it was so big and heavy that it trampled everything in its path, thereby helping the people to forge new trails through the dense forest. One day, so the legends go, the people became lazy and sluggish from drinking too much *chicha,* and the huge beast grew very angry and decided to leave. It opened its earlike wings and flew away, changing into the eagle. But it left its nose behind to become the serpent.

Our expedition into the Machenga range was cut short when I realized that Oswaldo was very sick. For two days in San Jose he tossed and moaned with a high fever, raving deliriously. It was impossible to travel with him in that condition. Finally, on the morning of the third day, the fever broke and Oswaldo woke up asking for food. Although he was very weak, he insisted he was ready to travel.

We had to retrace every agonizing step of our journey to San Jose, recrossing both the Rio Palmira on the bridge made of two poles, and the Rio Negro, where we left José and the horses and slung ourselves onto the cable for the crossing. José bade us goodbye, sad to see our friendship coming to an end. We had become very close during these last weeks. But he smiled when I promised that when I returned to this area I would get in touch with him again. The stories of the existence of a pyramid and a volcanic amphitheater in the area of San Jose had yet to be investigated. I knew I would be back.

When we finally reached Amaluza, Manuel Espinoza, the engineer in charge of the road project, offered us passage to Cuenca on the company Jeep that was leaving that night. Because the landslide still blocked the road, we had to walk the 5 kilometers to where the Jeep was waiting. Wet, cold, and exhausted, we crawled into it, and the next thing we remembered was the driver waking us up in Cuenca in front of Oswaldo's house.

Days later, as I flew back to the States, my mind was reverberating backward and forward—backward to the mountain jungle near San Jose where I had discovered significant leads in my quest, and forward to the uncertainties and complications of my September meeting with Mashutaka.

CHAPTER 13

The Curse

I landed in Quito early in the morning of September 3, 1970, with a vague, restless sense of foreboding. I then flew to Cuenca the next day, where Oswaldo was waiting for me. He had sent a message a week before to Mashutaka that we would be in Plan Grande within the first ten days of September. As he hadn't received any reply, we assumed that we were to proceed as planned. I felt relieved. But these feelings were short-lived when we learned that the only trail leading directly to Plan Grande—the Limon-Mendes pica—was completely closed. And because of the ever-present rain, there were no flights scheduled to the Puyomo landing strip.

While we waited in Cuenca, hardly an hour went by that Oswaldo didn't bring up the subject of the cueva and his dreams of a grandiose discovery. I could avoid it no longer; I had to tell him of Mashutaka's condition that he remain behind, as the "guest" of the Indians, until we returned from the expedition to the cueva. At first he was taken aback by this inexplicable demand. I could not explain it either, but for good reason or bad, I felt powerless to change it. Should we accept it? Oswaldo looked at the ground, then at me, and said, "But how will you feel traveling in there with those Indians, by yourself?"

I said, "Well, I was wondering more how you would feel. . . ." I had already made my decision. But I could hardly bring myself to contemplate the unknown risks and perils that lay ahead. Finally, in a quiet voice, Oswaldo said, "It will be all right with me, if it has to be that way."

We waited for three days before we could fly to Puyomo. There we had no way of knowing the condition of the trail to Plan Grande; two months ago, when we were on it, it had been in very bad shape. It was still in very bad shape, but by some miracle we arrived in one piece at Plan Grande by nightfall four days later, the first outsiders to appear there in almost three weeks. Zoila Gaiera had disconcerting news for us. She said she had not seen or heard from Mashutaka for fifteen days. We were two days late, and I thought he would surely have sent a messenger to inquire about us.

The next morning I sent a young Jivaro to El Pigos, through the heavy rain, with a message to Mashutaka that I had arrived in Plan Grande and was waiting for him. He returned the next day saying that Mashutaka was not there. He was out hunting; his wife would tell him on his return.

While we were waiting impatiently for Mashutaka, everyone in Casa Zoila had something to say about him. I heard that he had been in a fight with his brother, Kageca, over the 2500-hectare (6177-acre) tract inhabited by their clan. Mashutaka had laid claim to this land, formerly open domain, but he was taking title in his own name, not in the name of the family—and Kageca had resented this.

The people in Plan Grande were for the most part mestizos and were disinclined to concede that a "dumb Indian" could have accumulated so much property unaided. They related mysterious stories of a very important *padrino* (protector) who was the real authority behind Mashutaka, and who controlled all of his holdings. And there were many other stories, like the existence of a valuable mineral or crystal on Mashutaka's land that looked like diamonds. Obviously, among these people, Mashutaka was a powerful but enigmatic figure, and they were afraid of him.

We spent another night in Plan Grande, then I decided

to go to El Pigos myself the following morning. Oswaldo and I set out at dawn under clear skies.

The pica to El Pigos climbed upward through canyons in the range of the Cerro Crusado, twisting through bleached ravines, across rivers, and over luxuriant green plateaus. As we reached high altitudes, a bank of low clouds engulfed the land around us and we had the eerie feeling of stepping into a mysterious and unknown world. We climbed even higher above the clouds, and finally the pica snaked through a sea of tall grass toward an opening leading into a broad clearing. On the far side was a casa, and to the left a small wooden chapel no more than 10 by 12 feet, with a steeple and a bell. We had reached El Pigos—the home of Mashutaka, cacique of a Shuara clan.

The chapel was an indication of the degree of Westernization that Mashutaka had accepted, as was his house, a structure of board walls with a thatched roof, closer in style to the typical mestizo casa than to the slat-and-bamboo Jivaro chosa. Mashutaka's wife, Chicta Lachuncho, stood on the edge of the clearing. She had been watching us coming up the trail for the last hour. She said Mashutaka had not yet returned from hunting, but she knew where he was and agreed to send her two eldest sons to tell him that we had arrived and would wait for him in Plan Grande. The two boys, the oldest no more than fourteen, packed some food and machetes, and left the clearing.

I asked Chicta about her father, Vichuncho (the name by which Samakache was known), who had also agreed to accompany us on the expedition to the cueva. She said he was waiting for a message from Mashutaka before leaving his home. I sensed that perhaps our being late had caused some difficulty, but she seemed reluctant to say anything more. She didn't know what was on Mashutaka's mind, or perhaps didn't want to talk, and again I began to feel apprehensive about our journey.

Oswaldo and I started back to Plan Grande, hoping to reach it before dark. But once the sun set, we decided to pitch camp in a small clearing on the trail. I was sleeping soundly until, suddenly, I heard Oswaldo crying out for help in the darkness. I jumped out of my sleeping bag, grabbed my flashlight, and ran in the direction of his voice. There he stood, behind a clump of bushes, with his pants half down: under one boot was a squirming, writhing snake. It had struck and fortunately Oswaldo's boot had protected him from a very dangerous bite. But he was unable to move. If he shifted his foot, he would release the snake. I grabbed my knife and cut off its head. It was a ciega—about 35 centimeters long, white with random black spots over its entire body. Dormant during the daytime because it is blinded by light, it is a nocturnal creature, hence its name (*ciega* means "blind"). For Oswaldo it was a close call.

We waited another day and a half in Plan Grande before a messenger arrived with the news that Mashutaka would return to El Pigos tomorrow, and asked that I meet him there. I was puzzled by this change of meeting place. It seemed like an insignificant factor, but a Jivaro does not change a plan to which he is pledged unless there is a very important reason. But then I thought that the days of impatient waiting had undoubtedly fed our imaginations and increased our misgivings.

The next day, after a terrible struggle through the rain and mud with the horses and one mule we had brought for the journey, we again reached the plateau of El Pigos. And there, waiting in front of his casa, was Mashutaka, wearing a big smile. I realized that I, too, was smiling—my first smile in eight days. We took care of the horses and mule, and settled our gear into the chapel, which would serve as our quarters. Then we entered Mashutaka's casa for some chicken broth his wife had prepared for our arrival.

The Indians—even those who have been strongly acculturated—are not too concerned with sanitation. So I have found, over the years, that the only way to avoid getting sick on journeys into the interior is to shun the native food and stick to my tried-and-true diet of canned tuna and sardines. It's boring, but it's safe. But on this occasion, my first meeting with Mashutaka at El Pigos, I couldn't refuse the chicken broth Chicta had made for our arrival. To reject Mashutaka's hospitality in this fashion would have set up a certain barrier between us that would have been difficult to overcome. I tried the broth. It was hotly spiced with *aji* (peppers), but the rice with black beans and morsels of meat made it agreeable. A wooden plate of yucca with pieces of boiled chicken lay on the floor to be shared. We, the adults, ate on clay plates with wooden forks, the children on small wooden plates with their fingers. The silence in the room was interrupted only by the sound of gratified grunts as the food was savored. When we finished the meal, Chicta began disbursing cups of freshly brewed manioc beer.

Drinking down the last of the beer, Mashutaka gestured for me to look over his casa. It was not large, but had three quite comfortable rooms by the standards even of mestizos in the interior. We walked into his bed chamber where I saw a large *catre,* or bed platform, on which he and Chicta slept, probably with the younger children. Leaning against it was the ever-present muzzle-loading shotgun. Around the walls there were three *nankis,* spears made of chonta palm; three long *umis,* blowguns with a good supply of *ztinkztak* (arrows) in a bamboo quiver; and a *tundui,* a small ceremonial drum. There was also an elaborate tribal headdress, the *tawazap,* made with the feathers of the toucan, and to one side of it a small, colorful woven bag that caught my eye. Mashutaka opened it and, to my surprise, took out a *tsantsa,* a shrunken head. I asked him if he still practiced headshrinking. "No, not any more," he replied. But I felt sure that the atavistic concept of the *tsantsa* still lived on in his beliefs.

The Jivaro believe in the existence of two souls, the spiritual one and the *muisak,* the avenging one. This second soul leaves the body of a dead enemy through his mouth and will attempt to kill his murderer or a member of his family. Only by removing the head of the victim and shrinking it immediately will the *muisak* be trapped inside and powerless to seek revenge. Once trapped, the power your enemy possessed becomes yours, and by displaying the *tsantsa,* you become the powerful one, able to intimidate other enemies and ward off acts of aggression.

The preparation of a *tsantsa* is not a complicated process, although it is done over a period of several days. After the skin has been removed from the skull, it is simmered in plain water. Boiling reduces the size of the flesh, and by further treatment with hot stones and hot sand the head is shrunk to the size of a fist. As the skin dries, it is manipulated to help retain the features; and the incision at the back, the lips, and sometimes the eyelids are all sewn together with vine. No special vegetable astringent or plant extract is used during the entire process. Mashutaka's *tsantsa* reminded me of the many aspects of the decapitation ritual I had seen represented in the artifacts of South and Central America. That the tradition became widespread there is no doubt. Could its practice have originated with the ancient people of the Amazon Basin?

Mashutaka, Oswaldo, and I walked down to the small chapel to discuss the expedition privately. Oswaldo sat off a little to one side. He had been rather quiet through most of the afternoon; he obviously resented Mashutaka's condition that he remain behind. Perhaps his reason was a simple one. The Jivaros do not relate too well with the Spaniards; Mashutaka seemed more comfortable with me, a gringo.

He began by explaining why he had not come down to Plan Grande, as we had originally agreed. He had suffered a large wound on his foot caused by a slip of his machete eight days before. I had noticed he was limping around with some kind of packing on his foot. Otherwise, he said, the agreement reached at our first meeting remained unchanged, and I was very relieved to hear that. Mashutaka then added that he had visited Vichuncho a month before, and he had a new detail to report that he thought would interest me greatly. Vichuncho believed, in fact he was sure, that some kind of large animal now lived inside the cueva. Years ago he had seen the shadow of this creature in the darkness of the cueva, and had fired at it with his muzzle-loading shotgun. He remembered that just inside the entrance were six or seven large footprints. Vichuncho wanted to make sure we had adequate firearms. With that revelation, our expedition appeared even more intriguing, and in a flash I vividly remembered my encounter with the big mono in Venezuela.

Gradually, Mashutaka became more expansive and communicative as we discussed our destination. He told me that a short distance inside the cueva were gigantic statues, carved of rock, and that one chamber in the interior was illuminated with many different colors. He thought they might be reflections of light coming through clear crystal of various hues. From a leather pouch he then pulled out a fragment of clear crystal of extraordinary quality that he said he had found in the cave. As I examined it, I understood the rumors among the mestizos in Plan Grande that Mashutaka had a source of diamond-like material on his land.

After several hours of conversation I asked Mashutaka to show me the wound on his foot, and I offered to put on some of the medicine I had with me. Without ceremony, he removed the packing to reveal a greenish paste made from a plant called maiqua-guanto (known as "micquiti" by some of the other Jivaros), a preparation said to promote quick healing of broken bones. When we cleaned the paste off the foot, the deep wound seemed to be infected and the foot was very swollen. I applied iodine over all the raw flesh. Mashutaka didn't flinch. Then I covered the wound with a fungicidal salve and bandaged it. He seemed very satisfied.

The rest of the family watched the proceedings intently, and when Mashutaka leaned back and smiled, they all rushed forward. The mother-in-law had a skin rash and a headache—I gave her six Bufferins. Chicta had an intestinal upset and abdominal pains—I gave her some Maalox and Bufferin. Mashutaka's first son was complaining of indigestion—I gave him some Maalox. His second son had a pain in his shoulder—I gave him some Bufferin. They all seemed to have great faith in my healing powers, which increased later in the day when Mashutaka said that my medicine was very effective and his foot felt much better.

That evening I broached the subject of Oswaldo with him. I began by strongly objecting to his remaining behind. I then seized on the added fact of the strange creature said to inhabit the cueva and insisted that it was necessary to have Oswaldo along as additional protection. Further, I emphasized, if Mashutaka's reason for wanting him to stay behind was to guarantee that the compensation would be paid, I could assure him it would be paid on our return from the cueva. The responsibility for Oswaldo's safety was mine.

Mashutaka looked off into the distance, said nothing, then slowly began to walk back toward the casa, still without uttering a word. I felt he had tacitly acquiesced, but didn't want to say so.

He was nowhere to be seen all the next day. We heard him very early in the morning shouting at his children, but by the time we got up he was gone. Apparently upset by my reversing the condition that Oswaldo remain behind as a hostage, he had gone off into the brush, I sensed, to reflect on the matter. His sudden departure left us feeling uneasy and uncertain, but when the children showed up at our living quarters, as they customarily did, we took it as an indication that somehow our differences would be resolved. I knew that the mood of parents, especially the head of the clan, would be reflected in the children.

Later in the morning, the women and children left the compound for a nearby slope at the far end of the clearing to do their daily tasks. They gathered around a bamboo pipe from which a continuous trickle of water was pouring out to the ground below. The women washed their clothes, beating them on the flat stone beneath the pipe, while the children joyfully splashed themselves. Watching them, it occurred to Oswaldo and me that we could certainly help them by building a system to collect the water. There was plenty of wood available, and by mid-afternoon an oversized tub had been built out of double wooden planks with a layer of clay between to prevent the water from leaking through. Nothing elegant—certainly not suitable for Marie Antoinette's boudoir—but practical.

After it was installed beneath the trickling bamboo pipe, it quickly filled with water and Oswaldo decided he would initiate it with a badly needed bath. Being very modest, he tried to make an impromptu screen of his pants and shirt but was not too successful. The whole family watched with delight, and what they saw caused a certain amount of anthropometric consternation. To their amazement, Oswaldo's backside, usually covered by swimming trunks at the least, was white, whereas the remainder of his body was brown. They probably felt they had just seen *the* distinguishing racial characteristic of these strange foreigners who had come to their land.

Late in the evening Mashutaka suddenly materialized, and I saw that the swelling of his foot had gone down enough so that he was able to slip his boot on. He announced simply that tomorrow we would be leaving to make contact with Vichuncho in Pangi, somewhat northeast of Gualaquiza. He said nothing about Oswaldo, but we both understood that he would be permitted to come with us.

When we set off the next morning on horseback, Mashutaka was leading the way with myself and Oswaldo following. We were headed back to the Puyomo airstrip for a return flight to Cuenca; from there we would begin the difficult journey to Pangi. But the trail we took was not the one we had used to reach Plan Grande, nor was it commonly used by anyone traveling through this territory. It was Mashutaka's own trail, ideally hidden in the midst of the low-flying clouds, little more than scant tracks through the mud and foliage. Only he could find his way in this mountain jungle. We proceeded in silence, absorbed in our own thoughts, descending and ascending constantly on the twisting trail. From time to time, the sound of our voices urging or praising our mounts

Mosk.

blended in unison with the whistling and screeching of the birds perched high in the green canopy, and the muffled roars of the streams swollen from the last heavy rainfall.

By evening we reached Mosk, the compound of another Shuara clan, allies of Mashutaka. As in El Pigos, they too had a wooden chapel complete with steeple. There we were to spend the night, and later that evening, around the fire, Mashutaka asked me very penetrating questions about the country I came from and the way we lived. He then revealed a deep concern for the future of his own people. He talked at length about the changes that had taken place in the lives of the Jivaro since the missionaries and the white nationals had encroached upon their territory. The white man's diseases were now widespread, he said, carried by him wherever he went. Further, the missionaries were bad doctors and not equipped to cure. With all their prayers, the best they could do was prolong sickness; they did not have the power to reverse the disease.

In the old days, Mashutaka said, the Indians made war when their territory was threatened by outsiders. But now, the white man was too superior in numbers and weapons, and as a result, they were gradually losing control over their garden plots as well as their hunting areas.

Yet, all the while Mashutaka was speaking, I thought of the long-standing relationship he had had with the missions: the initiative he and so many of the other Indians displayed in building a small chapel or shrine on their land; the interest Mashutaka and the other Indians had in obtaining guns and machetes from the white man, wearing the white man's pants and shirts, and dealing with the white man's money; the willingness with which their own children were taken to the mission schools for education. Evidently, the situation had two faces—or did they have a choice?

Mashutaka went on, complaining that he only had one wife, and this made it harder to survive. One woman alone could not take care of the garden, raise the children, manage the household. Before his conversion, when he had had three wives, all captured during tribal raids, there were enough hands to share the labor, and everyone got along more easily. Although tribal warefare had declined in the border areas, where Indians were in closer contact with Western civilization, he said that deep in the interior it was still going on. The males were more frequently killed in tribal wars, by hunting accidents, or in raids to acquire new wives. Thus, in a certain sense, the practice of polygamy was a means to provide for the great number of widows and celibate girls.

Deep within the Amazon, he continued, in a little-known territory, there was a large "pueblo" that was occupied only by women. The only man in the settlement was their very old cacique, Makionjuy. Vichuncho and he had met him several times. Many years before, more of the men in the tribe had been killed as a result of revenge and clan wars among themselves. The women decided to put a halt to their grieving and stop this fratricide by expelling all the remaining males. They became proficient in the use of the blowgun and bow and arrow, and ever since have been ready to use them against whoever dares enter their territory.

The only exceptions to the regimen, Mashutaka said, are two periods during the year when young men could enter the territory for five days, once in the spring, the time of planting and fertility rituals, and again during the fall, the time of harvesting. The women consorted with these young men, and the resulting children, if they were male, were sent out of the territory to their fathers. The girl babies were kept in the village.

When he had finished this story, Mashutaka looked at me, probably expecting some comment. But the story was so unexpected that I was speechless. Its similarity to the fabled legend of the women warriors of Amazonia had immediately come to my mind. Perhaps seeing a look of disbelief on my face, Mashutaka emphasized again that as recently as two years ago he and Vichuncho had met with Makionjuy at a gathering of Jivaro caciques. And then he added that if I wished, they would take me to meet with him during the week that men can enter the territory with impunity. I lost no time in accepting his offer. If a clan of Jivaro chose to resolve such a situation with this radical social arrangement today, it certainly could have happened in ancient times, and could have given rise to the legends that have fascinated people ever since.

When we set out the following morning, Mashutaka warned us to be very careful with the horses. We were going to go through a territory that was very difficult, wet and deep with mud. He was right. In a short time we reached a point where the animals were simply unable to proceed through mud at least 50 centimeters deep. Laboriously, carefully, we turned them around, backtracked to safer ground, and looked for an alternate route. It was a continuous struggle to avoid sinking disastrously into some hidden hole or crevice.

Finally, several hours later, we were at the union of the Rio Namangosa and the Rio Paute. The vista before us was overwhelming. These two large rivers come together at a sharp angle, forming a huge waterfall, which thunders down wreathed in mist. The tremendous currents roiling and swirling below us looked like the waters of the Pacific in a storm.

Here we had to leave the pica and follow a narrow trail

that wound up the mountainside to a small plateau directly above the Rio Paute. When we reached it, we could see, 25 meters below us, a lone dead tree jutting from a crevice on a shelf of rock no more than 2 meters wide. Attached to the tree was a steel cable that stretched at least 200 meters across the river, and suspended from the cable was a small *taravita,* a wooden platform—the East Andean version of the cable car. This was to be our mode of transportation across the raging river.

There comes a moment when one loses one's assurance. To reach the tree to which the cable was attached, we had to slide down a depression carved in the mountainside, on our buttocks, in the hope that it would lead us straight to the tree. If we missed, we would become airborne before crashing into the river hundreds of meters below. Oswaldo, very apprehensive, said, "I don't think I'll be able to make it." I assured him that by tying a rope around his waist, we could guide him down slowly and safely.

As we discussed the situation, four Indians suddenly appeared on the trail, carrying on their shoulders a homemade litter covered with a sheet. A pregnant young women, very ill, was lying on the litter. They were bringing her to the mission clinic in Mendes. But even as they were telling us their story, we heard a loud, deep, rasping sound from under the sheet—then silence. One of the Indians moved the sheet aside and we looked into the girl's face. She was dead. Mashutaka asked if I would examine her, to make sure. I checked her pulse, respiration, and responses, then turned to him and said, "There is no question. She is dead." He spoke to the Indians in his tribal tongue. They crouched around the litter in silence. Then abruptly they began to cry out excitedly, covering their faces in both hands, howling louder and louder.

Their outcry was not one of sorrow, Mashutaka told us, but of anger and rage. He said that they believed the girl's death was the result of a spell cast by a *yahauci uwisin,* an evil shaman, hired by an enemy faction for revenge. The Jivaro do not accept death as occurring naturally, or by diseases, or accident. It is always the result of an evil spell put on the person by his enemy, and therefore regarded as an act of aggression that has to be avenged. The family of the dead girl had been feuding for many years with another clan over the capture of two young women. Their outcry was for revenge. Without emotion, Mashutaka said that she was his niece—one of the many children of Homero Kageca, his brother. I could not understand his complete detachment and equanimity until he told me that his family was not involved in the feud.

Oswaldo was very disturbed, and asked me if the death of this girl meant *mala suerte* (bad luck) for us. I persuaded him that it had nothing to do with us, and hoped he would not notice my own misgivings. And so we began the perilous crossing, relying on a tree whose roots we hoped were not too rotten and a cable that we hoped would support our weight.

Fortunately, with deep relief, the three of us and the Jivaro who were carrying the dead girl, no longer to the clinic but to the mission cemetery, all reached the other side safely. We continued down the trail on foot, our horses left on the other side to be taken back to Mosk where they could be cared for until our return. Disturbing thoughts of the sudden death still lingered as we trekked along a narrow trail for more than an hour. But the rest of our journey moved swiftly, and we arrived at the Puyomo landing strip just in time to board a plane for Cuenca.

Two days passed before we were able to organize our trip to Pangi. We would have to take an indirect route in order to circumvent the virtually impassable Saguerson range, and as we gathered information on the weather and road conditions, it began to seem an impossible task. But I knew we had to go on, to go forward, if ever the mystery of the cueva was to be unveiled. Vichuncho was the important link; only he could guide us to the cave.

The journey to Pangi took five days, three days by Jeep and two by foot, covering about 325 kilometers in a roundabout route. Finally, late on the fifth night, Mashutaka stopped on the trail and said, "Very soon we will reach the plateau where Vichuncho's house is." In the distance, we could already hear dogs barking. Mashutaka put two fingers on his lips and let out a very melodic, high-pitched whistle—three times. "Now we wait," he said. Three minutes, perhaps four, passed. I could hear only the loud barking of the dogs. Then, from the darkness in front of us, came the same tone—a very melodic, high-pitched whistle. The ritual had been completed.

We set off again, and within a few minutes reached a small plateau. At the far end I could see the silhouettes of two thatched-roof huts, which appeared to be a blend of the Jivaro chosa with the mestizo casa. The dogs were now barking furiously. Then the moon came out from behind a cloud, and I could see a man standing in front of one of the huts. We approached him slowly. "Vichuncho," Mashutaka said, and started to speak rapidly to him in his tribal tongue.

I looked at the figure standing in front of us and saw a man of strong build, but I was a little disappointed. From his reputation, I had expected Vichuncho to look like one of the powerful Indians I had seen many times in the Oriente, with toucan feathers around the head, and a necklace of stones and jaguar teeth. But in the play of light between the moon and the clouds I could see his two piercing eyes, shining and directed at mine. There was power in his gaze.

With a movement of his arm, Vichuncho invited us into his casa, and as we entered I noticed that a touch of modern living had been added—over one of the bed platforms was a spring and mattress. In the middle of the dirt floor, near the low fire, there were several stools, not just the usual one. Vichuncho pulled them up to the fire and motioned us to sit down. The only other light was an oil lamp hanging from the center pole of the hut. In the darkness of the far side I felt the presence of other people.

Vichuncho began speaking to Mashutaka, and Mashutaka was laughing. The conversation went back and forth for a few minutes, then Mashutaka turned to me and said, "He's very happy to see you."

"I come from very far away to see you," I said, looking

at Vichuncho, "and I brought you some presents." I
opened my pack and showed Vichuncho machetes and
boots that I had bought for him in Cuenca. Then I
handed him something else—a red wool stocking cap, the
kind worn by skiers or cherished by anyone living in cold
climates. Just the thing to wear when traveling in the high
Andes. Vichuncho took the cap, looked at it, started to
smile, and giggled, but apparently did not know what to
do with it. I took the liberty of rolling up the rim of the
cap and helped him put it on his head. He looked at me
and began talking so fast that I caught hardly anything.
Mashutaka translated. "He thanks you very much," he
said. "He likes it very much . . . he appreciates your gift."

With the cap on, Vichuncho looked like an entirely different person. Apart from the tribal tattoos on both his
cheeks, he took on the appearance of anyone's grandfather. He reminded me of the old men I knew in the Alps
as a boy, who wore these caps in the winter to protect
themselves from the cold. As I looked at him with these
benign images in my head, I thought, "How can this old
man be a famous cacique, a leader who fought so fiercely
in the jungle and spent most of his life leading warriors in
raids against other villages, for revenge against his ene-

Vichuncho.

mies or to steal their women?" It was difficult to fuse the reputation of this man, his character in the past, with the figure I saw sitting by the fire before me.

Not a word was mentioned of our reason for being there, but Vichuncho said that he would be ready to leave with us in the morning on our return trip to Cuenca, and from there back to El Pigos, where we would set out on our expedition to the cueva. The journey took almost a week and went exactly as planned. I did not relish crossing the roaring Rio Paute on the swaying *taravita*, but again we reached the other side safely, and the afternoon of the following day we arrived in El Pigos, too weary even to eat before we stretched our hammocks out in the little chapel and went to sleep.

Rain had again plagued us on our journey, but its unrelenting monotony was broken late the next morning by sudden cries and yells. Then I heard Mashutaka call me. I ran up to his casa and found everyone gathered around Urido, Mashutaka's eight-year-old cousin, the son of Vichuncho who had been living with Mashutaka's family for the last year. He had been looking for firewood in the bush and had been bitten on the leg by a snake.

Mashutaka and Vichuncho were talking excitedly to the eldest boy, who then hurriedly ran down the trail. I sent Oswaldo to get my medical bag, and when he returned I reached for my snakebite kit. After applying a tourniquet above the knee and cleansing the bite with antiseptic, I made two cross incisions over each fang mark with the blade of my knife. Urido was very brave; he didn't cry out and he even tried not to flinch. I applied a suction device, but it was not working properly, so I sucked at the incision, spat out the blood, and began massaging Urido's leg toward the incision to keep the blood flowing.

Two hours passed. Urido grew feverish, and I began to feel that my efforts might not have been in time to save him. Repeatedly I fed him goat's milk, hoping it would work as an antidote. Another hour passed and his condition remained unchanged. Then I heard a commotion outside. A few seconds later, Mashutaka and Vichuncho walked into the room followed by an old Indian. He crouched near Urido, looked into his eyes and mouth, and gave a sharp command to Chicta, who hurriedly left the room. Next he pulled from his sisal bag a small stone mortar with a pestle and a bunch of herbs and roots held together by a string. He meticulously selected several herbs and seed pods, and began to grind them in the mortar. When Chicta returned with a pail of hot water, he poured some of it over the crushed herbs, and as he mixed he would periodically dip the tip of his forefinger into the solution and savor it. The gesture reminded me of a French chef tasting his secret sauce. Minutes passed by, and after one more taste, he poured the contents of the mortar into a wooden cup carved with an intriguing geometric motif. Then he forced Urido to drink the dark liquid. Finally, after immersing a cloth in the rest of the water, he laid it over the bite. As Urido started to moan, the old Indian seemed satisfied, for he got up, walked out of the casa, and sat on the bench near the door.

Now I was able to see him in the light: an old, wrinkled face framed by jet black hair with the Shuara tribal tattoo markings on both cheekbones in the form of a triangle, and several dots on the tip of his nose. The old man looked at me with curiosity but said nothing. Mashutaka explained to me that he was the *curandero* they had sent for earlier, and the dark liquid he had administered was an antidote for snake bites.

Suppertime came and went. Urido was feverish but still alive. Repeatedly, the *curandero* would rise from the bench, enter the casa, and force the boy to sip more of the dark liquid. As time passed and he became aware of Vichuncho and Mashutaka's friendship toward me, the *curandero*'s aloofness lessened, and I sensed that I could now speak to him.

I told him about the attack by the aimara in Venezuela and said that my hand had been healed there by a shaman. But he immediately said, "I am not a shaman. I am a *curandero*." He made a very specific distinction between the two. The shaman is a mystic who draws on the spiritual relationship between man and the forces of the jungle. He takes *natema*—the hallucinogenic drug of the Jivaro—during the healing ceremony and may administer it to the patient in a ritual that may involve chanting and incantations. The *curandero*, on the other hand, is a jungle herbalist. He has broad knowledge of the jungle plants that are effective for various diseases, and he spends his "professional" time gathering these herbs and extracting the juices or processing the plants to make preparations suitable for ministration. He may administer hallucinogenic drugs, but does not have recourse to them personally. To the *curandero*, the drug will enable the body to recuperate, but it is not looked upon as a medium of communication with the spirits, as it is to the shaman. The *curandero* works more on a physiological plane. The Spanish word *brujo* (which translated means sorceror or magician) has been used since the time of the Spanish conquest to designate an individual who practices the art of healing, whether shamanistic or herbalistic. But as a tribe comes into closer contact with Western culture and becomes more acculturated, the tendency is for the influence of the shaman to diminish, and that of the *curandero* to increase.

Just before midnight, Urido opened his eyes and asked for food. When the *curandero* approved, the whole family rejoiced, knowing that the crisis had passed. Both the *curandero* and I had applied our particular brand of medicine to the boy's wound; I wondered which of our contributions had saved his life.

That night lying in my hammock, the image of the old *curandero* pouring dark liquid from a mortar into a cup brought to mind the many artifacts, both of stone and clay, in the form of mortars and cups, and human figures holding vessels, that I had seen recovered from ancient burials. No doubt they depicted the shamanistic concept, which played an essential role in the life of the ancient people. The shaman exuded his power from the visionary experiences he received, and the paraphernalia he used in the ritual became identified with this power as the inter-

mediary vehicles of communication between the shaman
and the jungle deities. The motif of a figure in an offertory pose with a vessel held at the chest or before the face
is seen with some frequency in the art of both South and
Mesoamerica.

The next morning Mashutaka arrived at our quarters
with a big basket of fruit, saying it was a present from the
family to the white doctor. Apparently, I was being given
some credit for Urido's survival. I was pleased, but at the
same time anxious to get under way. I asked Mashutaka if
the weather would clear. He wasn't sure, but said that if I
wanted to leave, he and Vichuncho were ready.

The horses and mule packed, we headed northeast
from El Pigos, with Vichuncho in the lead, and reached
the first major river we had to cross by mid-morning: the
Rio Shiru. We had not been traveling on a pica; there
wasn't a vestige of a trail visible. Only Vichuncho's sense
of direction and feeling for the land could guide us to the
cueva.

We studied the river. The current was very strong, and
I had no idea how we were going to get across. Vichuncho
took a gourd from his bag and offered us a drink from it.
It was *chicha* and he said it was very good against the cold
of the water. Then he walked up and down the bank, surveying the river, pointing out the way. He said he would
cross first and we were to follow with the horses. He told
us to wade carefully toward a large boulder jutting out of
the swift current halfway across, and then continue
straight to the other bank.

After guzzling down more *chicha*, he stepped into the
water. Fighting the current, advancing carefully, the
water almost up to his waist, he continued ahead slowly,
struggling until finally he reached the big boulder. He
climbed up on the rock. I waved an acknowledgment and
lowered myself into the water. Then I looked up to see
Vichuncho slip and lose his balance. He fell into the river.
I waited a moment for him to reappear, but there was no
sound and no sign of him.

I began forcing my way to the boulder as fast as I could.

*Figures holding vessels:
(top), Cañar; (center),
San Agustin; (bottom),
Olmec.*

The current was strong and almost swept me off my feet. Finally I thrashed my way to the big boulder and pulled myself up. Then I saw Vichuncho down in the current on the other side, desperately hanging on to a small rock a few feet away. I jumped in, struggled to reach him, and grabbed him by the shoulder. Then, with horror, I saw that the water around his leg was swirling with red. Desperately, I pulled him off the small rock and worked him back toward the large boulder. There I saw the reason for the blood. Vichuncho's machete, hanging from his waist, had cut a large, hideous-looking gash in his right thigh when he fell.

I shouted to Mashutaka and Oswaldo to come help me. They struggled across, reached the boulder, and between us we helped Vichuncho through the water, back to the riverbank. The blood was pouring out of his wound. Frantically, I looked for my medical kit. Mashutaka said he was going into the jungle to look for an herb he knew of that would stop the bleeding. Vichuncho said nothing. He just looked at me, and then at the sky. He began muttering something. I couldn't understand a word he was saying.

Mashutaka came back, unable to find the herb. And no matter what I did, I could not stop the bleeding—the blood continued to pour from Vichuncho's wound. I told Oswaldo to repack our gear and prepare the animals to leave immediately for Sucua, where there was a clinic and a doctor.

As we began the long trek, blood kept oozing out of Vichuncho's wound and he grew weaker. The trail was very rough, and he was being jolted on the back of his horse mercilessly. Mashutaka and I rode alongside him as much as the trail permitted, to help him stay on. At one point, Vichuncho turned and gave me a deep, meaningful look. He paused for a moment, then started talking. "That cueva," he said, "is protected by the spirits. Our legends tell us that only a white-skinned man can break this spell. When you came to Mashutaka, it made me think again of my desire to get into the cueva once more and learn its secrets. So we were going to let you enter first, to break the spell. And then. . . ." He didn't continue.

A horrible thought came into my mind but I pushed it aside. "Don't talk now. Try to save your strength," I said.

We stopped at nightfall. It was impossible for us to continue, at least until the moon rose. We helped Vichuncho off his horse and tried to make him comfortable. As we settled down to rest, my mind was racing and I felt the same sense of dread and apprehension that had haunted me ever since I returned to Ecuador to begin this expedition. The wound in Vichuncho's leg, with every passing hour, looked more ominous. And we all, I think, began increasingly to feel the presence of death.

Vichuncho began muttering in a delirium. I laid my hand on his forehead: he had a very high fever. I could not understand what he was saying; I picked up only a word here and there. But Mashutaka told me that Vichuncho was talking about destiny—that this had to be. The Indians are very fatalistic. They believe that any action invokes a certain consequence; any decision they make will involve specific aftereffects, and there is nothing they can do to alter the course of events once the wheels have been set in motion. The tribe of Vichuncho and Mashutaka believe, in their old legends, that to have revealed the secret of the cueva was a transgression against the will of the spirits. Vichuncho in his delirium was reminding Mashutaka of this. And although Mashutaka, in his life at El Pigos, had adopted much of the Western man's way of thinking, he now was considering very seriously what Vichuncho said, and was slipping back into the old tribal thought patterns.

Suddenly Vichuncho grabbed my hand and said, "Cumpal . . . you go to Cumpal, across the river two days' walk, on the left bank up the Rio Paute. . . ." He was telling me where the cueva was. Then he fell silent.

The sky was now clear, the moon up, and we could again see the trail. Mashutaka agreed that we should set out immediately. We followed the trail all night long, and by mid-morning we had reached the banks of the Rio Paute. Vichuncho had lost so much blood that he looked like a dead man. But still he stayed on his horse and never said a word. He seemed to be made of iron. After Mashutaka scouted the bank and found a suitable place, we forded the river; from there we traveled on the narrow pica that ended on the dusty and unfinished road leading to Sucua. I hailed a passing truck and the driver agreed to drive Mashutaka, Vichuncho, and me to Sucua. Oswaldo would take the horses and mule to Mendes, and rejoin us in Sucua as soon as possible.

We reached Sucua late that night and pulled up before the Hospital Pius XII, a kilometer outside the town. There we were told that an Indian could not be admitted without the signature of the chief of the hospital. Unfortunately, the chief, Dr. Raoul Contreras, was not there. I left Mashutaka and Vichuncho outside and ran to his house. It took me half an hour to persuade him to come with me and admit Vichuncho. If Vichuncho had any blood left by the time we got some medical care for him, it would be a miracle.

Mashutaka and I slept that night in the nave of the Salesian church. When the bells began to resound for the first mass at six the following morning, I woke up, looked around, and saw that Mashutaka was already gone. I walked quickly to the hospital. Mashutaka was there at the door. I sensed he had been waiting for me. Before I could utter a word, he said: "Vichuncho is dead."

I stared at him, not wanting to believe that the worst had happened. But Mashutaka looked at me and repeated simply: "Vichuncho is dead."

Stunned, I walked into the hospital and asked to speak to Dr. Contreras. He seemed embarrassed when he told me that Vichuncho had died earlier that morning of tetanus. He said that in the Oriente tetanus develops very quickly and can be introduced through the smallest of wounds. As I walked out of the hospital, I felt very depressed. All my feelings of apprehension and foreboding had been justified.

The following day Oswaldo arrived from Mendes and

we discovered that the shock of Vichuncho's death had affected Mashutaka deeply. He had decided to abandon the
whole expedition. He was convinced that I would be able
to find the cueva alone, from the information Vichuncho
had related to me before his death. But he told us he
believed now in the legend. No amount of persuasion on
the part of Oswaldo and myself could convince him otherwise. He remained adamant in his conviction that Vichuncho had died because he broke the unwritten law that no
Jivaro should divulge the secrets of his territory. Vichuncho's death was no accident. He was so experienced in
traversing the trails and rivers of the Oriente that even
making allowances for the *chicha* he drank, his fall off that
rock should never have happened.

Mashutaka tried to dissuade me from pursuing the
search further. He felt that some new misfortune was
bound to happen. But, after I had insisted that it was too
important to abandon, he said the only thing he would do
was send a message to the Indian clan living near the Rio
Paute not to interfere with our passing through their territory.

I saw sadness in his eyes when, the morning after, we
said goodbye. We shared a deep anguish, an inner knowledge that our destinies had taken an unexpected turn.

"Will you ever be riding back to El Pigos?" he asked.

"I hope to one day," I replied.

"I'll be waiting." He turned slowly and walked away.

A tremendous uncertainty overwhelmed me. The
search for the cueva had been long, difficult, and disap-
pointing. And now tragedy had struck. Was Mashutaka
right? Would misfortune follow us if we pursued our
quest? Were the legends to be believed, and if so, had the
spell now been broken? Conflicting arguments kept running through my head all the way back to Cuenca. Nevertheless, when it was time for me to board the plane for
Miami, I had formed a decision. "We must gird ourselves
to continue the search alone," I said to Oswaldo. "We
have endured too much to give up now. Myth or fact, we
must try to solve this riddle."

He nodded in agreement as we shook hands.

CHAPTER 14

Encounter at the Rio Paute

I returned to Cuenca one month after Vichuncho's death, determined to continue my search for the mysterious cave even though our first expedition had ended in tragedy. The words that Vichuncho had uttered as he lay dying were the only directions I had to go on, and Mashutaka's warnings still echoed in my ears. My friend Oswaldo again agreed to accompany me, but he too had many doubts. "From what we know, no one has ever attempted to explore that territory," he said. "What if another accident should occur? Look what happened to Vichuncho—we will be alone and nobody will know or care." His arguments had merit. It was not easy to discount them, but I could not accept the idea of abandoning my search.

Oswaldo and I pored for hours over a stack of maps, both old and new, looking for clues—some assurance that the terrain had once been charted and that it was not after all so mysterious and unknown. But it was in vain. We could find no pica on any map, no indication that the place we were looking for even existed. If Oswaldo suspected that I had completely lost my sanity, he kept such thoughts to himself as we completed our preparations for the expedition and waited for the weather to clear. We would travel by Jeep northeast from Cuenca on a trail that follows the side of the sierra Yausay, through the small settlements of Pan and Chuplan, to the remote outpost of Cumpal. It was the village closest to the area of the Rio Paute that we intended to explore; but there, as

272

nearly as we could determine, the known trails and settlements came to an abrupt end.

The Jeep took us only as far as Chuplan along a trail that was dotted with *pantanos*—huge pools of mud—and often skirted the edges of steep precipices. The journey took two days and most of the way, either Oswaldo or I was forced to walk in front of the Jeep to guide it from going off the side of the mountain. When we finally reached Chuplan, it was with a sense of relief that we left it in care of the owner of the local *bodega* (grocery).

The next day, with the help of two Indian porters to carry our gear, we proceeded on foot in the direction of Cumpal. The trail ascended steadily through fog, wind, and the never-ending rain. Through an occasional hole in the clouds, patches of blue sky framed the black peaks of the mountains towering all around us. Loose rocks frequently rolling down from the slopes above staved off our temptation to take a break along the trail. Soaked, frustrated, and miserable, we kept going, and night had fallen by the time we struggled up the remaining 100 meters to Cumpal.

The Teniente Politico, Nello Flores, offered us the hospitality of his house, one of the seven thatched casas of this settlement. We gathered around a crackling fire his wife had lit to dry us, and Flores was a genial host. But when he learned we intended to proceed into the Rio Paute area, his reaction was very discouraging and negative. Not only was the weather forbidding, he said, but also the territory itself—even the Indians feared and avoided moving in that direction. Flores's deep-set black eyes were very serious as he continued: "There are many stories of Indians disappearing, with no one knowing why or where. I can put you in touch with a family of Indians living near Cumpal who lost two sons in that area." I asked him repeatedly to tell me the cause of all this fear and his answer was always the same. He was sure a very bad spirit lived there.

The next morning the fog and clouds had lifted and the land appeared very different in the light of the sun.

Scattered through the green vegetation were patches of bright flowers, and hovering over them the colorful *colibri* (hummingbirds) that feasted on their nectar. Flores, however, was sure that it would be cloudy and raining again by eleven o'clock. Somewhat disconcerted but determined to proceed, Oswaldo and I left the settlement with three newly found horses.

Flores's prediction proved correct. Before we had climbed 1000 meters out of Cumpal, black clouds covered the mountain and rain poured down again. We picked our way through an unreal world, unable to see a thing, leading our horses by sound only and the feel of the trail under our feet. Everything was strange and ghostly. Above, around, and below us lightning flashed through the clouds. It was an eerie sensation. There was no way of knowing whether we would be hit, no time even to think about it as we just kept pushing up the trail.

In the early afternoon a thatched hut appeared through the clouds, seemingly hanging from the side of the mountain above us. And in front of it, peering through the veiled mist, was a man holding a shotgun. His name was Gonzales Cruz, the only inhabitant of this isolated, silent corner of the Andes called Paradero, where beams of sunlight rarely pierced the clouds to light the darkened shape of the jungle below. We were the first outsiders to have reached this place in years, and as we took the horses around to the rear of the hut, Cruz showed us the grave of a gringo he said had been killed by the Indians in 1958. From far below, we heard the muffled sound of a cataract that revealed the presence of the swift waters of the Rio Paute.

That evening, we shared a bottle of trago around the fire in a room filled with bales of seed, stacks of machetes, blankets, and rubber boots. Hanging on the wall were dozens of muzzle-loader shotguns. Cruz traded with the Indians and was familiar with their tales. At least we wanted to believe so. He told us that there were at least seven caves in the area we intended to explore, but no one dared enter any of them. Cruz believed there were crea-

View from Paradero.

tures living in the caves that attacked Indians and ate their flesh. He himself had heard many times a powerful howl in the night that was certainly not human. Looking up at the image of the Virgin Mary hanging on the wall, Cruz crossed himself and said he didn't like to talk about such things. And with that he emptied his glass and walked to the next room. Oswaldo and I gulped one more trago and lay down by the fire to sleep, with Cruz's tales hanging heavily in the stillness of the night.

When we awoke the next morning, Paradero was still floating in a sea of clouds, and as the hours passed, rain squalls grew more frequent. Cruz told us that we would be faced with increasing rain, mud, and unseen dangers if we attempted to reach the area of the caves. He believed, however, that in three or four weeks this constant downpour would eventually lessen into daily showers and conditions would be more favorable. Oswaldo and I decided to follow Cruz's advice, and when we left Paradero to return to Cumpal, we told him to expect us back in about a month. We had penetrated this far and now knew some of the hazards facing us. But we discounted his tales of man-eating creatures in the caves. If the natives were afraid to venture into the area, it was probably due to some other inexplicable incidents that had occurred there. Their fears may have been justified for some reason, but they did not alter our decision to search for the caves.

Oswaldo and I had no sooner arrived back in Cumpal when the news reached us that one of the bridges on the trail to Pan had collapsed and God knew when it would be repaired. We could not return to Cuenca by that route; after studying my map and other information, we decided to set out for Sucua. To the east the weather was improving steadily and an expedition to the Cordillera Cutucu and Quinta, site of the pyramidal tola Father Botazzo had mentioned, seemed to be the next logical step to take. I had never forgotten Father Botazzo's description of this pyramid and I was anxious to learn if such a structure actually existed. Moreover, the low pre-Andean range of the Cordillera Cutucu could yield important clues to population movements and possible migration routes in early times.

We made it to Sucua after a painful three days, crossing a landscape that alternated between dense mountain jungle and stark volcanic soil sparsely covered with yellow thorn shrubs where deadly spiders, the size of a fist, were lurking for an unwitting prey. Once in Sucua, on the advice of Raphael Garcia, the SAM dispatcher at the Puyomo airstrip who was by now an old friend, we decided to hire Samburasa, a member of the Jimbiquitir Jivaro clan, as our guide into the Cordillera Cutucu. Samburasa was skeptical of our plans. He must have been in his fifties, his intelligent face marked with tribal tattoos—miniature stylized butterfly wings—and fringed by unusually long black hair. After I had explained where we wanted to go, he looked impassively at us, pondering what he had just heard. "There might be a risk of confrontation with Indians that live there," he said finally, spitting on the ground. "They dislike strangers, especially white ones who are always trying to grab their land." Again he spat. It was his way of punctuating any comment that in his mind was important.

We were finally able to convince Samburasa that we were not land-grabbers and he agreed to leave with us the following day for Quinta—provided we could find fresh horses. That was not such an easy task even for the resourceful Oswaldo. That evening, as we ate our meal at a hostel, he initiated a chat with the daughter of the owner, a heavyset mestizo girl. When, at ten o'clock, the village generator was turned off and the lights went out, I left and went upstairs to our room. Oswaldo persevered with the girl in the romantic glow of candlelight until three in the morning, perhaps telling her how things are with gentlemen of adventure in the great world beyond. In the morning, when we arose, Oswaldo said, "I have the horses," and vouchsafed nothing more.

All went well on the first day of our journey into the Cordillera Cutucu, with the exception of an unexpected encounter, after fording the Rio Upano, with a hungry brown bear that frightened our horses. Only after we had fired several shots in the air did he decide to change direction. On the second day, by noon, after following Samburasa on a scarcely recognizable track, we reached the high ridge of the Cordillera Cutucu, and from this altitude (1800 meters), we could view the endless basin of the Amazon to the east, while to the west, in the midday haze, loomed the massif of the central Andean cordilleras. By late afternoon we had crossed the divide and descended the eastern slope where, on the south side of the pica, a small garden of cassavas, yucca, and banana trees betrayed the presence of an Indian compound. We followed the path through the garden to a clearing where three chosas stood, all empty. There were no dogs and only a few chickens scattered as we walked. But a burning log inside one of the chosas told us that the owner was not too far away.

Suddenly the usual late afternoon tropical rain came down in a deluge. We took refuge in an open thatched shed with our horses, and decided to camp there until morning. But that evening Oswaldo became ill with severe stomach pains and vomiting. By morning his condition had improved but not enough to continue. The sun was well up when furious barking dogs ran into the compound and we found ourselves facing a group of Jivaro—the men carrying muzzle-loader shotguns and the women

young babies on their backs. The encounter was very
guarded at first; we kept our firearms in clear view as they
approached. Samburasa spoke to them in their dialect and
learned that they were the owners of the chosas. We explained to the oldest, Suasy, that Oswaldo was ill and that
we had spent the night here. He, after consulting with the
others, said we were welcome.

Samburasa then asked if Suasy knew of a place called
Quinta. The Indians exchanged a few words among
themselves, then Suasy nodded and, with the classic gesture of his arm sweeping across half the horizon, said
something to Samburasa which he translated as *"Para
allá!"* I decided to show him one of the small stone pieces
I had received from Father Botazzo and asked if he had
ever seen similar ones. Suasy took it, and the Indians
looked at it with curiosity, chattering among themselves.
Then with Samburasa explaining, I drew on the ground
with my knife a truncated pyramid, the kind Father Botazzo had said existed near Quinta. The Indians looked at
my sketch and again began very excitedly to talk among
themselves and ask questions of Samburasa. Finally I could
stand the suspense no longer and yelled at Samburasa,
"What the hell are they saying?"

Translating as fast as he could, he said they wanted to
know how I had learned of the existence of such a tola.
They had never seen me before; how could I have seen it
without their knowledge?

I was stunned by their reaction. It meant that such a
truncated pyramid did indeed exist in the Oriente. As the
Indians continued talking to Samburasa, I tried to contain
my excitement. But then he turned to me and explained
what the Indians had said. "For many, many years a big
tola, like the one you drew, stood near Quinta plateau.
But about five years ago it was swept away and flattened
by torrential rainfalls and huge landslides."

I felt a tremendous sense of disappointment and frus-
tration, faced again with the destructive force of the inter-
minable rain, mudslides, and earthquakes so prevalent in
this land. How many other such tolas, I wondered, had

been lost to these natural disasters? Nevertheless, I wanted to study the site where the tola once stood; there might be vestiges left that would throw some light on its ancient builders. We asked Suasy if he would provide someone to guide us, and to my delight, he said he would be happy to take us there personally. Reassured that Oswaldo would be safe and watched over by Suasy's family, we set out immediately.

Four hours later we reached the Rio Pindu-Yacu, and after hiking along its west bank for at least another half hour, we arrived at the union of the Pindu-Yacu with the narrow Rio Pixana. As we stepped onto the open shelf between the two rivers, Suasy stopped, and with a semicircular motion of his arms said, "This is the place where the tola was washed away by the big flood years ago."

I looked at the grassy area around me. It was quite evident that it had gone through a drastic change in the recent past. The vegetation covering the terrain in the Y between the two rivers was young. There were no large trees or old underbrush, and it was difficult to imagine that a large tola had once stood on this site. But as I looked to the south, I could see that if a potent spiritual site was to have been selected for the erection of a tola, this would have been the perfect place. The valley cut between two cordilleras of the Cutucu, the Occidental that we had just crossed, and the Oriental, the last mountain range separating us from the Amazon Basin. And on the floor of the valley a large river snaked across its lush vegetation like a huge boa constrictor, slowly disappearing into the endless jungle beyond. The promontory on which we stood seemed to be floating in space between these two enigmatic ranges. It was a beautiful, awesome sight.

I explained to Samburasa and Suasy what we should look for—anything carved, anything with markings or designs—and we began to search, hacking our way through a tangle of jungle growth. We prodded for hours and it began to seem that after such a lapse of time, flood waters, and landslides, there was little hope of finding anything. But then, as we approached the eastern perimeter of the shelf, almost hidden by the heavy underbrush, I saw a group of boulders. Something about the way they were lying together caught my attention. I crawled down a few meters to them and called Suasy and Samburasa to come help me. We moved three of the boulders, stabbing and digging through the dirt underneath. But it was not until we moved the fourth boulder that I prodded something, and as soon as my fingers felt it, I knew it was not just a stone. I retrieved it from the dirt, brushed it off, and slowly the details became clear and alive.

Front and back views of figure carved from green stone. Quinta.

It was a small composite sculpture carved from a block of green stone. On one side was the figure of a seated man, with the features (square nose, heavy mouth, and oval eyes) typical of such pieces; but his face was upturned and he held to his chin a strange-shaped object that I could not identify at first. Later finds of similar figures would show conclusively, however, that this object was the representation of a bamboo, flutelike instrument. On the other side, a horned head of an animal was sculpted with the same blunt characteristics of the human face. Its front legs were elaborated into two small human figures, and circling the base of the entire piece was a caiman, a creature similar in appearance to a crocodile and one of the most important mythic animals in the Amazon. Beneath its tail was a small, lizard-like animal with a scaly spine, something like an iguana.

I could scarcely contain my excitement as I turned the piece over in my hands. And as this excitement transmitted itself to my two companions, in an emotional outburst, we started to laugh and slap each other on the back. We had found something important, and my companions now seemed to understand why I was making this search. I was particularly interested in the representation of the caiman, for its incorporation at the base of the piece was not only an indication that this animal was one of the fundamental mythic figures in the consciousness of an ancient stone-carving people but also that they were carrying on the tradition of the low Amazon, the natural habitat of the caiman. This legacy can be seen in the later cosmogony of both the Olmecs and the early Chavin culture of Peru, where in the beginning the universe was represented by a great caiman suspended in a sea that had no boundaries, and as such, embraced both constructive and destructive universal forces, the spirit of death as well as all the life-giving energies. Later, the great caiman became transformed into two dieties, which directed and moved all the events of the world. The first of these deities was the worldly caiman, associated with all the fertile forces of the sea and the land. The second deity was metamorphosed into a creature of the sky: a great predatory bird like the eagle or condor, the most awesome and powerful winged animals that are known in all the Americas. Further, as a figure of fundamental potency, the caiman became the character symbol for the first day of the ancient Mesoamerican calendar.

Stone fertility effigy. Quinta.

In the following days, as we dug into the Quinta plateau and became thoroughly familiar with it, our labors were often rewarded. The lack of heavy tools dictated the choice of places to dig, but I noticed that on the east side of the plateau these seemed to be the eroded remains of small mounds. They were covered by heavy underbrush and old tree stumps, and it was apparent that the trees that had once grown over the mounds had helped destroy them. Digging to remove the web of ancient roots, we discovered a number of carved stone pieces, one of which was a small fertility effigy showing two anthropomorphic figures in a position of copulation, a piece whose concept was strikingly similar to the stone carving I had discovered at San Jose. Another was a small offertory figure with an upturned face, holding a cup or ceremonial vessel at his chin. The nose and brow of the face were formed by a shape strongly suggestive of an ax, and this motif, combined with the offertory pose and the vessel held below the chin, reinforced my belief in the significance of the ax as a spiritual implement rather than merely a utilitarian one.

Stone figure with ax-shaped brow holding vessel. Quinta.

As we continued our search, I was puzzled by the lack of evidence of human remains. Perhaps this plateau had

Human skull. Quinta.

been used for ceremonial purposes only, rather than as a burial ground. But then one day, digging at the foot of a small cliff on the northwest side of the plateau, we exposed a crevice. It was low and narrow, and only by digging on my knees was I able to probe inside. Little by little, I withdrew rock debris and splinters of wood, carefully sifting the loose earth. Bits of bone came to light and when I dug further, I uncovered two small stone amulets. Their presence left no doubt that I was digging in an ancient grave. Excited by that discovery, I continued to probe deeper. My trowel struck something hard and I began to dig with my fingers. Suddenly I uttered a cry: I had discovered a skull, a human skull.

Slowly and very carefully I extracted the precious find, and when I examined it, the skull gave every appearance of being very old. I would later submit specimens from the skull to Dr. Jeffrey L. Bada, a geochemist at the Scripps Institution of Oceanography, University of California, who confirmed my belief that it was indeed very old (see Appendix).*

---

* Dr. Bada had discovered a new dating method—amino acid racemization—that did not require, as did the carbon-14 dating technique, the destruction of the entire specimen to provide enough samples for analysis. This method was based on the racemization (process of change) of the L-amino acid isomers found in living protein to the D-form after death. The rate of racemization can be measured and, hence, the age of an organism calculated.

When I again turned my attention to the amulets, I discovered that one of them had a lanyard hole and was carved with faces with the now-familiar blunt features, and a curious round patterned area on the chest below one face. The other amulet was in the shape of a human foot, with a carved bird head in place of the ankle. I pondered the significance of this piece for a long time. I reasoned that in ancient times any walk beyond the confines of a person's own immediate territory represented an event. It was never undertaken lightly and was always charged with significance. The representation of a bird, a creature that travels with such ease, fused with a human foot, was perhaps thought to bestow safety on its owner as he made a journey.

Carved stone amulet. Quinta.

Studying the unusual foot amulet, another thought came to mind. During my investigation of the coastal plain I had seen a variety of small vessels in the form of a foot, and these pots, found throughout South and Central America, serve to hold the juice of the lime, or powdered dried lime, which is taken along with coca to cut their bitter taste. Today, as in ancient times, the Indians chew coca leaves to provide them with strength and endurance on the trail. Thus these vessels, as with the Quinta amulet, probably represented a talismanic bestowal of the power necessary to complete a journey safely. The tradition of the foot-vessel spread to the later cultures both south and north of Ecuador, and, in time, its shapes changed to represent the feet of animals as well as human feet in various footwear.

Foot amulet. Quinta.

I was exhilarated by our discoveries on the Quinta plateau, restless with excitement, but too mentally and physically exhausted to untangle the many conjectures that were knotted deep in my mind. A pattern seemed to be emerging, but my discoveries were not yet sufficient to explain at once the significance of the menhirs of the Machenga range and the stone pieces from San Jose, Namangosa, Raranga, and now Quinta. Moreover, it was time to leave Quinta and return to Paradero for our rendezvous with Gonzales Cruz and another attempt to find the caves of the Rio Paute. I was still troubled by the un-

Pot in the shape of a human foot. Bahía.

certainties and dangers of the trip, but with such great success at Quinta, perhaps my luck would change at last.

Oswaldo and I returned to Sucua, pausing there only long enough to replenish our supplies, leave our findings with Raphael Garcia for safekeeping, and wait for the weather to clear before we set out for Paradero. When we finally arrived, and I spotted the lonely hut high on top of the mountain through a break in the clouds, I saw that our friend Cruz was again standing in front of it, firearm in hand. He shook our hands with his powerful grip and seemed glad to see us. Sitting around a fire in his hut that evening, Cruz told us that he had remembered an old Indian pica that led directly to another of the many places called "La Unión" where the Rio Balata enters the Rio Shiru. He said that this pica would greatly shorten our journey and he would guide us to La Unión, but he would go no further. His swarthy face then had a puzzled look as he mentioned that to his amazement it had been reported to him the Indians were already aware that we would be moving through their territory and that we were *tamay* (protected). I sensed from his gaze that he expected some explanation. As simply as possible, without elaboration, I said to him: "A Jivaro cacique has passed the word of our coming." Mashutaka had kept his promise.

We were on our way by 6:30 the next morning. It was a wet and somber day, but Cruz guided us skillfully through the mist and the mud of a series of narrow trails to the old pica that would take us directly to La Unión. It snaked up the wall of a steep canyon, and in order to climb it, we had to dismount and pull our horses up behind us. We reached a high, rocky plateau nestled just below Picco Chiumpi by late afternoon, and with darkness coming very quickly we decided to camp there for the night. Tomorrow, barring something unexpected, we should be at the cueva.

The tension and anticipation I felt kept my eyes from closing as I lay in my sleeping bag by the fire. The darkness was still and unseeing, the peace broken only by the mingling cries of the night creatures and the rhythmic beating of intermittent squalls on our tarpaulin shelter. Thoughts and images kept turning in my mind. Was it a coincidence that there were said to be seven caves in this area and the legendary *Chicomoztoc* (Place of the Seven Caves) mentioned as the place of origin of the ancient Mixtec and Zapotec peoples from the valley of Oaxaca, Mexico? Curiously, they also called themselves the "Cloud People" as, traditionally, the Indians living in this cloud-covered part of the Andes are also called.

What would we find tomorrow, I wondered; what would we see when we entered the cave? Caves all over the world have been discovered to be rich repositories of the art and artifacts of ancient peoples. And I remembered that Vichuncho had said his cave was the "guardian" of the past and its contents spoke of his people's ancestry. Now so close to the end of my search, I wondered if Vichuncho had not merely been repeating the old legends, and if I had not exaggerated their importance.

Next morning at the crack of dawn, we broke camp and soon reached La Unión, a savage but beautiful sight. As the Rios Balata and Shiru came together, they formed a spectacular waterfall at least 30 meters high before gushing down into an enormous cataract below. The roar was earsplitting and an atmosphere of unreality was created by the rising mist, which reflected all the colors of the rainbow. We threaded our way carefully down the bank to a place well below the cataract where the river could be forded safely. Cruz pointed out the vestige of a trail on the opposite bank and warned us not to trust the apparent placidness of the water; it hid a treacherous river bottom full of deep, dangerous holes. Then he said goodbye. As Oswaldo and I pushed our horses into the water, we heard him yell: *"Vaya con Dios, amigos!"*

We crossed the river without difficulty and began to pick our way through a canyon on a track that was no longer even a pica; it was just a slight, irregular line of different color over the rocks and through the mud. In places the canyon wall was almost vertical and it was an arduous effort for the horses to move ahead. The rain that had started early in the afternoon was coming down more heavily than before as we forded the turbulent currents of the torrent Chanci and heard the roar of the sweeping waters of the Rio Paute. Then suddenly, as we skirted a vertical cliff and rounded a bend on the trail, the entrance to the cueva loomed ahead of us. It was partially obstructed by loose rocks and debris that had fallen from the slope above, and all but hidden by a tangle of dangling lianas and creepers. We jolted to a stop and sat there on our horses, looking at it, almost hypnotized. We had reached our destination.

The only refuge from the downpour was the cueva. Oswaldo turned his glance to mine and without a word, almost in unison, we dismounted, tied our horses to a tree well below the cave, and started to clear the entrance with our machetes. I then dropped through the narrow opening to the ground inside, which was covered with rotting leaves and thick humus between lumps of dark and reddish stones shining here and there. I found myself in a small tunnel, able to stand upright at the far end where a heap of rubble nearly barred the passageway. Daylight penetrated not more than 15 meters of the passageway before it was swallowed up by the darkness beyond. Oswaldo, after passing the packs to me over the opening, joined me inside, and we stood there together for a moment, incredulous that we had finally found the mysterious cueva.

Then we began to look carefully around. Seen from within, the mouth of the cave seemed trapezoidal and the walls too regular and well formed to be a natural opening, but it was too dark to tell for sure. We pulled out our flashlights, but they did very little to dispel the blackness of the passageway. When we crawled over the rubble barrier, a stinking smell assailed us and, remembering Vichuncho's warning, we decided we had better check the interior of the cave further before settling ourselves in the passageway for the night.

I motioned to Oswaldo to come with me. Slowly we began to follow our beams of light into the darkness. The tunnel increased in height to at least 5 meters and surprisingly the air was not stagnant, but the smell seemed to grow more pungent. At times we stopped to listen, straining our ears to catch any sound that might betray what lay ahead. A ceaseless dripping was the only noise we heard. The uneven floor was scattered with rubble, rocks, boulders, and puddles of water. As we walked ahead slowly, our tension began to build, and no matter how we tried to control the impulse, our hands kept going to the grips of our guns. Oswaldo didn't say a word—his throat must have been as dry as mine. We could almost hear our hearts beat in this awesome silence.

We kept walking when, abruptly, my flashlight beam fell on a rock wall stretching across the tunnel directly ahead of us. "My God!" I thought. "After all this, the famous cueva turns out to be nothing but a small passage." But then, as we approached the wall, we saw that the tunnel took a sharp bend to the right. We made the turn, stopped, and directed our lights ahead of us. There we saw what appeared to be tracks of something having been dragged along the floor—a bear dragging his prey perhaps. Oswaldo was saying something, but I could not understand him. He was mumbling, not realizing that the sounds he made were not words, just sounds. We moved carefully along the right wall of the passageway as quietly as possible for about 25 meters. Then, suddenly, the tunnel opened up into what we sensed to be a huge chamber. We hesitated, hands on our guns, wondering whether to enter, our backs pressed against the safety of the wall. We stood there beaming our lights in all directions, unable to perceive the dimensions of this enormous black hole. There was no sound. After a few moments, we relaxed our nerves by lighting cigarettes.

This curious hiatus of darkness and silence must have lasted less than five minutes when it happened: an incredible, blood-curdling, howling roar, louder than the sound any man could make, coming from the depths of the cave. Then a crescendo of howls and paralyzing screams, higher in pitch and more intense. We stood there rooted with fear, our hearts hammering, staring in horror at the barrier of blackness, our lights making erratic patterns on the floor.

Oswaldo grabbed my arm and I felt a penetrating pain in my muscle. I tried to react, but then, amid the terrifying screams, a boulder smashed against the wall close to where we were standing. It crashed and splintered, jolting me out of my trance. In control of myself again, instinctively I dropped one of the flashlights to the ground, knowing it would continue to attract the attention of whatever was there, and leaped to the left. Oswaldo, still stunned, did not follow me. I shouted to him but he didn't move. Then he suddenly reacted; he pulled his gun out of his belt and with a yell started shooting into the darkness. The sounds of screaming and gunshots echoed through the cave as more boulders spun through the air and smashed against the wall. All the while Oswaldo kept shouting and stopped firing only when his gun was empty.

The howls continued as we fled, retracing our steps to the sharp bend in the passageway. But before we rounded it, I looked back toward the light left behind on the ground, trying to control my breathing and my heart's furious pounding. A tall, lumbering silhouette flashed across the shaft of light. The howls now became more intense, reverberating through the cave, and Oswaldo and I began to run toward the faint light of the entrance, splashing through the pools of water, losing our footing, stumbling over the rocks and rubble strewn in our path. At last—Oswaldo first, with me close behind—we reached the opening, grabbed our packs, and scrambled over the debris to the outside.

There I stopped and looked back. The roars and ear-splitting howls continued from within, then suddenly, silence. I looked at my watch. It read 4:25 P.M. And then I realized that tightly clenched in my hand was a small carved stone. I must have seen it one of the times I fell in the passageway and grabbed it instinctively.

When I turned around, Oswaldo was already on his horse racing down the trail. I wasted no time securing my pack, then followed him on my own horse, scrambling back down through the canyon. But it was not until after fording the Chanci and climbing up on the opposite bank that I finally caught up with him. I had somehow managed to conquer my fear during our hasty retreat, but Oswaldo was still in the grip of terror. He sat on his saddle, powerless to control his trembling and shivering, his wild eyes fixed in the direction of the cave. I looked closely at him and saw that a streak of his hair had a new color, light gray, almost white. I pulled him gently by the arm and told him softly, "Go ahead; we are not going back in again." He gazed at me, gave an almost imperceptible shrug, then, without a word, turned his mount and slowly started back along the pica that would eventually take us to the house of Cruz in Paradero.

We again spent the night just below the Picco Chiumpi, and after securing the horses and stretching the tarpaulin, I was able to kindle a small fire. The comforting smell of fresh coffee helped relieve some of our tension, but we had no desire to eat or sleep. We both sat staring at the fire, clinging to our warm cups, jerking at every unusual sound. Time seemed to be suspended. Surely it had all been a horrible nightmare. But we had been there; we knew it was reality. Yet who would ever believe that it had really happened, that it was not just a figment of our imaginations?

Jadeite amulet. Cueva de Rio Paute.

It was still too early for us to speculate about what we had discovered; we were too preoccupied with the experience to deal rationally with it. But in the recesses of my mind, abruptly, I recalled the small, carved stone I had picked up in the cave. I examined it closely by the light of the fire and noticed for the first time that it was green. It was a jadeite amulet depicting a soulful human face expertly carved on the surface of a stylized axblade. It had been a terrifying experience, yes, but I knew now for certain that there was something very important inside that cave.

It was the early afternoon of the next day when, with tremendous relief, we saw Cruz's house through the mist. But no barking dogs announced our arrival. The place was deserted, and we decided to continue on our way to Cumpal. There we found both Cruz and Flores. They were astonished to see us, but as we ate a nourishing dinner of pork and rice, they asked not one question, even though I knew they were eagerly waiting to hear what had happened to us. After dinner, over a bottle of trago, I began to relate the whole adventure, and as I talked I knew that my story would eventually reach the ears of every Indian in the area, adding immeasurably to their fear of the caves of the Rio Paute. Oswaldo fell asleep before I was halfway through the story; when I lay down later and saw his slumbering face, I hoped that the soul-scarring experience had not broken the spirit of my friend.

Early the next morning, after an icy, invigorating shower under a small waterfall nearby, we sat down to share breakfast with Flores and Cruz. It was then that Cruz suggested we take a route back to Cuenca that would bypass Chuplan, as the bridge was still down on the way to Pan. Cruz returned to Paradero, but Flores offered to travel with us as far as Gurainag where we hoped to find some kind of transportation back to Cuenca. We set off on a pica that zigzagged upward toward a high mountain pass, the morning mist so thick that I could see nothing other than the white tail of Oswaldo's horse not more than 10 meters in front of me. Just before noon, after we had crossed a very narrow passage between two mountains, our horses suddenly stopped in their tracks, uttering loud neighs. As I tried to rein in my mount and calm him down, I noticed that Oswaldo and Flores were also in the same predicament and it flashed through my mind that the horses had felt the presence of some wild animal or a snake further up the pica. Then suddenly, with a deafening roar, rocks and debris started rolling down from the slopes above, the earth trembled, and Flores shouted: *"Terremoto!* (Earthquake!)"

We quickly dismounted. Flores and Oswaldo, pulling their horses, ran toward a huge rock overhang on a bend of the pica further up. The tremors became more violent and I tried to pull my horse ahead quickly, but the packs he was carrying scraped against the wall of rock that bordered the narrow pica on one side and there was no room for him to maneuver. Rocks were now crashing down very close. I dropped the horse's reins and ran ahead to take shelter under the overhang with Flores and Oswaldo. It was then that the mountain trembled violently and a landslide of rocks and earth swept across the pica from above. I looked down the trail and saw only two horses. My horse was gone.

As abruptly as the earthquake started, it stopped, and we cautiously moved out of our refuge. I walked to the edge of the precipice and, peering over it, saw far below, perhaps 100 meters down, my horse crushed to death on a rocky streambank. The packs he was carrying had split open and my cameras, film, and gear had all been swept away by the raging current. I stood there stunned, chilled with horror. Every record of our expeditions to Quinta and the cave of the Rio Paute had been destroyed. There was no time for regret. Flores took my arm and said, "We have to leave immediately. There may be more landslides."

With only two horses for the three of us, we had to take turns until we reached the pass and began our descent. Then I climbed up behind Flores and as we rode, my mind went back to the terrifying sounds of the crashing boulders and howls I had heard inside the cueva. Perhaps there was another explanation for that experience. I asked Flores if he had felt any tremors two days previously. Thinking for a moment, he nodded, and said, "The land trembles quite often here." Then, in an ironic aside, he added, "God has not yet decided what to do with our land. That is why it has yet to settle down." I wondered then if we had not, by a mere stroke of fate, entered the cueva at a most inopportune time. Perhaps whatever beasts were there had sensed the tremors and had been fleeing in terror when they were unexpectedly confronted by our presence. As I was pondering this, the howling pitch of their screams reverberated again in my head. I had heard it before, but where? Then I remembered. Of course, on the Chiquao plateau in Venezuela from the creature known as *el Mono Grande*.

We reached the village of Gurainag without further mishap, but we had to linger there for two days waiting for transportation to Cuenca, in one way grateful for the time. The stress of our expedition had taken its toll. On the morning that Oswaldo and I left, we were saddened to have to say goodbye to our new friend, Flores. We wanted to pay him for the lost horse, but he adamantly refused, saying that the earthquake was the wish of God and we were not responsible for that.

It took one week for the pack of specimens we had left with Raphael Garcia in Puyomo to arrive in Cuenca. At the same time a very important event occurred. Oswaldo's father invited all the family, and myself, to the best restaurant in town for a special celebration. Everyone wondered at the reason for his invitation; not a birthday or an anniversary, past or present, was in sight. But at the appointed time all the guests were present, dressed in their finest. The food was superb and the Chilean wine served at the right temperature. I could sense, however, that the entire family would soon collapse from exhaustion and tension if the host didn't say something.

Finally, the tall figure of Señor Mora stood up at the head of the table, his thumbs in the pockets of his vest and his eyes scanning the expectant faces of his family. He cleared his throat, then announced, "I have bought a business, a travel agency, and Oswaldo will be the manager!" The suspense was broken. Applause, congratulations, good wishes, and *abrazos*—Oswaldo was the hero of the moment. The family head had spoken, and the family had approved.

A few days later at Cuenca airport on my way to Quito, Oswaldo and I sadly shook hands for the last time. For him, his adventures in the mountains of the Oriente were ended. Considering what we had been through together, I regretted that our parting had come so suddenly and before we had discovered reasonable proof of the ideas he had also come to believe in. But I wished him well in his new venture.

When I returned to Quito, I visited the National Library to see if, by chance, there were any old newspaper accounts of strange events similar to our encounter in the

Oriente. Dusty yellow papers were stacked against the walls all the way to the ceiling; they were not filed in order or indexed, and I found nothing. But the next day at a cocktail party given by my old friend Major David McLaughlin, attached to the U.S. Military Mission in Quito, I met Colonel Oswaldo Espinoza, an officer in the Ecuadorian army. I told him of my experience in the cueva and he showed no amazement. "From time to time reports are received from the Oriente of Indians that have disappeared, and of animal screams and howls during the night," he said to my surprise. Occasionally, such accounts appeared in official reports but, he emphasized, he did not know of any stating that someone had actually seen one of the "beasts." "They may be just the superstitions of the Indians," he said with a smile.

That was the official opinion; but for me the reality was there in a cave near the Rio Paute and my terrifying encounter remained vivid in my memory. True, I was tired out, tired of rain and mud and all the risks I had run with no reward. Death had passed me very close, and now my friend Oswaldo had left me. I had the urge to walk away and never set foot again on this land. But my despair always receded when I looked again at the mysterious jadeite amulet I had found in the cave. Its ax-shaped form stood out vividly, and the sadness of a doomed race was reflected in the face carved in the polished green stone. Who were the ancient people who had carved this beautiful piece? Thus the least expected discovery triggered my strength and desire to continue my quest.

PART V

Legacy of the Ancients

CHAPTER 15

The Andeolithics

Early one morning in May of 1972, Henrique Euse and I left Quito behind and were driving south. Our first destination was Ambato, capital of Tungurahua Province, and as we traveled along the road, Henrique tried to control his Latin temper while maneuvering his Jeep through the maze of traffic bringing produce to the Quito markets. Short, lean, and square-shouldered, he was an engaging young man who spoke English quite well. But his shy and reserved manner was the antithesis of the flamboyant Oswaldo. We had met a few years before and had become good friends. In the year since Oswaldo and I parted company, he had occasionally joined me on my travels to break the monotonous existence, he had said, of life on his family's hacienda.

The past year had been a very profitable one for me. My search had taken a new direction when Serafin Correa, a landowner from Pillaro—a small town north of the Pastaza Valley on the slopes of the strange and forbidding range of the Llanganates in the province of Tungurahua—told me that a carved stone representation of a corncob had been recovered from an ancient burial mound in the nearby Huagrahuasi Mountain. The implications of such a find were far-reaching. For the only reference to maize cultivation in the uplands of the sierra that I was aware of had come from Jijon y Caamaño, the Ecuadorian investigator of the early 1900s, who reported that in one excavation in the Pillaro area, which he labeled

297

Ceramic figurines representing a parrot (top), an iguana (center), and a caiman (bottom). Tungurahua.

the Panzaleo culture, he had uncovered corn seeds in a refuse pit of an ancient settlement. Without doubt, an artifact that depicted a corncob indicated that cultivation of a dependable food staple had been known and relied upon by an ancient people living high in the sierra. And if this was so, it could explain the cultural development and expansion of the Chorrera people, mountain dwellers of the Andes, who had reached a spectacular level of achievement earlier than any other culture in the Americas.

Consequently, I decided to investigate the Tungurahua region, and when I visited Correa at his home in Pillaro, he took me into a large room containing a most impressive collection of vases, statues, bowls and plates, whistles, pipes and amulets, including the tiny stone representation of a corncob I had come to see. I was struck by the profusion of styles of the artifacts in his collection. Many of the bowls and vases were painted with the same iridescent schema—ocher, red, and black—that I had seen in the artifacts of the Chorrera culture, and would see again in many other sites of the Oriente, and north in the Rio Pisco area. There were also a number of ceramic figurines of unfamiliar creatures with a strange, very distinctive quality. They were not painted, although some were glazed. Most of the animals, interestingly, were depictions of creatures of the Amazon rain forest—parrots, caimans, monkeys, and jaguars; others seemed to depict prehistoric animals.

Serafin Correa's collection was not unique in the region. His friend Cesar Piedra had even more pieces. Piedra's land lay to the northwest, further up the slopes of the Huicotango (part of the great mountain system of the Llanganates) above San Jose de Poalo, and closer to the pass leading eastward into the Llanganates. Where Correa was able to pack his collection into one room, Piedra needed a barn. During the years he had been digging, he told me that probably as many as 20,000 pieces had passed through his hands. "Whenever we put down a shovel," he said, "we come up with *infieles*." The abun-

dance of pieces in his collection showed, indubitably, the richness of the Tungurahua region, and many of them showed stylistic traits of the Chorrera culture. I was particularly interested in the stone pieces in his collection. The oval shape and characteristic features of so many of them, whether they were sculptures with a single image or multiple figures, were similar to the carved stone pieces I had seen from the south. That there was a relationship could scarcely be doubted.

Most of the pieces I had seen in both these areas were carved from stones found in abundance in riverbeds or in exposed geological stratas at all elevations of the Andean mountain ranges. Early sculptors apparently found a ready-made shape in these oval stones. An ancient legend of the Andes recounts that one day in the distant past, the Creator became disenchanted with the continuous strife among his children on earth, and during a big storm he changed the hail into round and oval stones to punish them. Many died, but those who survived changed their ways and began to carve on the stones from heaven the images of those who no longer were there. To the shaman, the stones became the recipient of the forces of the universe, and ever since then they have been used in healing rituals.

Ovoid stone sculptures. Tungurahua.

I learned that some of the pieces I saw in collections in the Tungurahua area had come from shaft tombs. Many others came from small tolas, which often had the major burial in the center, or from larger tolas whose burials were always around the base, possibly indicating that a kind of shrine or funerary monument had once stood at the top. Strange funerary figures with an abstracted torso formed of a spiral or ringed shaft were also uncovered in many of the burials; and later, significantly, I was to see comparable stone funerary pieces in the south Oriente.

The abundance and concentration in a single area of all these pieces seemed to provide further substantiation for my belief that a stone-carving culture had evolved in this region with its roots in the Amazon Basin. For most of the

Funerary shaft figure. Tungurahua/Pillaro area.

artifacts had come from a triangular area lying between
San Andres, a small settlement a few kilometers north of
Pillaro; Poalo, lying northeast higher on the slopes of the
Huicotango; and Laguna Yambo, lying west on the far
side of the Rio Cutuchi. And Poalo is situated at the entrance of a pass through the Huicotango, one of the two
passes into the Llanganates, the other being further
south, along the Rio Verde Chico deep in the valley of
Tungurahua, not far from Baños. Both routes of access
join together to become one with the valley of the Rio Pastaza, which eventually empties into the Amazon Basin.

Now Henrique and I were on the trail of another clue.
His aunt, Doña Aida Euse, had invited us to her hacienda
to see her collection of artifacts, among them a ceramic
representation of a corncob. We also planned further investigations in the Tungurahua region. But our first step
was Ambato, and the convent of the Josefinos Order,
where there was a large collection of artifacts from many
locales throughout the Tungurahua region and the Napo
area in Oriente on display.

Dr. Alfredo Lorio, the unofficial keeper of the collection, welcomed us when we arrived at the convent. An ar-
ticulate and cooperative man, his deep interest in the past
of his country was evident as he showed us around. He
confirmed that the Cutuchi Valley, down to the Rio Pastaza, was very rich in artifacts. Moreover, there was abundant evidence of a very old culture along the Pastaza, with
characteristics similar to the ancient Chorrera culture. He
pointed out several stone and ceramic pieces that had
been excavated from different burial grounds in the Pastaza Valley, extending east to Mera and beyond, into the
Amazon Basin, to Indillama.

Many of the stone pieces were similar to the Andeolithic
artifacts I had become familiar with, where the natural
shape of the material dictated the stylistic traits of the
limbs. But other stone pieces were carved in a very distinctive style. Their faces and chins were V-shaped, and
sometimes the mouth was given the same shape as a V
paralleling the lines of the chin. I had seen this same V-

Two stone sculptures.
Ambato Museum.

shaped characteristic in a stone piece from the south Oriente, at Quinta, and in clay figurines from Pillaro and the coastal plain. One of the artifacts with a V-shaped face in this collection was strikingly unique: a large, bell-shaped stone piece from Indillama. It had a round hole on one side just above the carved image of the sun, whose purpose neither Dr. Lorio nor myself could explain. Dr. Lorio suggested the object might have been used as a bell. I thought that by blowing a whistle through the hole into the chamber, the sound would become magnified as through a megaphone. On the opposite side, prominently carved on the face was, significantly, the ax-shaped nose and brow. A serpent with anthropoid faces on both ends of its body became the rim of the artifact. Another intriguing stone piece displayed an ax-shaped headdress.

Front and back views of a bell-shaped stone sculpture. Indillama.

There were scores of magnificent clay vessels: bowls decorated on the inside by iridescent painting, zoomorphic and spouted jars combining human head features with animal bodies, and anthropomorphic jars with bulging cheeks that unmistakably represented the chewing of coca. The red and white stripes artistically embellishing many of the anthropomorphic vessels displayed, undoubtedly, the characteristic style of body painting worn by the Indians of the Amazon Basin, which can still be seen today. In many, the "coffee-bean" eye trait of the Chorrera was very evident.

Among these clay and stone artifacts, perhaps most interesting of all was a mastodon bone—a tibia—and several large fragments of mastodon teeth. Dr. Lorio said they had come from the valley of the Rio Pastaza, to the southeast, but no studies had been made to determine their age. However, their discovery suggested, like the discovery of the mastodon tooth in the Namangosa Valley, the possibility that the Pastaza Valley may have provided a natural route of migration for prehistoric animals from the Amazon into the sierra.

Stone sculpture with ax-shaped headdress. Indillama.

The following day Henrique and I drove south from Ambato and after crossing the Rio Patate, we entered the Cutuchi Valley where twenty-five years ago devastating

Anthropomorphic vessel with "coffee-bean" eyes and red and white stripes. Panzaleo/Tungurahua.

earthquakes had destroyed most of its small villages. We moved at a leisurely pace along the primitive road winding up the slope of the Llanganates. When the magnificent view of Volcan Tungurahua loomed in front of us, Henrique stopped the Jeep and pointed to the green valley spread below between the slopes of the Tungurahua and the Llanganates. "That is Doña Aida Euse's hacienda," he said.

Doña Aida was at home and welcomed us warmly. Her collection was large and I noted the wide variety of stone and pottery pieces. There were bowls, vases, and pots, small amulets, and carefully carved human animal figures similar to the ones I had seen at Pillaro and Ambato. But my expectations were fulfilled when I was shown the piece I had come to see. It was a pottery representation of a cob of corn, about 15 centimeters long, with the kernels very carefully delineated, and with a row of three kernels, spaced down one side, made very much larger than the others. This piece, like most of the others in Doña Aida's collection, had been found in the vicinity of Pisabo along the bank of the Cariyacu River, an affluent of the Rio Pastaza.

Pottery representation of high-yield corn. Tungurahua.

If, according to my belief, an early people had come out of the Amazon during the postglacial period, moved westward through the passes in the cordilleras up into the Mesa, then developed a complex, multi-faceted culture, there had to have been cultivation of staple crops in the Mesa. And here in my hand, in the form of this pottery corncob, was possible corroboration that such an agricultural/social development had occurred.

The corn represented in this artifact was probably an early form of "flint corn," a high-yield, large-kernel variety, far removed from the primitive, grasslike plants that are the ancestors of corn. This, in turn, presumed a preceding stage of development, experimentation, and botanical evolution lasting at least 2000 or 3000 years. Flint corn was grown in Ecuador in the millennia B.C. when low-yield varieties were widely cultivated in Mexico and Peru. However, the origins of corn in the Americas are quite a controversial subject even today. Some scholars assign the early cultivation of high-yield corn to the eastern slopes of the Andes, others to the highlands of Mesoamerica. But there is evidence indicating that, along with the varieties of food plants such as manioc, chili peppers, and peanuts, the early domestication of corn was also carried from the Amazon westward into the highlands of Ecuador and Peru. In fact, in Ecuador a variety of high-yield corn has been excavated from sites of the ancient Valdivia culture (3500 B.C.) both in Cerro Narrio, on the slopes of the western Andean range, and on the coast.

Whether in the Amazon itself or in the mesas, the development of high-yield varieties continued until a strain known as *kcello ecuatoriano* appeared. This strain is probably the ancestor of the very efficient varieties seen in the Peruvian Andes (culminating in the giant corn of Cuzco), and possibly of the corns grown for flour in west Mexico today.

During the following weeks, Henrique and I investigated the many sites in the Pisabo area where most of the artifacts in Doña Aida's collection had been excavated. The burials were rectangular graves, 1.5 to 2 meters deep, covered by capstones and then earth. The campesinos who had done the digging reported that they rarely found bones and only occasionally a few teeth. The terrain was saturated all year around by the constant rain, and bones deteriorated rapidly.

Artifacts uncovered in the Pisabo area seemed to provide further evidence of a relationship between the cultures of the high sierra and the coastal plain. Stone-carved statues found west of Pisabo displayed flat headdresses similar in style to those of the Manteño culture. It was significant, I thought, that this coastal culture flourished on the same latitude as the culture of the Tungurahua but at a later time (ca. 500 B.C.), and the Manteño culture is known to have made extensive use of stone. I was also struck by the number of similarities between the artifacts of the cultures of the Tungurahua area and the Chorrera. They could be seen in the whistles and seal stamps, in the incorporation of animal and human forms into pots and vessels, and in negative molds for casting, an advanced pottery technique that appeared as early as 1800 B.C. in the Chorrera culture.

The concept of a negative mold for casting one or a number of objects was a brilliant technological advance which in Ecuador, obviously, occurred at a very early date. And I came to believe that this leap forward was made by a transitional people—the people who effected the advance from stone to pottery as they moved west into the Mesa from the Amazon Basin. I further came to believe that, among several possible equatorial cultures of

Negative molds: (top), Tungurahua; (bottom), Chorrera.

Ecuador, the Chorrera is a very good candidate for consideration as the culture that had its beginnings in the Mesa and then extended itself, carrying Ecuadorian traits to the coastal plain, Peru, Colombia, and Mesoamerica. There is evidence to substantiate this belief. For example, pottery with a red iridescent finish, which appeared without prior local antecedents at the Ochos site in the La Victoria area on the Pacific coast of Guatemala, is identical in style and finish to the iridescent Chorrera ware. The La Victoria area has been extensively excavated, and if the iridescent red Ochos pottery had evolved locally, so that the similarities to Chorrera were coincidental, prior stages of development would almost certainly have been found. This, however, has not been the case at Ochos. Furthermore, the Chorrera seemed to be a dynamic, mobile people. In contrast to many other ancient Ecuadorian cul-

Necklace of mold-made figurines. Bahía.

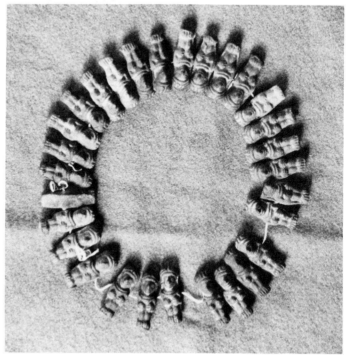

tures, like the Valdivia, that seem to have remained rather stationary and self-contained, the Chorrera ranged over a wide area, extending their distinctive culture over a broad expanse and influencing the rise of other cultures both in the south and the north.

Other parallels between the Chorrera and the cultures of Peru and Mesoamerica have been reported in recent years by some scholars. And the ground has just been broken. Clearly, we have much yet to learn about the origins and influence of the powerful, energetic Chorrera culture. But from my investigation of the Tungurahua area, it seemed clear that a technologically advanced society had established itself in the upper lands of the central range by the beginning of the postglacial period, a society which may well have had its roots in the Amazon Basin, and which, in turn, was linked to the Chorrera culture.

I was anxious to discover if evidence of a transitional culture could also be found in the valleys of the Rio Chota and Pisco in the north Mesa; so, after leaving the Tungurahua Valley, Henrique and I drove first to Cayambe, a small town perched on the foothills of Volcan Cayambe. From there we moved on north around a great spur of the Cordillera Central into the valley of the Rio Chota, then east through the valley to the village of Pimampiro. Behind this village, to the west, rises the northern spur of the Cordillera Central, terminating in a peak called El Redondo. Across the Rio Chota, to the east, rises Mount Olivo, southernmost peak of the Cordillera Pimampiro, which stretches northeast and is the last bastion before the Amazon Basin. I knew that this chain of mountains had yielded many striking artifacts over the years. But I had no way of knowing, as I gazed up toward this range, that hidden within it lay a most important and exciting site that I was shortly to stumble upon.

Arrangements had been made for me to meet Gabriel Roman in Pimampiro. He was a wealthy landlord renowned in the area as a successful hunter of ancient burial grounds. However, being a secretive man, he rarely, if ever, spoke on this subject. It was only through

*Seated coca chewer.
Pimampiro/Pisco
area.*

his friendship with Henrique's family that he had finally agreed to a meeting. When we entered his house, I could see that Roman had prepared well for our coming. Arranged on a large table were several stunningly beautiful ceramic pieces in the style that is labeled as Carchi, after the Carchi Province, which covers a broad area of the northern sierra. There were iridescent painted bowls and plates of various sizes with colorful designs, involving geometric motifs with stylized monkey, bird, and other animal forms. There were also cups and vases of all dimensions, and several of the mugs were rendered in the form of human heads whose faces bore the familiar vertical painted stripes typical of the rain forest inhabitants and were similar to artifacts I had seen in the Pillaro region of Tungurahua.

Male figures seated on benches were especially striking. Most of them were coca chewers, as evidenced by the bulge of the cheeks. The female figures, on the other hand, showed no distortion of their cheeks, indicating that coca chewing was a male tradition. I noted, too, the smooth, skullcap treatment given the hair in most of the male figures, which was a tradition derived from several of the Indian tribes of the Amazon where the hair is smoothed down over the head with pitch from a certain plant. This stylistic trait, plus the spherical handling of the heads and the barrel shape given some of the torsos, was strongly similar to that of ancient figurines of the Panzaleo region of Tungurahua.

The figure of a coca chewer seated on a bench fashioned in the form of a jaguar's body further reinforced the link between the Pimampiro cultural area and the Amazon Basin. The figure is holding a small pot which contained the lime used to cut the bitter taste of the coca. The bench itself also had great significance; without doubt, it represented the seat of authority. Even today in every Indian chosa, a wooden bench is the only piece of furniture aside from the sleeping platform. This bench is for the exclusive use of the head of the clan, and if he, as a hunter, has killed a jaguar, the bench is covered with its skin and his status as a leader is then heightened. The tradition of the jaguar bench and the power it represents can be clearly discerned in ancient artifacts of many cultures and, unquestionably, goes back thousands of years. The coca-chewing tradition also goes back thousands of years and expanded from the highlands to the coastal areas at a very early date. Artifacts depicting coca chewers recovered from ancient sites all along the coast indicate that continuous trade was carried on with the peoples of the sierra through all ages, since the coca plant cannot be grown further than the western slopes of the Andes.

I stood for a long while, my gaze going from one to another of the extraordinary pieces in Señor Roman's collection. What sort of burials had they come from? In the succeeding weeks my investigations and excavations would reveal a system of burials I had not encountered elsewhere: shaft tombs with one or more radiating chambers. A skeleton was found in each chamber with a certain number of artifacts, and that number, I suspected, varied according to the status of the individual buried there. The entire burial was always mound-shaped and covered with cangahua, a hard volcanic aggregate. It was difficult to dig through it. The cangahua was dense and hard; over the centuries, as it settles and periodically becomes soaked with water, it solidifies into a mass sometimes as hard as concrete. I could readily understand why several of these burials had never yet been entered.

The pottery ware uncovered in these tombs was both for ceremonial and everyday use. I was particularly intrigued by a bowl decorated with a pyramid-shaped body and geometric designs of the step-spiral or "meander" motif. Another fascinating piece was a volcanic grinding stone with pestle containing chunks of yellow and red ferruginous clay and white kaolin. This smaller version of the *metate* was obviously used for the preparation of colors that are seen on painted artifacts and not for the grinding of food.

After further investigations of the region around Pimampiro, it seemed to me that three specific geographic

Coca chewer seated on jaguar bench. Pimampiro/Pisco area.

Bowl with monkey and step-spiral design. Pimampiro/Pisco area.

Grinding stone and pestle with chunks of ocher pigment and kaolin. Pimampiro/Pisco area.

areas in this region had evolved into a culture that I came to refer to as Pisco. The first of these areas, the closest to Pimampiro, was the "Olivo," in the immediate environs of Mount Olivo, the southwest terminus of the Cordillera Pisan. The second was the "Mirador," on the slopes of the great mountain of that name at the northeast end of the Pisan. The third was the area around Picco San Jose, the middle of a chain of three great peaks in the Cordillera de las Juntas, which runs north-south, east of the Rio Pisco. I would return to all these areas in the following years for additional exploration and excavation.

On this trip, however, one site in particular caught my attention. It was a small plateau on the slopes of the Cordillera Pisan which, to my eyes, looked too symmetrical and level in comparison to the steep, rugged surrounding terrain. "What do the natives call this place?" I asked Henrique.

" 'La Mesita'—the little plateau," he answered.

It was a difficult climb to La Mesita, but when we finally stood on the broad green expanse covered with grasses and broad-leafed shrubs, my eyes were drawn toward the east. There across the canyon, through the mist of the morning fog, soared three towering peaks that in the shimmering light took on the outline of three great pyramids. It was a spectacular site. Then my eyes were diverted by a flickering light between scraggy shrubs where deep erosion of the land had taken place. We probed carefully with a steel rod, and when we struck something hard below the surface, we began to dig with our small army shovels. In a few minutes we had exposed a flat mica slab whose characteristic sparkling, reflective quality had attracted my attention.

We scraped and dug some more, in the grip of a strange mixture of feelings. Slab after slab came into view, and we began to consider the possibility that they might be a part of a carefully built structure. Soon a row of eight slabs had been uncovered, of different widths but of the same length. From their arrangement and cut, we were sure that they had been deliberately placed there. They were laid regularly, side by side, like paving blocks. As I surveyed the plateau, I could see that one stretch of grass had an unusual lighter yellow color that seemed to extend north from where we stood for quite a distance. It was an indication that most probably more rows of slabs lay underneath.

Over the next eight days, with the help of a hired crew of local campesinos, we cleared away the shrubs and soil, exposing the entire structure. There were no signs of walls, no indications of a superstructure. Unmistakably, it was a platform composed of carefully crafted rectangular stone slabs, placed side by side thirteen to a row, each ap-

Mica slab platform. Pimampiro/ La Mesita.

proximately 2 meters long, 60 centimeters wide, and averaging 15 centimeters thick. The long axis of the stones was oriented from north to south, and at both ends there were three rows of small stone slabs that appeared to finish off the structure with a "fringe." The size of the entire structure was 8.5 meters wide and 28 meters long.

The structure was bowed, the center being perhaps 1 meter higher than either end. Three different types of stone had been used: mica, a greenish igneous stone, and a sort of sandstone. The mica slabs were scattered in what seemed to be a random pattern among the igneous and the sandstone slabs. But they apparently had a special significance in that each of them bore a carved relief across the top surface depicting animal forms, some of which appeared to be representations of the tapir or monkey, others of a mythical double-headed scorpion. Here again was a provocative link to the lowlands of the Amazon, for these creatures are not seen in the Mesa where the platform was built.

We were clearing earth and plant cover away from the west edge of the platform when we encountered a stone projecting upward. I wondered at first if this might be the remains of a wall. But as we worked, we found that the stone slab was only about 2.5 meters long, and was squared off on both ends; there were no other stones on either side projecting above the platform surface. A 16-centimeter semicircular depression had been carved in the middle of the top surface of this slab, and as I pon-

Relief carvings on the mica slabs. Pimampiro/ La Mesita.

dered its significance and reasons for its construction, a
story Gabriel Roman had told me came back vividly to
mind. Several years before, he said, a landslide had uncovered a small grotto that contained hundreds of skulls
but no skeletons on the slopes of the Picco San Jose, the
tallest of the three peaks visible from the platform and
which today is an inactive volcano. Perhaps in time past
there had been large-scale sacrificial decapitation performed on this site to placate the deity the natives believed lived inside the volcano. I knew that both ritual and
actual decapitation was widespread throughout South and
Mesoamerica. Had we uncovered a sacrificial platform? I
knelt down and placed my neck in the notch carved in the
stone. It fitted perfectly.

Sacrificial headstone. Pimampiro/ La Mesita.

After the platform had been completely exposed, we probed between the slabs with a rod. We encountered nothing to indicate that burial chambers existed beneath; however, during the excavation, I noted natural erosion under the southwest corner of the platform where it appeared that a cave-in had taken place. I decided to probe deeper. The following week we carefully excavated a pit to a depth of 3 meters below the surface, and inward, under the platform itself, to an extent of about 2 meters. As we painstakingly dug and sifted the soil, a steady progression of artifacts came to light. From the lowest level, we uncovered three projectile points and a scraper fashioned from obsidian, a volcanic glass. They resembled the points, scrapers, and other stone tools discovered near the gorge of the Inga River in the Cordillera Central in Ecuador by Allen Graffham, an American geologist, in 1956. Later, this carefully studied site, dating from 7500 B.C., was proved to be an ancient center for the production of obsidian tools due to a large deposit of volcanic glass nearby. Significantly, projectile points of a style similar to those in the Inga deposit were uncovered in 1937 at Palli Aike and Fell's Cove, Chile, by Dr. Junius B. Bird of the American Museum of Natural History. The remains of prehistoric animals found associated with these obsidian tools yielded at the Palli Aike site a carbon-14 date of 11,000 years, and at the Fell's Cove site a date of 8760 B.C. When these dates were reported by Dr. Bird, they became very controversial and were first regarded by the scientific community as too early for man's presence on the tip of South America. However, they proved that man was already established at the tip of South America toward the end of the last continental glaciation.

From the intermediate level of our excavation under the platform, four small stone amulets were unearthed that again revealed a veneration toward the traditions of the Amazon to the east: the first and second were a stylized monkey and a parrot; the third was a highly polished axhead; and the fourth a figure with an anthropoid head and a torso formed of spirals carved with the character-

Obsidian projectile points and a scraper. Pimampiro/La Mesita.

istic traits of stone-carving people. An extraordinary skull
was also uncovered at this level of our excavation. Paleon-
tologists of the Smithsonian Institution, through the good
auspices of archaeologist Dr. Betty J. Meggers, have
judged the skull to be that of an adolescent human. But
the anatomy is so unusual that some specialists I have
shown it to have hesitated, giving it considerable study
before pronouncing it human. Viewed from the front, the
principal impression is of a pronounced tapering. The
upper aspect of the skull is very wide and the cranial capacity is relatively large. But the sidewalls, the temporal
areas, taper inward markedly, giving the structure a triangular character. The orbits are also triangular in character
and do not have the floor seen in most human skulls.
Completely missing is the zygomatic arch—the bridge of
bone seen in most skulls that starts at the cheekbone,
below the eyes, and loops around to the side of the skull,
enclosing a hollow space in the temples which is filled with
important blood vessels and nerves. The absence of this
distinctive bony arch gives such a different appearance to
the skull that one cannot help but think this creature must
have appeared to the other ancient people as a being

Small stone artifacts.
Pimampiro/La Mesita.

Tapered skull with triangular orbits. Pimampiro/ La Mesita.

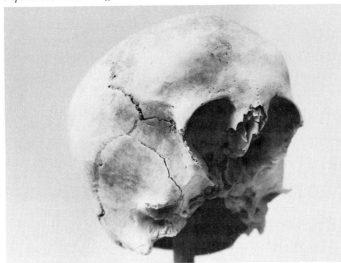

Green stone figurine.
Pimampiro/La Mesita.

from another world. No information has come to light since its discovery that would help answer the question whether this creature was an anatomical oddity or a member of an unknown and now extinct race or tribe in some way related to the ancient cultures of the Mesa.

Buried hardly ½ meter beneath one of the large slabs of the platform, we recovered a figurine of a male of beautifully carved highly polished diorite stone. The features bore some of the familiar traits of a stone-carving culture: flat square nose, slanted bulging eyes and mouth, truncated arms over the stomach, and rudimentary legs.

I was exhilarated by what I found at La Mesita. The discovery of a structure of cut stone slabs with carved reliefs and the excavation of sculptured artifacts in this remote and mysterious region high in the Cordillera intimated to me once again that a stone-carving culture must have flourished in the Andean highlands. In the south, in the central Mesa, and now in the north, I had discovered artifacts that, despite regional differences in style, revealed definite similarities, tying these geographical areas to a single cultural complex that seemed to extend down the eastern slopes into the Oriente. To simplify references to it, I have designated this stone-carving complex "Andeolithic," from Andes plus *lithos,* the Greek word for stone. I had also noted that stone figurines from the northern highlands showed an interesting progression in style. In some respects—the multiple figure design-in-the-round and the handling of some of the facial features—they seemed clearly to have been influenced by the Andeolithic. But in other respects they were more advanced and closer in aesthetic effect to the more sophisticated pieces of the Mesa cultures further west. This seemed to indicate that the area around Pimampiro was a transitional one between the early Andeolithic influence that may have come from the east, and the later cultures of the sierra. Certainly the prominence of jungle creatures in the art of the ancient people of this area seemed to suggest an influence whose roots lay deep in the Amazon, and whose traditions were carried to the uplands by the early settlers.

Pursuing this belief, I later extended my investigations further northeast into the Cordillera Pisan, the valley of the Rio Pisco, and across the Cordillera de las Juntas into Colombia. This region—from San Gabriel to the Colombian border and west—has been a source of a great variety of beautiful artifacts displaying an astonishing level of development, including human and animal figurines, pots, bowls, plates, and vases with elaborate multi-colored designs of extraordinary subtlety and refinement. They have been classified under a number of terms: Cara, Carchi, Capuli, El Angel, and others. But the area eastward, including the Cordilleras Pisan and de las Juntas with the Pisco Valley in between, had been very little explored. This was the area where I concentrated my efforts.

A wealth of material emerged from my explorations, and it soon became apparent that stone artifacts with characteristic Andeolithic traits were not restricted to the eastern edge of the Pimampiro region but were also to be found in this northern part of the sierra which, via the Cordillera del Due Pass eastward from the Pisco Valley into the valleys of the Rios Cofanes and Chingual, was linked to the Amazon Basin. Moreover, carved stone sculptures found in this region bore a marked resemblance to early stone figures from Chavin de Huántar, Peru, Tiahuanaco, Bolivia, and San Agustin, Colombia. But as yet I had discovered no animal or human remains that might provide a date for the presence of early man in this region. Thus it was with great excitement that I learned much later of the recovery of part of a mastodon tooth on the bank of the Rio Cuché, a small river that flows from the Cordillera Pisan. Cesar Tocain, an old campesino who had accompanied me on several expeditions into this northern region, had stumbled on it after a landslide and immediately sent word to me.

It was a cold rainy day in February of 1975 when I arrived in the small village of La Paz to meet again with Tocain. In addition to my interest in the mastodon tooth, I had learned that some workmen digging for limestone

Stone sculptures: (top), Andeolithic/ Cordillera de Pisan; (bottom), Chavin, Peru.

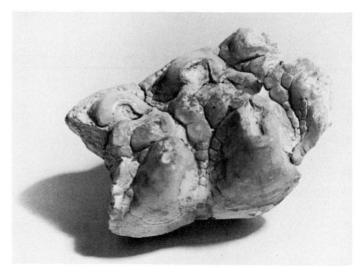

Mastodon tooth. Rio Cuché.

had found bones that looked as if they might be human in a cliff in the Cordillera Pisan, a little southwest of Mirador, overlooking the narrow canyon of the Rio Cuché. A previous reconnaissance of this highland area had led me to believe that it might be one of the locales where an ancient people coming from the Amazon had originally established themselves, for it was dotted with caves for shelter and protected from the cold winds by surrounding mountains. Now I was anxious to explore the area more carefully.

After a hazardous Jeep ride one morning, Cesar and I had to continue on foot along a steep, twisting trail to the banks of the Cuché, turbulent and roiling from the heavy rains. Then, after a long walk on a narrow ledge that separated the river from the vertical face of the mountain, we reached the place where the workers had reported finding human bones. The natives called it Calera.

The geology of the mountain strata was clearly evident, and at many points, from ground level to the top of the cliff, large crevices extended deep into the face of the cliff between the strata. In some of the crevices, small stalactites could be seen suspended from the crevice roof. There it was clear that the structure had been undisturbed for thousands of years, while at another point, along the northern reach of the cliff face, a large landslide had completely altered the entire face of the cliff.

The cliff itself was about 100 or 120 meters high; and not far away, behind a bend in the river above a small hill, were two huts that provided us with shelter for the next few nights. The two shepherds who lived there were most willing to help with the dig.

We spent what little daylight remained surveying the layout and geology of the area, and the following day we began to dig at various sites along the base of the cliff. The second day, we made an important strike. Digging behind a boulder, not far from where the workers had reported finding bones, we found several that appeared to be human but they disintegrated as we tried to recover them. Among them, however, were several obsidian artifacts. These were the tools used by ancient people for thousands of years for cutting and carving designs on stone and bone surfaces. Shaped into projectile points, they also became weapons for hunting: long flakes struck from obsidian blocks became knife blades, and notched and bifacial blades become scrapers and chisels.

Obsidian flake knives and scrapers. Calera.

The cliff at Calera above the Rio Cuché.

The following day we attempted more digging, but the rainfall, which had begun during the night, became torrential and we decided to leave the site. We were not able to resume work for a week and a half, and when we returned to Calera, I was particularly anxious to examine the crevices higher up on the cliff. I had noticed that some of them were closed off with adobe and stone, which indicated that they might have been constructed as burial sites. Workers had reported finding bones within the low crevices of the cliff; clearly, the best way to determine whether these were burial sites was to check crevices that were high enough above the ground so that it was more likely they had not been disturbed.

I selected for the first try a crevice that was almost horizontal, had an opening around 1 meter high, and was about 30 meters above ground level. It was a very difficult ascent. The limestone of which most of the cliff was composed was weak and crumbly, and it broke apart repeatedly under my weight. But slowly, I made progress. Finally, I reached the crevice and the opening was just wide enough for me to work my way in by lying on my stomach. Before me I found a barrier of loose-packed stones that had been layered to seal the crevice completely. Through the ages, it had hardened into a solid wall, but I pulled out my knife and found I could break through it. Behind the barrier there was a great amount of lime powder mixed with leaves and sticks. Moving this material out of the way, I found pieces of bone. Then I encountered a long bone—probably a femur. But as I attempted to remove it, it crumbled into pieces. Most of the other bones did the same.

I continued to dig, looking for evidence, either in the layout of the bones or in the presence of artifacts, to indicate whether this was a deliberately performed human burial. But I found nothing. Then in the low light filtering into the crevice, I realized that part of the crevice roof had collapsed. As I carefully removed this debris, I came across what appeared to be blocks of material which, on later examination, proved to be fossilized leaves and bark.

The author climbing into a crevice at Calera.

Then I saw something with a smooth curved surface and a brownish color. When I was able to get my fingers around it and pull it toward me, I realized it was a skull; and as I slowly pulled it closer, I saw the face, with the upper teeth in place. The lower jaw was missing. I reached back into the cavity where the skull had lain, and right where I expected to find it, my fingers touched the lower jaw. I pulled it out and saw that it, too, had teeth.

I lay there in the crevice for a few moments, turning the precious bones over and over in my hands, feeling a flush of excitement and satisfaction. But I needed more light to see clearly what sort of skull it was. The problem now was to carry it down. I slid toward the edge of the crevice and called to Tocain: "Cesar, I found a skull! I need something to lift it down safely!" One of the shepherds went to his nearby hut and soon returned with a basket and a long rope. He climbed expertly toward me and after the third try, I was able to grasp them. Carefully packing the skull and jaw with loose earth inside the basket, I lowered them to the ground below, then slowly climbed down myself.

When I was able to examine the skull more closely, it appeared to be very ancient. But it was the teeth that roused the most daring hope in my mind. They were worn flat, and the ground-down surfaces were almost polished, a sign, I believed, that possibly what I was holding in my hands was a specimen of an early settler in the An-

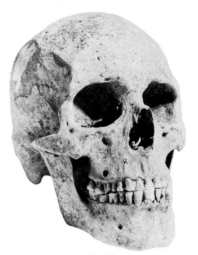

Skull from the Calera site, dated ca. 10,000 years old.

dean range—Andeolithic man. For ancient man evolved from the predominant occupation of hunting, which required constant travel in pursuit of game, to a more settled, semi-migratory existence in which the collecting of plants for food consumed the major part of his time. After gathering hard seeds and the kernels from predomesticated corn and grains, he ground them in mortars fashioned from volcanic rock, or on slabs of rock (the forerunner of the *metate*), in the process adding grit from the grinding stone to his foodstuffs. Years of chewing fine grit along with his food wore his teeth down, providing us today with a distinctive clue to his stage of development. Could I dare to hope that the abraded teeth of the skull I held in my hand identified it as belonging to a man who had lived at this time in prehistory?

We were able to spend only a few more days investigating the Calera area before torrential rains again drove us away. But before we left, we dug into what appeared to be an ancient refuse pit a few kilometers from the cliff. Our labors were rewarded when, between rubble and broken shards, I recovered a well-preserved androgynous clay figurine dressed in what seemed to be a heavy garment and headgear. Was the stocky broad-shouldered figure a possible depiction of Andeolithic man?

I returned to Miami with the precious skull in my possession and later sent a specimen to Dr. Bada of the Scripps Institution of Oceanography for evaluation and amino acid racemization dating (see Appendix). I also submitted samples from the strange tapering skull found under the sacrificial platform at La Mesita, and part of the mastodon tooth that was found on the banks of the Rio Cuché.

While waiting for the results of the tests, I reflected on the history of these early settlers of the upper Andes who, forced to cope with the rugged terrain of the sierra, had found in natural geological faults or crevices a ready place for the burial of their dead. For the primitive tools at their disposal at this time in history most probably could not have provided any other alternative. But what were the dates of these early settlers? I did not know the answer to that question until several months later, when Dr. Bada's scientific analysis and conclusions yielded an age of "10,000 years or slightly less for the Calera skull." For me it was a crucial date, which helped put to rest any misgivings I might have had about my theory of the antiquity of Andeolithic man.

Androgynous clay figurine. Calera.

CHAPTER 16

The Corridors

It was September 1972 and I was sitting near a large window overlooking the ornate courtyard of the Presidential Palace in Quito. A few minutes after 10:30 A.M. a military aide entered the room to announce that the President would arrive shortly.

Two days before, a phone call had informed me that I was summoned to the palace for a meeting with General Rodriguez Lara, the new President of Ecuador. I had been in this room once before over a year ago when another President, Velasco Ibarra, and his wife Doña Corina had invited me for afternoon tea. It had been during this informal meeting that I sought help in overcoming the bureaucratic maze that was standing in the way of a careful scientific investigation of Tolita Island. At that time, an important archaeological site on the island lay completely abandoned and was subjected to continuous plunder, not only from Ecuadorian treasure hunters but also from grave diggers from nearby Colombia. President Velasco had listened with interest as I described the immeasurable archaeological potential of Tolita, and had nodded with understanding and sympathy as I tactfully explained the lack of headway I seemed to be making with government officials. Then he said casually, "Go ahead and dig. If you get into any problems, come and see me," a remark that convinced me that for him, archaeology was only a historical hypothesis, not a political reality. Time had passed, the political fortunes of Velasco

324

declined, and in February 1972, he was overthrown by a military coup. But at least one suggestion I had made to him came to pass. The Tolita archaeological site now had an army patrol guarding against plunderers.

The sudden call of my name brought me back to the present. "The President will see you now," the aide announced, then preceded me into the quiet, somberly decorated presidential suite. Behind a massive ornate desk, General Lara was leaning back in a brown leather chair speaking on the telephone. Dressed in the uniform of the commander general of the army, he somehow gave the impression of a man not yet at ease with his new authority. "Sit down, sit down," he said brusquely as he hung up the phone.

Again I was seeking official recognition of the value of the archaeological exploration of his country, and as our conversation turned to my years of research, he mentioned that on his hacienda in Pugili, in the central Ecuadorian province of Cotopaxi, workmen digging a well had uncovered an ancient burial ground from which some artifacts had been recovered. He suggested that I might be interested to look at them. I accepted his invitation and promised that after my return from the Mojanda region, situated northwest of Cayambe in the Cordillera Central—the area I had planned to investigate during the next few weeks—I would stop in Pugili. Before our meeting ended, I reasserted my belief that the government had to support legislation to preserve the ancient legacy of Ecuador, and should also help to expand the fledgling museum sponsored by the Banco Central in Quito.

A few days later, Henrique and I climbed into a Jeep and started north again. We reached the Rio Guayllabamba several hours later, and after crossing it, left the paved highway to drive onto a dusty dirt road that followed a northwesterly direction. As we wound upwards, a sheer mountain wall rose on our right for thousands of feet, and on our left the precipice dropped hundreds of feet below. It had not rained for weeks in this part of the sierra and volcanic white dust became a floating wall behind us. We drove for hours on the side of the steep slopes until we reached an altitude of 3400 meters, where the dirt track became little more than a deep rut between torn trees and scrub. We finally reached our destination by late afternoon: the settlement of Kuuchazqui, an isolated, privately owned enclave perched high on the slopes of the Mojanda Mountains.

A year before, I had found a most interesting reference to the ancient inhabitants of this region in an old Spanish chronicle. Every year, the report said, virgin girls were sacrificed on top of a "step-built tola." Somehow this description seemed to differentiate such a tola from the "mound with steps," a description that I had come to believe referred to a big mound with remains of a platform on its summit reached by a circular ramp or stairway. One such "mound with steps" is found in Rumicucho, built on the flat plain that the ancient inhabitants of the region believed marked the center of the world.

Henrique and I explored the area in the next few days, hoping to find the remains of a "step-built tola." One day, after crossing the divider above Kuuchazqui, we were walking across country into Malchingui, skirting brush-covered knolls that looked like rolling dunes at the sea's edge, when bits of clay lying in a shallow pool of water caught my attention. I stopped and picked some of them up.

"Every time after heavy rains we see hundreds of these," said the Indian guide who was accompanying us. It was apparent that we were walking on mounds of all sizes, and that these bits of clay were pottery shards washed down from the eroding terrain.

But by far the most interesting and imposing sight was a flat-topped hill surrounded by a line of tall trees that overpowered the landscape. My initial vague curiosity turned to excitement when I discovered that the hill was covered with cangahua, and in the days that followed, with the help of local campesinos, we removed a layer of cangahua from one side where deep erosion had taken place. To my astonishment, behind the cangahua rubble,

Pyramidal mound at Malchingui.

Hewn stones of the pyramidal structure at Malchingui.

cut stone blocks were revealed; and as work progressed and more rubble and vegetation were cleared, a surprising structure emerged. The stones had been hewn, fitted and erected without mortar or cement, into what appeared to be a pyramidal mound, rising in tiers to a truncated summit.

Built at an altitude of close to 4000 meters (12,000 feet), on harsh, arid land where farmers struggle with the rocky soil, such a structure had almost certainly required careful planning on a huge scale. And although it was not as high or as massive as those in Mesoamerica, it and the smaller

Pottery representation of pyramidal mound. Jama-Coaque.

mounds disposed around the complex covered a large area. Only a systematic, orderly excavation requiring months, if not years, of labor would be able to ascertain whether there was elaborate stonework on the façade and tombs underneath. But as I surveyed the portion of the structure that we had exposed, notwithstanding the fact that information was sparse as to when or by whom it had been constructed, it seemed apparent to me that the ancient Andean highland people who had inhabited this region had developed the concept of pyramid building. It was a concept that would evolve through successive cultures in South and Mesoamerica from a simple mound topped with a small structure for the tribal shaman, to larger mounds with more elaborate temples on their summits reached by stone stairways, and, finally, to truncated pyramidal mounds built with tiers of stone platforms sustaining on their summits temples and sacrificial altars.

Depictions of the pyramid are clearly seen in the artifacts of later cultures of the highlands, the Mesa, and the coast. And the pyramid is frequently symbolized in the "fret" or step-spiral motifs carved in stone, painted on pottery, hammered on gold ornaments, woven in baskets and clothing, and used as an architectural decorative element. Its profusion of uses shows persuasively the central position this symbol held through the millennia in the cultures of the Americas. But as I gazed at the mound we had excavated at Malchingui, the great question and unsolved puzzle became: Why had the ancients covered this pyramid with cangahua, thereby making it invisible? What mystical beliefs were behind such burials? And have other

Compotera with step-spiral motif symbolizing the pyramid. Pisco region.

pyramid-shaped constructions in South America eluded investigators because they were camouflaged or buried under rubble, cangahua, or earth as part of a ritual after they had served their purpose?

Bad weather plagued our excavations at Malchingui. On the last day of work, before the rains arrived in full force, we were digging on the west side of the complex in a small tola that had been opened by *huaceros* in the past.

A deep trench had been dug through the middle, but for some reason the two sides had been left untouched. Carefully sifting through the packed earth, we uncovered dozens of shards from broken vessels and plates of dark and reddish fired clay. None displayed any decorative design. Then, suddenly, one of my helpers shouted to attract my attention and excitedly handed me two small objects he had found. As I carefully brushed off a coat of dirt from one of them, intricate carvings came to light on the flat surface and it became apparent that it was a seal stamp. The other object was a figurine.

Solid clay figurine. Malchingui-Chorrera (?).

The fury of the rain increased and we had to leave Malchingui and return to the hacienda at Kuuchazqui. There I was able to examine the two artifacts more carefully. I saw that the figurine was of solid clay and the triangular shape of the head reminded me of figurines I had seen in Venezuela. The "coffee-bean" eye treatment, I noticed, was also similar to the figurines of the Chorrera. When the seal stamp was cleaned further, I saw that the design was a raised pattern of swirling lines around a circular center. The short, sturdy handle had a hole through it, and the stamp was obviously meant to be worn around the neck. I was immediately struck by the similarity of the abstract pattern on this seal to the designs of early Chorrera flat stamps, evidence, perhaps, of the expansion of the Chorrera culture into this part of the highlands.

Seal stamps are found in abundance throughout Ecuador, as in Mesoamerica. They are made of fired clay, although carved stone specimens have also been found. They generally take two forms: a flat stamp with a grip; or a cylinder, intended to be rolled. A tremendously wide range of designs is seen, including abstract geometric motifs and animal forms, either naturalistic or mythic. And it is the accepted belief among archaeologists that these stamps were used to decorate the body, pottery, or fabrics. But I had come to challenge that belief. For if this had been the case, then the thousands of figurines, human or otherwise, that have been recovered from

Seal stamp. Malchingui/ Chorrera (?).

Cylindrical stone stamp with zoomorphic design. Manteño.

burials would bear testimony to this practice. Apart from a few exceptions, however, the decorations on pottery artifacts are not similar to those seen on stamps. And when depiction of body painting is displayed, the patterns are comparable to the traditional body painting seen, still today, on the aborigines of the Amazon forest—vertical and horizontal lines, not the swirling designs and other motifs of the seal stamps. Furthermore, archaeologist Frederick V. Field, in his investigation of thousands of pre-Hispanic clay stamps from Mexico, found that the few pieces of textile that have survived climatic destruction had been hand-woven, not stamped. And this coincides with textile remains found in both Ecuador and Peru.

Thus, seal stamps apparently served some other purpose. Field postulated that the designs on the stamps "are the motifs of magic, the symbol of mythology, the talismans of religion," and that they were used by the shaman, who distributed their impressions to the people. This interpretation, I found, agreed with my own observations and study of innumerable stamps from Ecuador. However, I came to believe that because of their incredible number and wide distribution, and the variety of symbols on the stamps, they could not have been only in the exclusive possession and control of the shaman, but were obviously in everyday use. They may have been worn as amulets by the people or hung in dwellings. And by imprinting the "magic" symbol—a bird, a serpent, a jaguar, a monkey, flowers, or abstract figures and patterns—on the adobe of their house, they appeased or called on a specific deity for help and protection. A Chorrera stamp of a foot, and another from Esmeraldas with the same motif but ending with the fret design, suggested that seal stamps may also have been used to bestow a safe pilgrimage to a holy center by imprinting the ideograph on the trail to ward off any attack by enemy or beast.

Seal stamp depicting the step motif. Jama-Coaque.

A stamp that I recovered on the slopes of Quinnaloma, which depicted a chain motif similar to the one carved on the gunwales of the stone canoe found at Intihuatana, led me to speculate on the possibility that many stamps may have symbolized the ceremonial centers where they, or their impressions, were distributed by the shaman to the faithful as an extension of this power. Another stamp depicting the step motif reinforced this belief.

I also found that, in many instances, symbols expressed in the stamps preceded by hundreds of years similar symbols seen in pre-Columbian cultures in both South and Mesoamerica. On an earlier dig in the mountain region of the coastal plain, Montañas de Convento, near the edgewaters of the Rio Mongolla, I had unearthed a stunning cylindrical stamp. Rolled on clay, the stamp's impression revealed two distinct panels. One contained triangular shapes, together with heavy bars, interspersed with rows of dots. The second consisted exclusively of bars, dots, and bars with varying numbers of projections. I was struck by the remarkable resemblance of this impression to the Olmec-Maya dot-bar system of numeration. The Olmecs, considered the mother culture of Mesoamerica, are believed by many authorities to have introduced the counting system. Later, by the Mayan era, the vigesimal system (as it became known because it is based on 20 as opposed to our decimal system based on 10) developed into a sophisticated method of numeration allowing computation that, in some respects, was as efficient as the Arabic system used in the modern world. But I found that the artifacts of many earlier Ecuadorian cultures portray dots in their decorative motifs, some associated with bars,

Cylindrical stamp with its impression displaying dots, bars and geometric motifs. Jama-Coaque.

and in many instances they seem to follow a mathematical order in their manner of presentation.

The reason for early man's use of the dot and bar symbols is open to many varied interpretations. Most probably, however, it had a very simplistic beginning. Observing modern-day Indians in the marketplace squatting near their supply of goods and engaging in trade presents an insight. They do their counting over a stretch of soft earth,

Ceramic compotera with dots and bars. Pisco region.

pushing in a fingertip and leaving a hole, or dot, to indicate a unit; when they reach the desired number of units, they draw a vertical line, or bar, that then represents the sum of dots. In ancient cultures, dots inevitably became a means of recording periods of time, specific events, and celestial happenings, and associated with powerful symbols took on a mystical meaning. Dots associated with the jaguar and snake are seen frequently in bone carvings and in the ceramic and stone pieces of many cultures. One of the most impressive applications of the symbolic and spiritual meaning of this characteristic trait I have encountered was displayed in a *compotera* (bowl) recovered in the Pisco region. The inside of the bowl is painted with nine encircled dots enclosed between two bars, and above each bar the cosmic symbol of the universal forces revolving clockwise endowed the piece with a powerful mystical meaning.

But by far the most intriguing find was unearthed in an excavation near the summit of Paragachito Hill during my investigation of the Pimampiro area, an area that was occupied in pre-Columbian times by the Paragachi Indian tribe, now almost extinct. After excavating a vertical shaft tomb, practically destroyed from seismic earth movements, that contained countless numbers of shards from broken vessels, a seal stamp in the form of a tablet came to light. This astounding tablet, which I would rank as one of the most important artifacts from the north Mesa that I have encountered, indicates an extraordinarily high level of development on at least three grounds: the incorporation of the feathered serpent, which stands as one of the most prevalent and powerful deities in the mythology

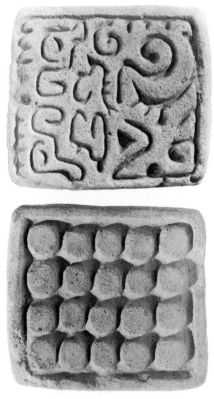

Clay tablet with stylized head of a feathered serpent on the front and twenty dots on the back. Paragachito Hill site.

of the Americas; the subtle, skillful aesthetic sense with which the design was worked out and accommodated to the confines of the rectangular space; and the twenty dots appearing on the back, indicating use of the vigesimal numbering system.

I had long been intrigued by the frequent depiction of both the serpent and the jaguar in the artifacts of the early cultures of Ecuador. I discovered one sterling example on the banks of the Rio Tiaone, near Esmeraldas, which depicts a human figure whose face is peering from the mouth of a jaguar mask with the characteristic trait of the "speech balloon"—a flat hanging tongue. This was manifestly the symbol of the jaguar deity speaking through the shaman. Other masks I have seen depicted the same concept but with a serpent mask. Clearly, both the serpent and the jaguar were endowed with mystical

Ceramic representation of a shaman peering through the mouth of a jaguar mask. Esmeraldas.

Stone sculpture of jaguar and serpent. Cordillera de Chanchan.

and magic powers; but whatever their meaning to the men of these early cultures, their choice of symbols provides us with an important clue as to their origins. And the jaguar and serpent are the two natural powers of the Amazon Basin. Their portrayals, singly and in combination, on the artifacts of both early and later cultures, are many and varied in South and Mesoamerica. In fact, I had found that cultural traits of unparalleled diversity had developed within the narrow limited boundaries of the Andean highlands of Ecuador itself. Yet the dominance of jungle deities, the similarity in burial practices and mound-building techniques, and the continuity of many cultural traits and symbols all bore evidence of a common ancestor.

Another artifact and its symbolic representation that pervade the early cultures of South and Mesoamerica is the axhead, whose meaning and significance I had long pondered. Ecuador is rich in ax manifestations, from the Oriente to the highlands and down to the coastal plain, and the stone axheads that have been found range from miniature amulets to large pieces weighing hundreds of kilograms. The copper pieces are of two basic types: the familiar crescent-shaped axhead; and those with almost parallel sides like a chisel, or with thin crescent-shaped blades and narrow shafts that probably fitted into handles carved of wood or bone. These blades clearly functioned

Chisel-like and crescent-shaped copper blades. Milagro.

as knifelike tools, and there is a strong suggestion that they were also used in sacrificial rituals and trephination, a highly skilled surgical operation on the skull that reached its highest form during the Inca Empire. But what of the larger crescent-shaped blades?

It would be logical to assume that they, too, were used as weapons or tools. Thus I was puzzled by the results I had received from the chemical analyses and laboratory tests of a small metal axhead found in Bahía. The spectographic method used to determine the composition of this piece showed that its major component was pure copper, with 1 percent arsenic and 6 percent impurity traces. The arsenic content was appropriate for copper in its natural state; and Dr. Ronald Hawke, of the Lawrence Livermore Laboratory, University of California, after subjecting the specimen to hardness and conductivity measurements and radiographic inspection, stated that the method that had been used to make the axhead was a casting process, followed by light pounding and hammering for hardening. However, the hardness was not such that one could consider this to have been a utilitarian tool because, unlike bronze tools, it could not withstand continuous stress.

Nor was it likely that this and similar copper axheads had been used as weapons. In a society where warfare was an everyday occurrence, the possession of a weapon like a hard copper ax would certainly have assured supremacy in any contest. But the metal ax is never depicted, either as a weapon or as a utilitarian tool, in any of the artifacts of the ancient cultures of Ecuador, as the stone ax, club, mace, *atlall* (spearthrower), and sling are. Clearly the copper ax had some purpose beyond use as a weapon or tool, or as a medium of exchange, the conventional explanations of its use. But I was unsure what that purpose might be until the discovery of giant copper axes, weighing more than 20 kilograms, on the west side of the Central Cordillera, crystallized a theory I had been formulating for a long time. Both surfaces of these axes bore images of human figures with elaborate supporting geometric

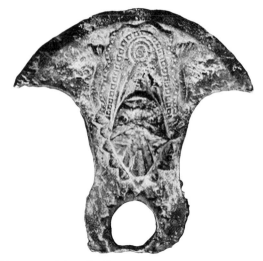

Large copper ceremonial ax. Gualinag.

motifs and sunburst designs. Unquestionably, they had a ceremonial purpose.

With this realization, I came to believe that the wide, crescent-shaped blade and rectangular shaft of the metal ax had religious and mystical significance to the Andeolithics, and that the manner in which it was portrayed in their artifacts was an important clue as to its meaning. The crescent shape and rectangular shaft were carved as the brow and nose on the faces of many of their stone figures. In others they were incorporated into the headdress or head crown, or a crescent-shaped pendant was worn around the neck. And in time, in the later cultures of South and Mesoamerica, the symbol of the ax was depicted on ceramic figurines, vases, gold masks, and, most importantly, as a representation of the knife used in sacrificial rituals and trephination, all of which bore further testimony to its ceremonial purposes.

Ceramic figurine with ax-shaped pendant. Bahía.

The emergence of this symbol in the mind of man at a very early stage, its omnipresence in his artifacts, and its subsequent dispersal over the South American continent and Mesoamerica through the course of millennia, is eloquent evidence of its importance, even if its fundamental significance remains hidden. It would seem apparent that the crescent shape of the ax represented a number of potent natural and spiritual forces to the Andeolithics and

Stone carved figure with an ax on its brow. Chavin.

Ceramic figure with ax on
its headdress. Mochica.

later cultures. The path of the sun is crescent-shaped, for
example, as are the phases of the moon. And the bril-
liance of copper, and later gold, crafted into this shape
might have been an important aspect of this symbol. The
crescent shape may also have represented the power of
the ax itself. Hence the incorporation of this shape with
the human brow, and its use in headdresses and other
ceremonial objects, pendants, amulets, and decorative motifs. Not surprisingly, the crescent shape is often combined with representations of other powerful forces like
the jaguar and the snake. It is also the natural shape of
the mushroom, and such a symbol on ceremonial objects
might have represented the power of that source of hallucinogenic drug.

In the artifacts of later cultures throughout South and
Mesoamerica, the crescent shape becomes very elaborate
and sophisticated. But in the light of my speculations
about the origins of these cultures, I was particularly intrigued by the discovery of a much earlier piece in the
Cordillera de las Juntas of the north Mesa of Ecuador. It
was a slate ax head with a crescent-shaped cutting edge,
that bore on one side a carved stylized figure of a monkey
and on the other a serpent, thus linking the symbols of
the Amazon with the tradition of the ax.

He was an old, ex-Salesian missionary who preferred to

Slate axhead with carved stylized monkey. North Mesa.

Pottery bowl fragment with stylized serpent motif. Napo region.

travel alone, on foot or horseback, through the jungle forests of the Oriente in search of *huacas* for what they could offer in knowledge and history. Short, black-haired, incredibly thin, he carried within his soul an inextinguishable energy that was reflected in his compulsive verbosity. To everyone he was "the Professor," but to me he had introduced himself simply as Mario Zanetti. Born in Italy sixty-eight years before, he arrived in Ecuador at the age of thirty as a missionary. It was love at first sight, he told me, "not only for the land and the *Indios* to whom I spoke of Jesus, but for the archaeological richness of the country."

Padre Zanetti's collection of ancient artifacts from the eastern slopes of the Andes and beyond in the lowlands of the Amazon Basin was invaluable to me for comparison studies with my own findings, as these areas were almost unknown archaeologically. And here again in the vast Zanetti collection—much of which had been recovered from burial sites along the banks of the Rios Napo and Coca—I found that numbers of artifacts displayed connections of one form or another to the Chorrera culture, strengthening my belief that the Chorrera had its roots deep in the Oriente. Among the traits linking the Napo region to the Chorrera were the tradition of the clay stamp, polychrome decoration, figures in the form of a

Figurines with representations of an obsidian mirror: (top), Napo region; (center), Tolita; (bottom), Olmec.

seated male with a barrel-shaped body, the distinctive fret or "step-spiral" decorative motif, and characteristic eye treatment and spool earrings. The level of aesthetic sophistication achieved in some of the pottery was as stunning as that seen in the Pisco region and the coastal plain.

One of the pottery pieces in Padre Zanetti's collection generated a strange effect as I gazed at it. It was a figurine of a man, about one-quarter of which had been broken away and lost, but it was still evident that he was holding at his chest a polished black disk. I had seen a similar piece at the Casa de la Cultura in Quito. To me the representation was obvious: there was a clear parallel with the black obsidian mirror I had seen in the Yannuzzelli collection in Esmeraldas, and the ones I had unearthed in the Pisco area in the north Mesa. Similar mirrors made of obsidian, pyrite, or mica have been found throughout the sierras and in some areas of the coastal region. In Peru, the Chavin culture employed polished anthracite mirrors; and in Mesoamerica, the Olmecs crafted polished obsidian pyrite and hematite mirrors. From close study of these artifacts and their representation in pottery figurines, it would seem that polished stone mirrors were the precursors of disks made of gold and other metals, and were associated with shamanistic traditions that survived as late as the Inca civilization. Here again, I had found a fragment of evidence indicating the continuity of Ecuadorian culture.

From Padre Zanetti's collection and from my own investigations, I found that another important cultural area producing highly refined pottery of ancient origin lies on the westernmost end of the Napo Basin, in the valley of the Rio Quijos. This complex—designated the Cosanga by Padre Pedro I. Porra, professor at the Universitá Catolica in Quito—reflected a span of cultural development from early stone sculpture to more sophisticated ceramic pottery. And again, it appeared in many respects to be a transitional culture, with its early roots in the Amazon Basin and its later branches in the adjacent Andean highlands. The pottery of the Cosanga, for example, includes

pots, bowls, and vases of skillful design frequently involving tricolor decorations of red, white, and orange pig-
ments, and distinctive human figurines with faces painted
with horizontal or vertical stripes very similar to designs
seen on pottery figures from Pillaro in the Tungurahua
area, and in Pimampiro and the Pisco Valley of the north
Mesa. Thus it seemed, chronologically and geographically, that this distinctive Amazonian trait became extraordinarily widespread.

In spite of their extensive use of pottery, stone remained an important element in the art and building
practices of the Cosanga. The application of the lithic material in their burials shows a unique level of sophistication. Carefully prepared interior vaults were created by
using large unshaped stone slabs to form walls separating
two chambers and to support the roof. After interment of
the corpse and artifacts, the vault was enclosed by massive
stone slabs on sloping angles. In turn this entire structure
was covered with earth, resulting in what appears from
the exterior to be a simple tola. On top, however, a stone
menhir was often erected with arms bent at right angles
and hands placed on the chest.

The discovery that the technique of covering funerary
monuments with earth was similar to the schema used by
the highland people, and later by civilizations in Peru,
Colombia, and Mesoamerica, and the use of funerary
menhirs having Andeolithic traits with incised arms bent
at the chest or over the upper abdomen in the chevron
shape—a trait seen also in all the cultures of the
Americas—bolstered my belief that in times of great antiquity, man had lived and prospered in this region. Evidence of the antiquity of the Cosanga complex was obtained by Father Porra by submitting samples of material
recovered in the burial grounds to the Smithsonian Insti-
tute. The oldest carbon-14 dating yielded an age of 1495
B.C.—a very early date indeed for such a level of development in this eastern region. My investigations of the
Napo and Coca areas seemed to offer further
confirmation of my belief that an early people, following

Stone menhirs. Quijos Valley.

routes blazed by prehistoric animals through the natural corridors provided by river valleys and mountain passes, had migrated from the Amazon Basin to the Ecuadorian highlands. I had had this same impression of natural corridors in my earlier investigations of southern Ecuador, in the valleys of the Rios Zamora, Santiago, Namangosa, and Paute, the natural routes leading to the highland passes of Loja, Matanga, and Cañar into the Mesa; and again in the north, investigating the valleys of the Rios Cofanes, Chingual, Pisco, and now Coca. This corridor fanned out from south of the Colombian border to as far as the Volcan Sumaco southwest, then through the passes of Huaca, Pimampiro, Guamani, and de Due that provided ready access down the valleys of the Rios Pimampiro, Pisco, and Apaqui to the northern section of the Mesa. Ample archaeological evidence of progressive stages of cultural development from east to west enhanced the plausibility of this theory. Moreover, the richness and profusion of archaeological finds made it quite evident that the Pastaza Valley must also have served as a major corridor—the middle corridor from the Amazon, with access into the sierra through the Chalupas, Angamarca, and Pastaza passes.

Thus it seemed that three natural corridors formed by great rivers flowing eastward from the Andes into the Amazon, cutting east-west canyons into the otherwise impenetrable sierra, allowed the migration of ancient animals and men from the Amazon Basin to the sierra. As a general pattern, fossilized bones of extinct animal forms, including mastodon, horse, and camel, have been recovered from along all of these routes.

A remarkable geological coincidence that I noted and began to associate with my theory was the occurrence of natural hot springs in the important intermontane valleys of the Ecuadorian corridors. Surely, at 20,000 and 15,000 B.C. when the glaciers descended to a low of 3000 meters, these springs must have been a welcome oasis to the fauna, and to the hunters, as well as to the people of later cultures who followed them. Deep in the Pastaza

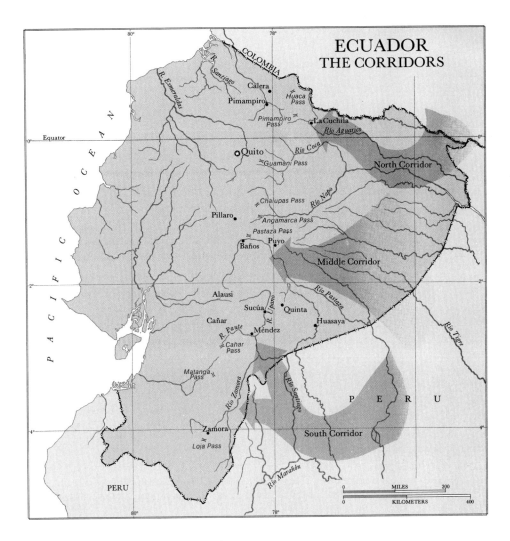

Valley, between the Llanganates Mountains and Volcan Tungurahua, such an oasis was to be found at Baños, the oldest settlement in this region.

I traveled to Baños, hoping by further exploration in the area to find confirmation of my belief that the Pastaza Valley had served as a middle corridor from the Amazon to the sierra. When I reached the picturesque small town, traditionally a center for seekers of health from the hot baths and for bargain-hunters at the extensive Indian market, my first stop was the home of Padre Ramon Perez, a missionary who had spent many years in the Oriente. At seventy, the padre still impressed one as a man of outward simplicity and imposing personal presence. True to the pattern, he had amassed over the years a considerable number of artifacts both in stone and pottery. And in many instances I had the sensation, while examining these pieces during the next few days, that I was looking at highland material. For some of the pottery cups and bowls were decorated in a style similar to that of the Pillaro and Tungurahua areas. Yet these pieces had all been recovered in the Pastaza Valley, well into the east.

I pursued my exploration of the Pastaza Valley on a journey southeast of Baños, across the Cordillera de Huamboya, deep into the lush jungles of the Oriente in the territory inhabited by the Yumbo Indians. With the cacique of a small Yumbo village as my guide, I explored a number of mounds in the jungle nearby. There were six of them, each about 12 meters long and 3 meters high, overgrown with short underbrush and trees. But to my dismay, I saw that they had been devastated by the Yumbos in a futile search for gold. Shards were scattered everywhere—the remains of cups and bowls broken in the frenzy of their search.

I explored the burial mounds, hoping to salvage some pieces that had escaped destruction, and uncovered one small, reddish vessel with an ornate appliqué of a frog figure on its rim and a miniature black jaguar head inside. Part of a crudely hewn grinding stone also came to light, an indication that the ancient inhabitants of this region had progressed to a stage of planting seed-producing crops, for the *metate* is considered contemporaneous with the evolution from a migratory hunting and food-gathering existence to a more sedentary lifestyle. Mound building also seems to be related to the beginnings of this new pattern of living which, in turn, brought about the transition from stone implements to pottery.

Later study of a number of exceptionally artistic pottery shards from the site revealed that their distinctive decorations, incisions, and geometric designs corresponded closely with those Padre Porra had collected from the Huasaya site, an earth-built terrace east of Taisha near the Rio Pastaza, deep in the swampy lowlands of the Amazon. Material associated with the findings yielded the remarkable date of 2000 B.C.

Bone carved head, the gift from Kashiwa.

My exploration of the Yumbo site, as well as of a number of other locations in the Oriente, also refuted the assumption that mound builders proliferated primarily in the uplands and on the coastal plain. The Amazon lowlands are dotted with innumerable mounds that clearly are of very ancient origin. I was given a small bone-carved head that had been recovered from one of the ancient Yumbo mounds, and was struck by the similarity of the eye treatment to the coffee-bean style of the Chorrera. Finding an artifact bearing Chorrera traits in this area was not surprising, however, for near the Tres Cruces Pass, in the Cordillera de Huamboya, whistling bottles characteristic of the Chorrera culture were also uncovered. And this pass, significantly, provides access from the Pastaza Valley, through the Palora Valley, to the central Mesa. I left the Yumbo village convinced that the Pastaza Valley had been a major corridor for the migrations of an ancient people from the Oriente to the high sierras.

Yet when I returned to my home in Miami, I knew that I had found no final answers to the provocative questions that inspired my years of research and exploration in Ecuador. Speculation as to the age of man's arrival and the origin of his cultural rise in South America has been rampant in archaeological circles for years. The most accepted theory suggests that man migrated from Asia to the New World about 12,000 years ago, at the end of the Pleistocene epoch, which lasted roughly 2,500,000 years, ending about 10,000 years ago. This epoch is often referred to as the Ice Age due to the extensive ice sheets and glaciers that were recurrently formed on the earth during this time. Water frozen into the ice sheets lowered the sea levels by about 100 meters, causing the appearance of land bridges that connected major land areas. In North America the Bering Strait became a huge low-lying, dry region connecting two unglaciated areas, northeastern Siberia and western Alaska. Periodically, over the millenniums, during the advance and retreat of the glaciers, a north-south ice-free corridor opened up through the North American continental ice sheet connecting Alaska to the fertile southern plains. It was during one of these periods, about 12,000 years ago, that it is believed man gradually migrated southward. But a manmade scraper of caribou bone found in the Canadian Yukon Territory in 1972 has yielded a radiocarbon date of 27,000 years, which suggests that man at that time was already moving south. Other evidence of man's early presence in North America well south of the Asian land bridge was that of a skull discovered near Los Angeles reputed to be 23,600 years old, and probably older; and in southern California, on Santa Rosa Island, the discovery of remains of charred mammoth bones believed to have come from a manmade fireside, which revealed a carbon-14 date of 29,000 years.

Many scholars are puzzled and disturbed by these dates, for in the framework of the accepted theories, they push man's presence on the continent and his southward migration back many thousands of years. But it is entirely conceivable that man found his way to the New World and began his southward trek at an earlier time when other glacier-free corridors south from Alaska were still open. It is to this theory that I subscribe, for the results I received from the analysis of the last two specimens I sent to Dr. Jeffrey Bada reveal that man was present on the equator as early as 30,000 B.C. Although the specimens, human teeth, were from two different geographical areas—the Quinta site in the Cordillera Oriental, and the La Cuchila site on the eastern side of the Cordillera de Pimampiro—the racemization analysis for both of their aspartic acid ages was 23,000 to 32,000 years (see Appendix).

These dates and the locations in which the specimens were found—both sites lie in the east-west corridors of Ecuador: Quinta in the central and La Cuchila in the northern—seem to substantiate the theory of man's early presence in the Amazon lowlands, for they predate by thousands of years his known presence in the central highlands and the coast of South America. The El Jobo sites on the coast of Venezuela, for example, considered one of the oldest, have yielded a radiocarbon date of 14,920 B.C. Moreover, the dates of these specimens and the artifacts associated with them presuppose a period of cultural development that could only have taken place under favorable climatic conditions. And during the last glacial age while the rest of the planet was still quite cold, temperatures within the narrow equatorial belt were high enough to permit the evolution of the rudiments of culture. In South America this seems to have occurred particularly in the Amazon Basin, where the ecology was lush enough to provide secure food sources from game and plants, thus eventually permitting man to drop his nomadic lifestyle and begin to live in semi-stationary settlements where large numbers of the tribe could devote considerable time to activities other than food gathering. These two factors, stability and a secure food supply, made it possible for the early people of the Amazon to develop the beginnings of complex social systems.

At a later period, however, the melting of the mountain glaciers caused a drastic change in the temperature of the lowlands. The soil, inundated by the flooding rivers and increased rainfall, could no longer produce the food necessary to nourish both animal and man. It is therefore reasonable to assume that migration, from the Amazon westward into the Ecuadorian sierra, began as early as

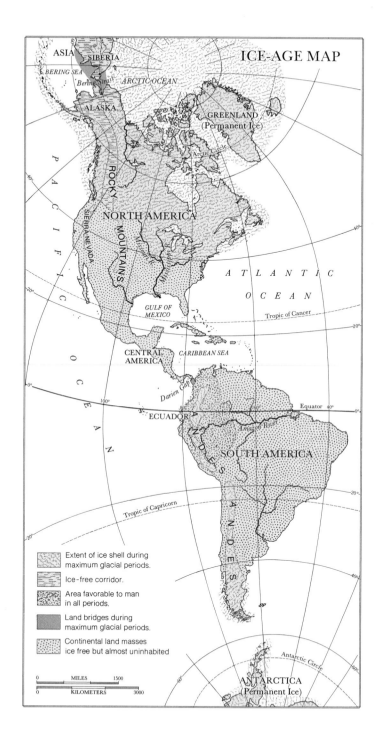

ICE-AGE MAP

ASIA
SIBERIA
BERING SEA
Bering Strait
ARCTIC OCEAN
ALASKA
GREENLAND
(Permanent Ice)
Arctic Circle

ROCKY MOUNTAINS
NORTH AMERICA
SIERRA NEVADA

ATLANTIC

OCEAN

GULF OF MEXICO
Tropic of Cancer

CENTRAL AMERICA
CARIBBEAN SEA

Darien Gulf

ECUADOR
Equator

Amazon River

ANDES
SOUTH AMERICA

Tropic of Capricorn

Extent of ice shell during
maximum glacial periods.

Ice-free corridor.

Area favorable to man
in all periods.

Land bridges during
maximum glacial periods.

Continental land masses
ice free but almost uninhabited

Antarctic Circle

0   MILES   1500
0   KILOMETERS   3000

ANTARCTICA
(Permanent Ice)

PACIFIC OCEAN

15,000 B.C. It is my contention that this migration took place through the three natural corridors leading from the Amazon into the north, central, and south portions of the Ecuadorian Andes. And following these corridors, the ancient people seem to have been taking the same routes established by the large animals. To be sure, such a migration was a complex process that took thousands of years and probably involved numerous cross-contacts and reversals.

I found abundant evidence of the presence and evolution of these early cultures as they advanced from stone to pottery as a medium for producing artifacts, and metallurgy, too, was developed to an astounding level of technical accomplishment. Indeed, some of these cultures left legacies of exceptional richness. During this period a great number of traits were developed that can be seen 1000 or 2000 years later in the great cultures of Peru and Mesoamerica: the feathered serpent, which ultimately became the Mexican Quetzalcoatl; pictographic writing, seen first in Ecuador in the very early seal stamps; the mathematical numbering system, which became fundamental to the Olmec and Mayan civilizations; the serpent and jaguar

Extensive ice sheets and glaciers repeatedly formed on the land during the ice age (known as the Pleistocene epoch, lasting roughly 2,500,000 years, ending about 10,000 years ago). In North America, at the height of the glaciation periods, the Bering Strait became a broad land bridge connecting Siberia with Alaska due to the lowered sea level. Ice covered a large part of the continent, reducing the average temperature by ten to twenty degrees centigrade. In the Rockies glaciers descended below the 3,000 meter level. But in the periodic warming up of the climate, during which the glaciers partially receded, an ice-free corridor connected Alaska with the heart of America, generally following the alignment of the Canadian Rockies. Through this corridor man and mammoths, mastodons, camels, giant ground sloths, bisons, and other animals fanned out into the American plains. With the return of a glacial age the corridor was closed once more, the changing climate forcing animal and man to move to more hospitable lands. The migration was gradual, spreading to the equatorial region. At the height of the glaciation periods, ice covered most of the southern part of South America due to the spreading of the Antarctic ice sheet. The Andes Mountain Range was covered by separate groups of glaciers that descended down to 3,000 meters and extended to the Caribbean Sea. But in the equatorial region favorable climatic conditions prevailed during all cold epochs, making it possible for early man and animal to survive. The expansion of the glaciers transformed the rain forests into drier regions, which, over time, fostered the development of more progressive cultures.

deities; pyramid-shaped burial or ceremonial structures; the meander, or step-spiral graphic device; the "Greek-key" decorative motif; various pottery devices such as the stirrup vessel, iridescent painting, black plumbate ware, whistling figures and jugs, the tradition of the ax; and many more. Finally, one of the most important revolutionary events of all the Americas—the domestication of corn—appears to have begun on the eastern slopes of the Andes sometime between 5000 and 10,000 B.C., and then to have been carried westward into the central Mesa and further, down into the coastal plain, where it appeared in the Valdivia culture by 4000 B.C.

The rise and later influence of the Valdivia and Chorrera cultures in Ecuador are well documented. So, too, is the decline in their creative force as the torch of high cultural creativity passed to the inhabitants of Peru and Mesoamerica, where the great American civilizations as we know them came to the fore. Yet still ignored and virtually unexplored are the earlier cultures of Ecuador, which contributed so much to the greatness of these later civilizations. One day, perhaps, they will be given the careful study that they deserve, and will no longer be regarded—in the words of the old priest I met on one of my first journeys to Ecuador—as the work of little more than "a bunch of savages."

Appendix:

Racemization and Radiocarbon Dating
of Specimens Found at Ecuadorian Sites

University of California, San Diego
Scripps Institution of Oceanography

La Jolla, California 92093
July 19, 1978

DEAR MR. TUROLLA:

I have completed the racemization analyses of the . . . samples you sent me. The results and the estimated ages are listed in the enclosed table. The ages should be considered as only rough estimates due to the lack of reliably dated samples to use for "calibration."

This appears to be an extremely interesting series of samples which I think could make an important contribution in answering the question of the antiquity of human beings in the Americas. . . .

I'll be looking forward to hearing from you.

Sincerely,
JEFFREY L. BADA

SAMPLE NO.	LOCATION, ELEVATION, AND TEMPERATURE	D/L ASPARTIC ACID	ASPARTIC ACID AGE (YRS.)
1	San Jose/Quinta Site elevation = 2750 m. avg. temp. = 12.5°C.	0.36	23,000* to 32,000†
2	Pimampiro/La Cuchila Site elevation = 2400 m. avg. temp. = 14°C.	0.35	23,000* to 32,000†

*Calculated using $k_{asp} = 1.3 \times 10^{-5}$ yr^{-1}, deducted from racemization results at Riobamba (temperature 13°C., elevation 2795 m.) ; see letter to P. Turolla, Nov. 30, 1976.
†Calculated by dividing above k_{asp} value by 1.4 to account for Holocene/ Pleistocene temperature differences.

University of California, San Diego
Scripps Institution of Oceanography

La Jolla, California 92093
November 30, 1976

DEAR MR. TUROLLA:

I have carefully evaluated the racemization results of the Calera tooth and I believe it is possible to at least make a rough age estimate. The measured D/L aspartic acid ratio for the tooth was 0.20.

351

In order to estimate a value of k_{asp} for the site, I have used some results we have obtained for a skull from Punin (near Riobamba, Ecuador). The value of k_{asp} at Punin has been calculated to be 1.3×10^{-5} yr^{-1}, based on a measured D/L aspartic acid ratio of 0.112 and a C^{14} age of 3,190 years. Using this k_{asp} value yields an age of $\frown$ 10,000 years for the Calera skeleton.

Using the Punin k_{asp} value to deduce an approximate age estimate of the Calera material seems valid because the temperature at Riobamba (13°C, elevation 2795 m) is about the same as that at Tulcan (11°C, elevation 2949 m), the locality closest to the site where temperature information is available. (The difference in temperatures of these two locations can probably be attributed to elevation.) Since the elevation of the Calera site, obtained from R. Hawke, is 2400 m, and thus lower than Riobamba, the actual temperature may be slightly higher than Riobamba. This temperature difference (if it exists) would tend to make the racemization age of the Calera skeleton somewhat less than 10,000 years.

The racemization results and my interpretation thus suggest an age of $\frown$ 10,000 years or slightly less for the Calera skull.

I'll be anxious to hear your comments on this.

Sincerely yours,
JEFFREY L. BADA

University of Miami
Department of Geology

April 4, 1975

DEAR MR. TUROLLA,

Following are the results of radiocarbon activity measurements made on...samples submitted by yourself. Apparent age was calculated relative to 0.95X of NBS oxalic acid radiocarbon dating standard. Quoted precisions are one standard deviation and includes only the counting precisions of the unknown sample, background, and modern standard. The samples were thoroughly inspected and cleaned prior to chemical conversion.

LABORATORY NO.	DESCRIPTION	APPARENT AGE YEARS B.P.
UM-425	#3 (Mastodon Tooth)	5480 ± 120

Sincerely,
Koneta L. Eldridge, (Mrs.)
Asst. Director
Radiocarbon Dating Laboratory

Bibliography

Bada, Jeffrey L. "The Dating of fossil bones using the racemization of isoleucine," *Earth and Planetary Science Letters*, vol. 15, Amsterdam, 1972, 223–231.

———. "Amino Acid Racemization Dating and their Geochemical Implications," *Naturwissenschaften*, vol. 62, Springer-Verlag, 1975, 71–79.

Bedoya, M., and Angel, N. *Aspectos de la Arqueologia en la Region de Cañar*. Quito: Editorial Casa de la Cultura Ecuatoriana, 1965.

Bell, Robert. *Investigaciones Arqueológicas en el Sitio el Inga, Ecuador*. Quito: Editorial Casa de la Cultura Ecuatoriana, 1965.

Bennett, Wendell C. *Ancient Arts of the Andes*. New York: Museum of Modern Art, 1954.

———, and Bird, Junius B. *Andean Culture History*. Garden City, New York: The Natural History Press, 2nd revised edition, 1964.

Bernal Andrade, Leovigildo. *San Agustín, Testimonio de Piedra Sobre el Origen del Hombre*. Bogata: Graficas Leipzig, 1976.

Bernal, Ignacio. *El Mundo Olmeca*. Mexico City: Porrúa Hermanos, 1968.

Bersoe, Paul. "The metallurgy and technology of gold and platinum among pre-Columbian Indians." *Ingenierviden skabelige Skrifter*, no. 44, Copenhagen, 1938.

Bushnell, G. H. S. *Peru*. London: Thames and Hudson, 1956.

Cevallos, P. F. *Compendio de la Historia del Equador*. Guayaquil: Imp. de "El Telégrafo," 1885.

Cieza de Leon, Pedro de. *Crónicas del Peru, Historiadores Primitivos de Indias*. Madrid: Imp. de M. Rivadeneira, 1853.

Cline, R. M. and Hays, J. D., eds. *Investigation of Late Quaternary Paleoceanography and Paleoclimatology*. The Geological Society of America, memoir 145, 1976.

Coe, Michael D. "Archaeological Linkages with North and South America at La Victoria, Guatamala." *American Anthropologist,* vol. 62, 1960, 393.

———. *The Maya.* London: Thames and Hudson, 1966.

Collier, Donald, and Murra, John V. "Survey and Excavations in Southern Ecuador." Anthropological Series, vol. 35. Chicago: Field Museum of Natural History, 1943.

Cossio Del Pomar, Felipe. *Arte del Peru Precolombino.* México: Fondo de Cultura Economica, 1949.

Covarrubias, Miguel. *Indian Art of Mexico and Central America.* New York: Knopf, 1957.

Dockstader, Frederick J. *Indian Art in South America.* Greenwich, Ct: New York Graphic Society Publishers, 1967.

Estrada, Emilio. *Ultimas Civilizaciones Pre-históricas de la Cuenca del Río Guayas.* Guayaquil: Publicación del Museo Víctor Emilio Estrada, No. 2, 1957.

———. *Los Huancavilcas, Ultimas Civilizaciones Pre-históricas de la Costa del Guayas.* Guayaquil: Publicación del Museo Víctor Emilio Estrada, No. 3, 1957.

———. *Prehistória de Manabi.* Guayaquil: Publicación del Museo Víctor Emilio Estrada, No. 4, 1957.

———. *Las Culturas Pre-clasicas, Formativas o Arcaicas del Ecuador.* Guayaquil: Publicación del Museo Víctor Emilio Estrada, No. 5, 1958.

———. *Arqueologia de Manabi Central.* Guayaquil: Publicación del Museo Víctor Emilio Estrada, No. 7, 1962.

Estrada, Emilio, Meggers, Betty J., and Evans, Clifford. *Cultura Valdivia.* Guayaquil: Publicación del Museo Víctor Emilio Estrada, No. 6, 1959.

Fawcett, Colonel P. H., D.S.O. *Exploration Fawcett.* (Arranged from his manuscripts, letters, log, and records by Brian Fawcett.) London: Hutchinson & Co. Ltd., 1953.

Field, Frederick V. *Pre-Hispanic Mexican Stamp Designs.* New York: Dover Publications, 1974.

Gonzalez Suarez, Federico. *Historia General de la Republica del Ecuador* (Atlas Arqueologico). Quito: Imprenta del Clero, 1892.

———. *Los Aborígenes de Imbabura y del Carchi.* Quito: Tipografia Salesiana, 1908.

Heuvelmans, Bernard. *On the Track of Unknown Animals.* New York: Hill and Wang, Inc., 1965.

Holm, Olaf. Las Hachas—Monedas Ecuatorianas. Guayaquil: Pieza 3, Exposición presentada por la Sección de Antropología Cultural, Casa de la Cultura Ecuatoriana, Núcleo del Guayas, 1975.

Homet, Marcel F. *Sons of the Sun*. London: Neville Spearman, 1963.

Jijon y Caamaño, Jacinto. *Contribución al Conocimiento de los Aborígenes de la Provincia de Imbabura*. Madrid: 1914.

———. *Antropología Prehispánica del Ecuador*. Quito: La Prensa Católica, 1952.

Klein, Richard G. "Ice-Age Hunters of the Ukraine." *Scientific American*, June, 1974.

Lathrap, D. W. *The Upper Amazon*. London: Thames and Hudson, 1970.

MacNeish, Richard S., Peterson, Frederick A., and Flannery, Kent V. *The Prehistory of the Tehuacan Valley*, vol. 3, *Ceramics*. Austin: University of Texas Press, 1970.

Mangelsdorf, P. C., MacNeish, Richard S., and Galinat, W. C. "Domestication of Corn." *Science*, Vol. 143, no. 3606, 1964, 538.

Matovelle, J. Julio Maria. *Cuenca de Tomebamba*. Cuenca: Publicaciones del Centro de Estudios Historicos y Geograficos del Azuay, 1921.

Maudsley, Alfred P. *The True History of the Conquest of New Spain*. London: Hakluyt Society, 1908.

———. *Collection of Maya Sculptures from Central America*. British Museum Publication, 1923.

Meggers, Betty J., Evans, Clifford, and Estrada, Emilio. *The Early Formative Period on Coastal Ecuador: The Valdivia and Machalilla Phases*. Washington, D.C.: Smithsonian Institution Press, 1965.

Meggers, Betty J. *Ecuador*. New York: Frederick A. Praeger, 1966.

Meggers, Betty J., and Evans, Clifford. *Archaeological Investigations on the Río Napo, Eastern Ecuador*. Washington, D.C.: Smithsonian Institution Press, 1968.

Morley, Sylvanus Griswold. *Introduction to the Study of Maya Hieroglyphs*. Washington, D.C.: Smithsonian Institution, Bureau of American Ethnology, Bulletin 57, 1915.

———. *The Ancient Maya*. Palo Alto: Stanford University Press, 1946.

"New World Archaeology: Theoretical and Cultural Transformations," W. H. Freeman, *Scientific American*, San Francisco, 1974.

Paddock, John, ed. *Ancient Oaxaca: Discoveries in Mexican Archeology and History*, 2nd ed. Stanford: Stanford University Press, 1970.

Piña Chán, Román. *Las Culturas Preclásicas de la Cuenca de México*.

Mexico: Fondo de Cultura Económica, 1955.

Porra, Pedro I. *Fase Cosanga.* Quito: Ediciones de la Universidad Católica, 1975.

————., and Piana Bruno, Luis. *Ecuador Prehistorica.* Quito: Instituto Geografico Militar, 1976.

Prescott, William H. *History of the Conquest of Peru.* New York: The Heritage Press, 1957.

Ralegh, Sir Walter. *The Discoverie of the Large, Rich, and Bevvtifvl Empyre of Gviana.* London: Robert Robinson, 1596.

Reichel-Dolmatoff, Gerardo. *San Agustín.* New York: Praeger, 1972.

Ribadeneira, Captain Jorge A. *Estudio Geologico de la Población Prehistórica la Tolita, Provincia de Exmeraldas.* Quito: Talleres Gráficos del Colegio Militar, 1941.

Rivet, Paul. *Les Origenes de L'Homme Americain.* Paris: Gallimard, 1943.

Rouse, Irving, and Cruxent, José M. *Venezuelan Archaeology.* New Haven: Yale University Press, 1963.

Sampedro V., Francisco. *Las Cuevas de los Tayos.* Cartillas de Divulgacion Ecuatoriana, no. 15. Quito: Editorial Casa de la Cultura Ecuatoriana, 1977.

Santiana, Antonio. *Nuevo Panorama Ecuatoriano del Indio,* Vol. 1, Quito: Editorial Universitaria, 1966.

Sauer, Walter. *Geología del Ecuador.* Quito: Editorial del Ministerio de Educación, 1965.

Saville, Marshall H. "Antiquities of Manabi, Ecuador." Contributions to South American Archaeology, New York, 1907.

Smith, G. Eliot. *Elephants and Ethnologists.* New York: E. P. Dutton & Co., 1924.

Tello, Julio C. "Discovery of the Chavin Culture in Peru." *American Antiquity,* vol. 9, no. 2, Salt Lake City, 1943, 135–160.

Uhle, Max. "Späte Mastodonten in Ecuador." New York: Proceedings of the Twenty-Third International Congress of Americanists, 1930, pp. 247–258.

Verneau, R., and Rivet, Paul. *Ethnographie Ancienne de L'Equateur,* Paris: Gallimard, 1912.

Verrill, A. Hyatt, and Verrill, Ruth. *America's Ancient Civilizations.* New York: Capricorn Books, 1967.

Wicke, Charles R. *Olmec, An Early Art Style of PreColumbian Mexico.* Tucson: University of Arizona Press, 1971.

Zevallos, Carlos. *La Agricultura en el Formativo Temprano del Ecuador (Cultura Valdivia).* Guayaquil: Editorial Casa de la Cultura Ecuatoriana, Núcleo del Guayas.

Acknowledgments

To the many people who, directly and indirectly, contributed to my research, I am most grateful, particularly those Indian friends who shared a style of life at times too dynamic for comfort. I wish to express my personal appreciation and thanks to New Horizon Research Foundation for their valued support; to Mark Diamond for his care in the production of some photographs; to the Universidad Catolica library and museum for the use of their facilities; to the Instituto Geografico Militar for their assistance; to Señor Hernan Crespo Toral, Director of the Museo del Banco Central, for the courtesies he extended; to Doña Lola Gangotena de Ponce, Señor Oswaldo Guayasamín, and Doña Teresa Duran Restrepo who brought me fresh insight by allowing me to study their invaluable private collections. I am also indebted to Peter Tompkins for alerting me to the importance of writing this book. Finally, I would like to express my gratitude to M. S. Wyeth, Jr., Editor-in-Chief of Harper & Row, and Burton Beals, for their continual encouragement and assistance throughout the production of this volume.

PHOTO CREDITS

All photographs were supplied by the author except those listed as follows. To those institutions and individuals I wish to express my sincere thanks: Museo del Banco Central, Quito, 49 top, 58 top, 67 bottom right, 173 top, 328 top; Cuzco Museum, 50 top; Museo Nacional de Antropologia, Mexico City, 51, 68 right, 224, 267 bottom, 341; John Paddock, *Ancient Oaxaca: Discoveries in Mexican Archaeology and History*, published by Stanford University Press, 75 left; Courtesy of Museum of the American Indian, Heye Foundation, N.Y., 58 bottom, 107, 129 top, center, bottom; François de Loys, 134; Museo del Oro del Banco de la República, Bogota, 157; Richard S. MacNeish, *The Prehistory of the Tehuacan Valley*, Volume III, *Ceramics*, published by The University of Texas Press, 174 bottom; Ceturis of Ecuador, 186; Hamlyn Group, 317; Courtesy of the Trustees of the British Museum, 337 bottom; Eugen Kusch, from Huaras Museum, 337 top; Casa de la Cultura Ecuatoriana, Quito, 340 top.

Index

Page numbers in italics refer to illustrations.